IMAGES
of America

SPICELAND TOWNSHIP

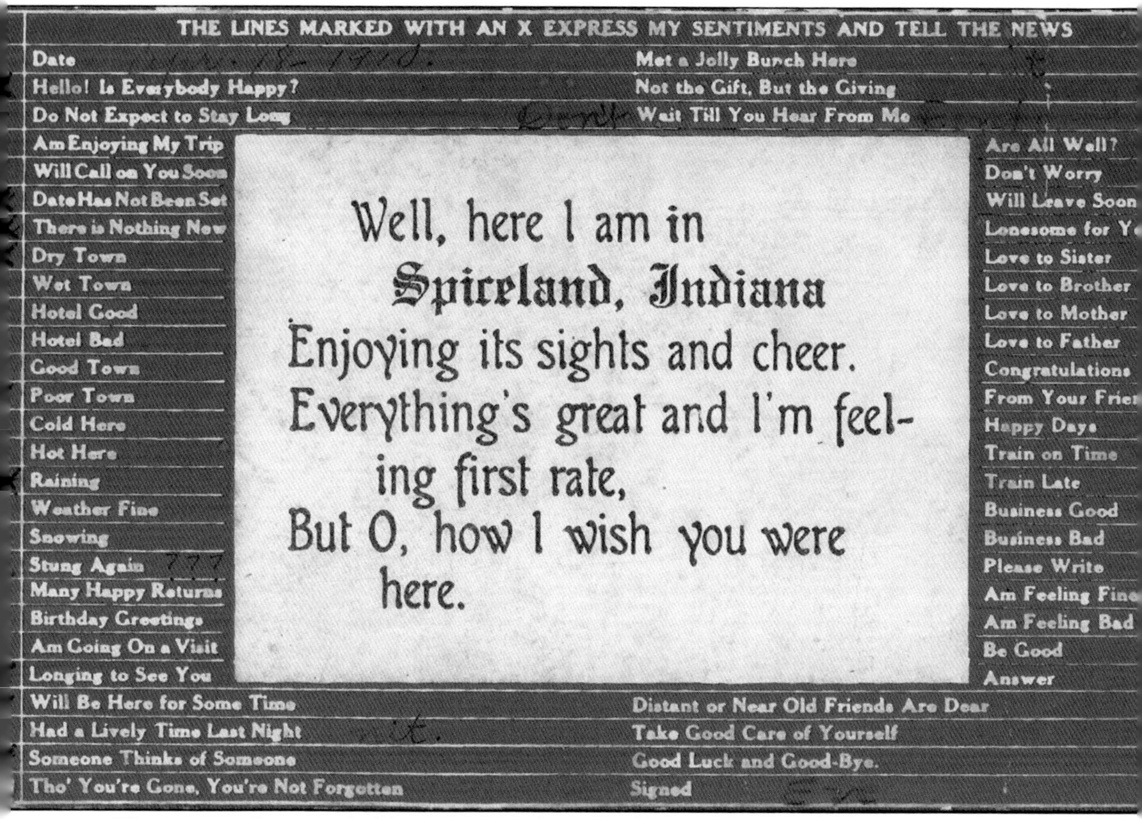

This postcard was mailed from Spiceland on April 10, 1910, to a resident of Straughn, Indiana. The sender did not sign their name. The inscription on the back is lighthearted: "Do you know anything of interest? I have something silly to show you. The news is beginning to leak out. Company downstairs and I'm cold. Where is the robe?" (Courtesy of the author's collection.)

On the Cover: Members of the Spiceland Cornet Band pose in this 1892 photograph. The band members are, from left to right, Tom Taylor, Orestus Mote, Harry Emminger, Harry Pike, Bill Butler, John Thompson, and Leslie Beach. Clifford Porch and J.M. Emminger are on the back cover. (Courtesy of the author's collection.)

IMAGES
of America

SPICELAND TOWNSHIP

Richard Pickering Ratcliff

ARCADIA
PUBLISHING

ISBN 978-1-4671-1254-3

Published by Arcadia Publishing
Charleston, South Carolina

Printed in the United States of America

Library of Congress Control Number: 2014944247

For all general information, please contact Arcadia Publishing:
Telephone 843-853-2070
Fax 843-853-0044
E-mail sales@arcadiapublishing.com
For customer service and orders:
Toll-Free 1-888-313-2665

Visit us on the Internet at www.arcadiapublishing.com

To Ralph Hawkins and Erma Anora Pickering,
Jesse Cook and Lillian May Ratcliff, my grandparents.
Though gone for many years, precious memories still linger.

Contents

Acknowledgments

For over 50 years, I have been collecting photographs pertaining to Spiceland Township. Countless citizens of the township, many of them now deceased, have been very generous in adding to my collection, assuming I would be a good steward of their possessions and knowing of my interest in local history.

Certainly I am not the first resident of the township to realize the importance of preserving photographs and other items from our past. Earlier historians and collectors led the way. I am only following in their footsteps, picking up where they left off. Those early preservers of the past include Daniel Lawrence (1839–1924), Henry W. Painter (1848–1923), Charles L. Stubbs (1868–1955), Sylvester Lykins (1878–1963), Thomas C. Evans (1907–1983), and C. Frederick Poer (1912–1990). To them I owe a debt of gratitude for collecting and preserving photographs and other items of interest.

Many years ago, I was given 407 original glass-plate negatives taken by Cephus M. Huddleston, a photographer who had a studio in Spiceland from about 1890 until 1909. Many of the images in this pictorial history were taken by Huddleston. By the use of his camera lens, Huddleston has allowed us a rare look at how the citizens of Spiceland and Spiceland Township worked, lived, and played. In 2007, I gave this collection to the Indiana Historical Society in Indianapolis. There, the negatives were cleaned and catalogued, and they are now available to anyone doing research on the small-town America of an earlier period.

Unless otherwise noted, all the images in this history are courtesy of my collection. However, I would like to thank Charlene Williams; pastors Mark Herbkersman and Larry Delon; John D. Pidgeon; the Henry County Historical Society Museum in New Castle, Indiana; and Martha Resler, Sylvia Salanitro, Dr. Thomas D. Hamm, and William Ed Pierce for providing 12 additional photographs.

Introduction

Even though Spiceland Township was not organized until 1842, settlement began in the early 1820s. From the uplands and tidewater areas of the South came movers—among them Quakers, members of the Religious Society of Friends—disgruntled with drought, slave competition, the institution of slavery, the expansion of the plantation system, and the fact that the soil was sandy and worn out. These Quakers, mainly from North Carolina, became especially numerous in southwestern Henry County, mainly in what became Spiceland Township and neighboring Greensboro Township.

Desiring a distinguishing name for their settlement in the growing township, the pioneers turned to a form of vegetation in naming their principal town and the township itself. Both were named for the spicebush, which once grew in abundance in the area. Pioneers often partook of the savory and pungent tea brewed from the spicebush. The beverage was believed to possess medicinal value. One pioneer suggested that he was attracted to the place because of "the abundance of springs that gave forth good, cool water, the enticing odor of the aromatic and ever-present spicebushes, the many sugar trees, the undulating surface of the ground, and the quietness that seemed to be a part of the place."

Although there had been a settlement at what became the town of Spiceland at an earlier date, it was not until 1847 that the town was officially laid out by William R. Macy and Aaron Lancaster Pleas. That same year, Driver Boone (1796–1881) began to sell land for building purposes. A post office had been established on April 10, 1838, and the town was eventually incorporated in 1869. The 1880 population of the town was 527; in 1930, the number stood at 722; and the 1970 census listed 957 residents.

The village of Ogden, in the southwestern portion of Spiceland Township, was laid out and platted by Hiram Crum in December 1829 and is located on the Old National Road. It was named in honor of Hiram Ogden, a US engineer engaged in the construction of the famous road, once nicknamed "Main Street, USA." The village was originally called Middletown because it was the halfway point between Richmond, Indiana, and Indianapolis, but when the application was made for a post office, a new name was given, as another Middletown already existed in Henry County.

The town of Dunreith is located along the National Road (now US Highway 40) and State Road 3 in south central Spiceland Township. It is believed that a tavern was first built in the vicinity to accommodate westward travelers. Tradition also suggests that the earliest cluster of houses was called Crum's Springs. A few years after the Indiana Central Railroad passed through the township in 1851, a stop known as Coffin's Station was established. The name came from Emory Dunreith Coffin, the leading proprietor of the town at the time. In 1863, Coffin, a rabid abolitionist, made plans to sell his store and move to Kansas with his family to take part in the state's increasingly heated struggle over the issue of slavery. Unfortunately, he died on the Fourth of July that year. To honor Coffin's memory and to retain the connection of his name with the town, the name Dunreith was chosen as the new name for the town. In 1861, a post office was established, and the town was formally platted in 1865. By 1870, there were 180 residents in the community. The 1960 census listed 236 residents, and the figure for 1990 was 205.

The National Road (US 40), Indiana's Main Street, has become a side street because of the superhighway known as Interstate 70. No other transportation route had more to do with the settlement of Central Indiana, which would include Spiceland Township, than did the National Road. Both Ogden and Dunreith were founded as a result of their proximity to the famous road. Construction of the interstate across Indiana took place during the 1960s and 1970s. This superhighway roughly parallels US 40, and, today, nearly all the trucks and automobiles that once used the National Road use the interstate. Many restaurants, service stations, and motels that once greeted weary travelers have either lost business or gone totally out of business because of Interstate 70.

The area of Spiceland Township is 22 square miles. It is drained by the Big Blue River, which forms the northwestern boundary of the township. Buck Creek, running in a southwesterly course, eventually flows into the Big Blue River. The classic little stream named Brook Bezor rises near the center of the township and flows north before emptying into the Big Blue River. According to the 2010 census, there were 2,270 residents of Spiceland Township.

For over 50 years, the Spiceland community was known for its academy, the next-to-last Quaker academy to close in Indiana. The Spiceland Sanitarium and Mineral Springs attracted visitors from all over the United States until it was destroyed by fire in 1913. In the pre–Civil War days, Spiceland and Spiceland Township were hotbeds of abolitionist activities, with many residents doing all they could to assist escaped slaves from the South.

The former Spiceland Academy and Spiceland High School turned out a number of outstanding graduates, including a Broadway playwright and lyricist; USO performers during World War II; a director of the Mayo Clinic in Rochester, Minnesota; the founder of the Carnation Milk Company, known for its "milk from contented cows"; the developer of the nation's first citrus concentrate and the head of the Minute Maid Corporation; the man often referred to as "The Dean of American Historians"; and numerous authors, college professors, and college presidents. At one point in the 1880s, the Spiceland Friends Meeting was the largest Quaker congregation in the United States. Draper, Inc., located in Spiceland, is a manufacturer of window shades, movie screens, and gymnasium equipment. With over 500 employees, it is the largest factory of its kind in the United States, and the largest industry in Henry County.

Hopefully, by examining the images presented here, readers will have a better understanding of what life was like in a bygone era for the people of Spiceland, Dunreith, Ogden, and all of Spiceland Township. The images are varied, but so were the people. While some of the photographs might bring on a chuckle, some might rekindle similar memories of your own, and some may surprise you. Even though these images can only capture brief moments in time, they are but a small fraction of the incredible story of the people of Spiceland Township. If you would like to learn more about the history and people of the township, perhaps you might plan a visit to Hoover Hall, the home of the Spiceland Preservation and Tourism Society, located at 103 East Main Street in Spiceland.

One

They Came, They Saw, They Conquered

The "Daniel Boone" of Spiceland Township was Levi Butler, a veteran of the War of 1812 who squatted on land with his wife, Elizabeth, in 1816. Other settlers came in 1820, 1821, and 1822. Daniel Jackson came with his wife, Prudence, in 1821, but he fell victim to yellow fever in 1824 while taking a flatboat full of produce to New Orleans. He reached home only in time to die.

Then, between 1822 and 1836, came the great influx of Quakers. Some migrated from Georgia, Tennessee, Pennsylvania, Virginia, and South Carolina, but the vast majority had been residents of North Carolina, mainly from Guilford and Randolph Counties. In order to reach their new home in the Indiana wilderness, it was necessary for them to cross the Appalachian Mountains using Boone's Wilderness Road, follow the Kentucky River, cross the Ohio River, and then travel on to their new home. While some walked, others came on horseback or in wagons. However they traveled, the journey was long and hard. These Quaker families would be the founders of the Spiceland Friends Meeting.

Some thought of children as economic assets. Others took seriously the injunction to be fruitful and multiply. There was work to be done in clearing the wilderness, and young hands could help. Large families were usually followed by a depressing record of early deaths. The Friends cemetery at Spiceland is filled with many pioneer offspring who never reached the age of 21.

The cholera epidemic of 1839, which struck Indiana and Spiceland Township, was a prime example of the hardships of pioneer life. The 12 to 15 plague victims are buried in a row in the Friends cemetery at Spiceland. Only the names of two are known. But the majority of the first settlers withstood hardships and exposures, had strong constitutions and temperate habits, and reached old age. Nearly all died in the home of their early choice—the place where they had spent years of honest toil and where God had bestowed many blessings upon them.

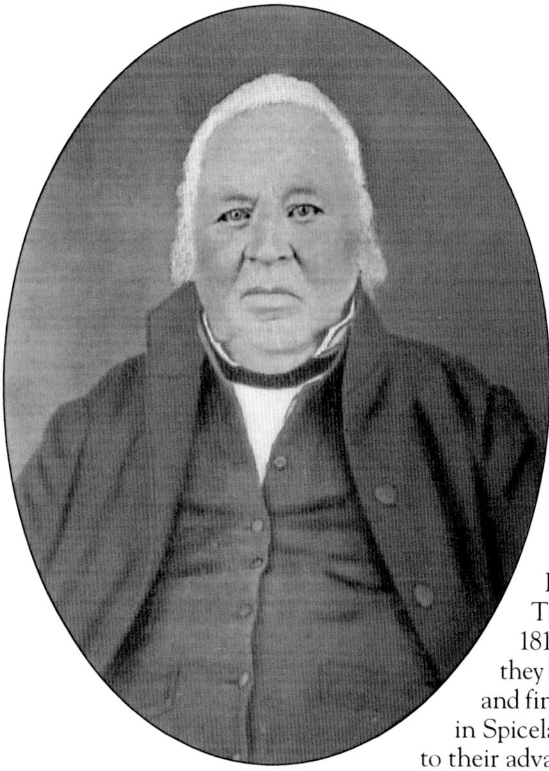

Thomas (1782–1865) and Hannah Symons (1788–1873) were both born in North Carolina. After their marriage in 1811, they moved to the Indiana Territory, but they were soon forced to go to Ohio, as the Indians made life uneasy for frontier settlers. They did not return to Indiana until the War of 1812 ended. Finally settling in Wayne County, they first lived in a cabin, then a hewed-log house, and finally a brick house. By 1852, they were living in Spiceland with their son and daughter-in-law due to their advanced age and feeble condition.

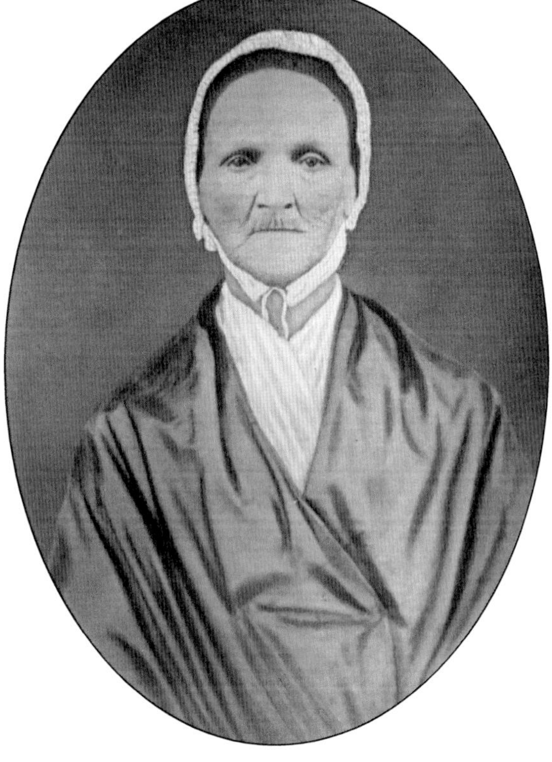

Thomas Scattergood Teas (1794–1850) was born in Philadelphia. About 1815, he started on foot for the Indiana Territory, going by way of Niagara Falls. In a few years, he loaded a flatboat in Cincinnati with bacon and other produce and headed for New Orleans, selling what he could along the way. Upon reaching the city, and still in possession of many items, he sailed to the island of St. Thomas, where he disposed of the remainder of his cargo. Coming to Spiceland Township in 1835, he built and operated a mill along the Big Blue River. He was a prolific letter writer, and many of his letters have been preserved at Haverford College in Haverford, Pennsylvania.

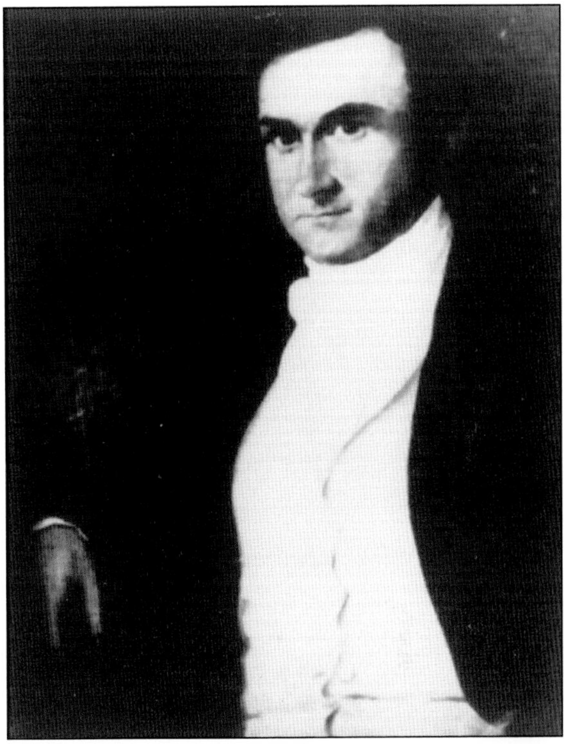

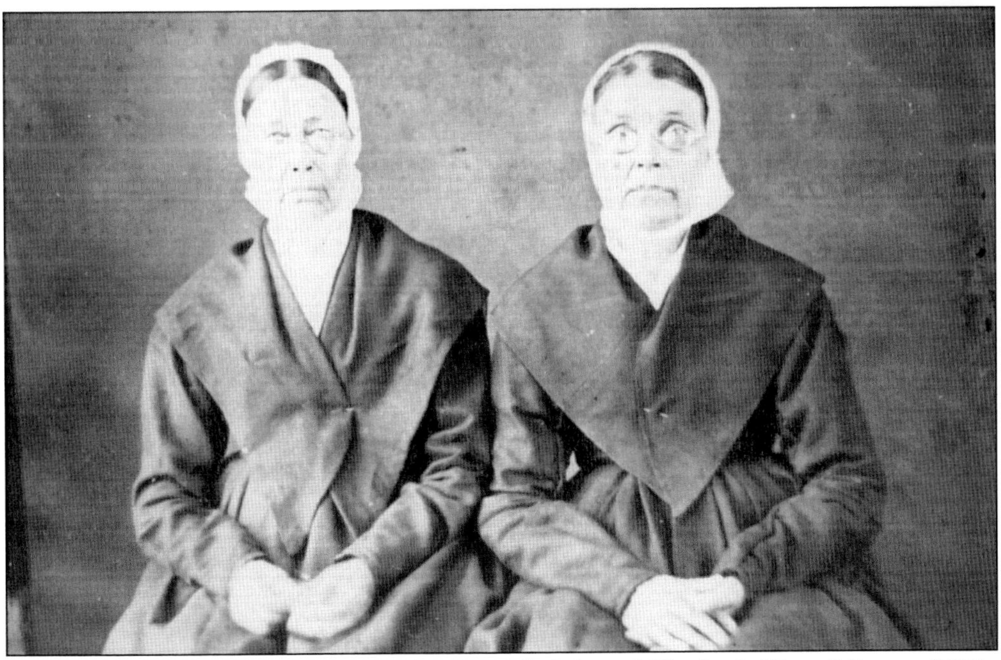

These maiden ladies, Dorcas Boone (1807–1875), left, and Elizabeth "Betsy" Boone (1803–1869), were born in North Carolina and were the younger sisters of Driver Boone (1796–1881), Spiceland's second postmaster and the town cobbler. They resided in Spiceland with their bachelor brother Charles (1801–1878) and their mother, Dorcas Boone (1765–1848). (Courtesy of Dr. Thomas D. Hamm.)

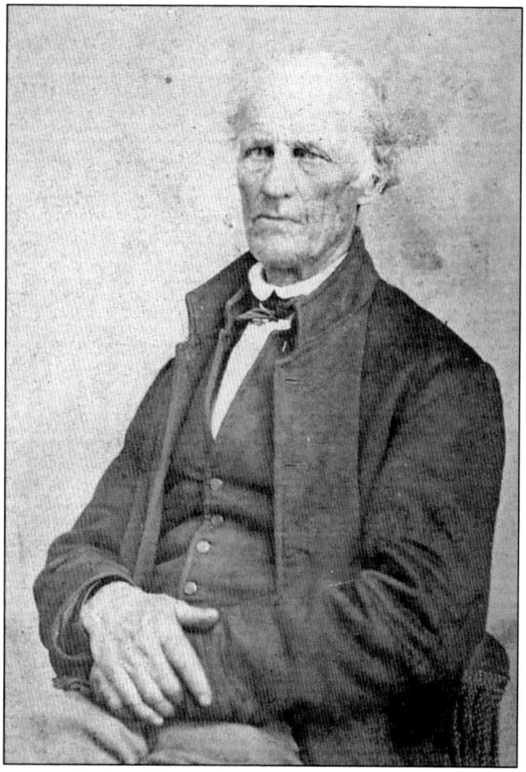

Joel Cloud (1800–1883) was born in Sevier County, Tennessee, and Anna Cloud (1798–1859) was born in North Carolina. Both were founding members of Spiceland Friends Meeting. From the beginning of their membership, the Clouds were profoundly interested in seeing that suitable educational facilities were available for their children and other youth in the meeting. (Both courtesy of Sylvia Salanitro.)

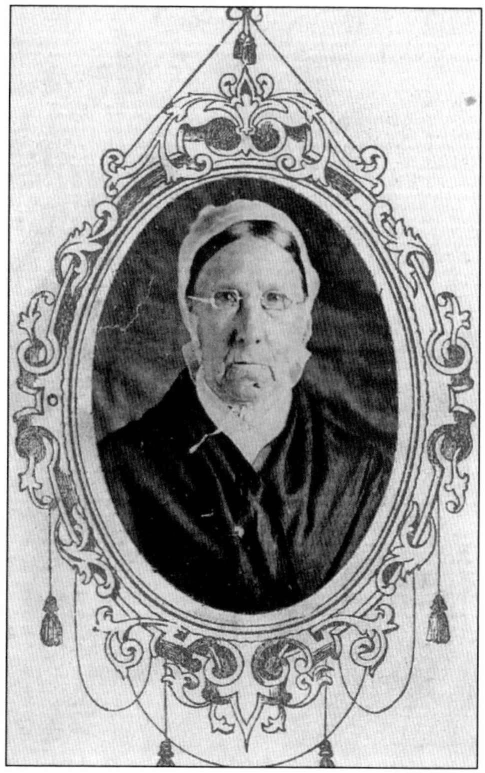

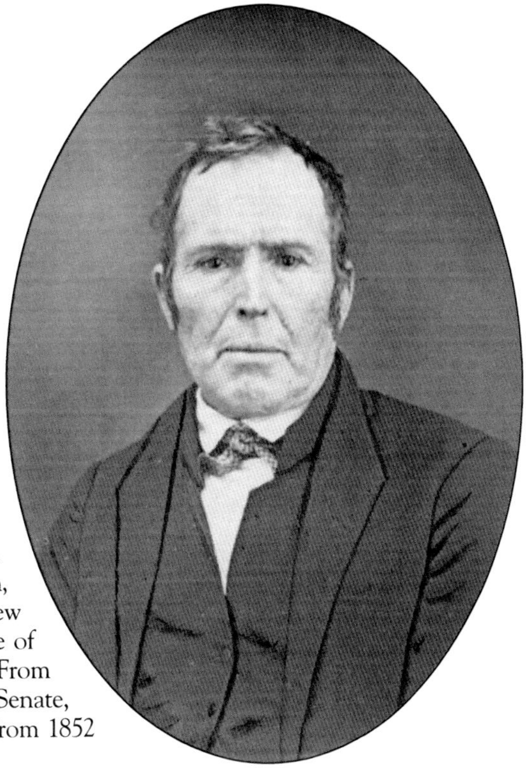

George Evans (1802–1863) was born in South Carolina, and Mary Evans (1798–1859) was born in North Carolina. They were original members of Spiceland Friends Meeting, and George served as the first clerk (or head) of the meeting. In 1839 and 1840, he made a trip on horseback through northern Indiana, Michigan, and Canada to Boston and back, by way of New York City and Philadelphia, for the purpose of visiting as many Friends meetings as possible. From 1848 to 1850, Evans served in the Indiana State Senate, and he was a trustee of Indiana University from 1852 until 1857.

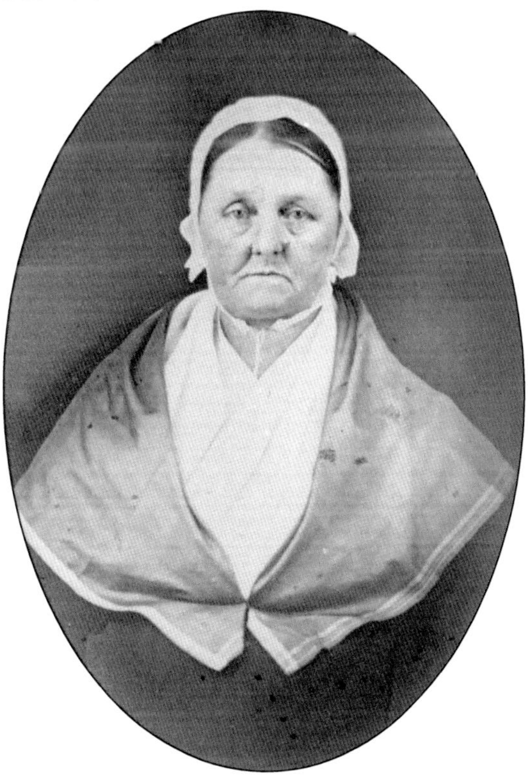

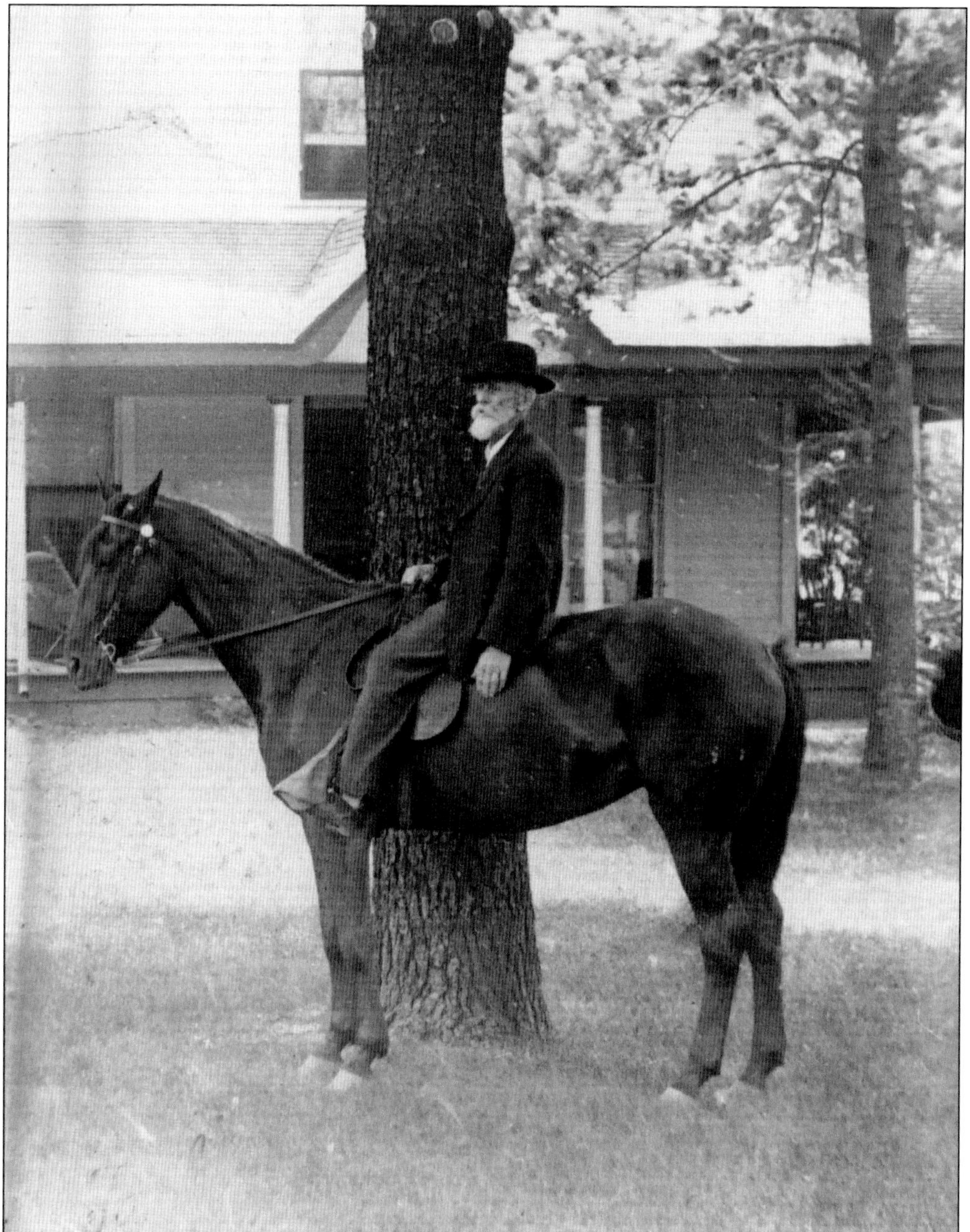

Jesse Gordon (1832–1917) is shown here in 1912 on his way to the Friends meeting in Spiceland. His parents, Charles Gordon Jr. (1804–1855) and Lydia R. Gordon (1804–1846), and his grandparents Charles Gordon Sr. (1766–1844) and Ruth Gordon (1768–1855) were among the founders of Spiceland Friends Meeting.

Two

To God Be the Glory

The early history of Spiceland Township is to a large extent the history of the Society of Friends (Quakers), whose members were among the earliest settlers. As early as 1824, they were holding "meetings for worship" (to use their terminology) under the trees in what soon became a thriving village that they named Spiceland.

"Campbellites" (Disciples of Christ) were holding meetings along Buck Creek at present-day Dunreith as early as 1838. Not to be outdone, Methodists, the followers of John Wesley, established churches, first at Ogden during the Civil War and then at Spiceland in 1870.

Baptists and Nazarenes did not start churches in the township until the mid-20th century. Today, all of these congregations have impressive houses of worship and are about the business of winning souls for Christ. Members strive to be more like Jesus Christ by loving God, loving people, and serving their world.

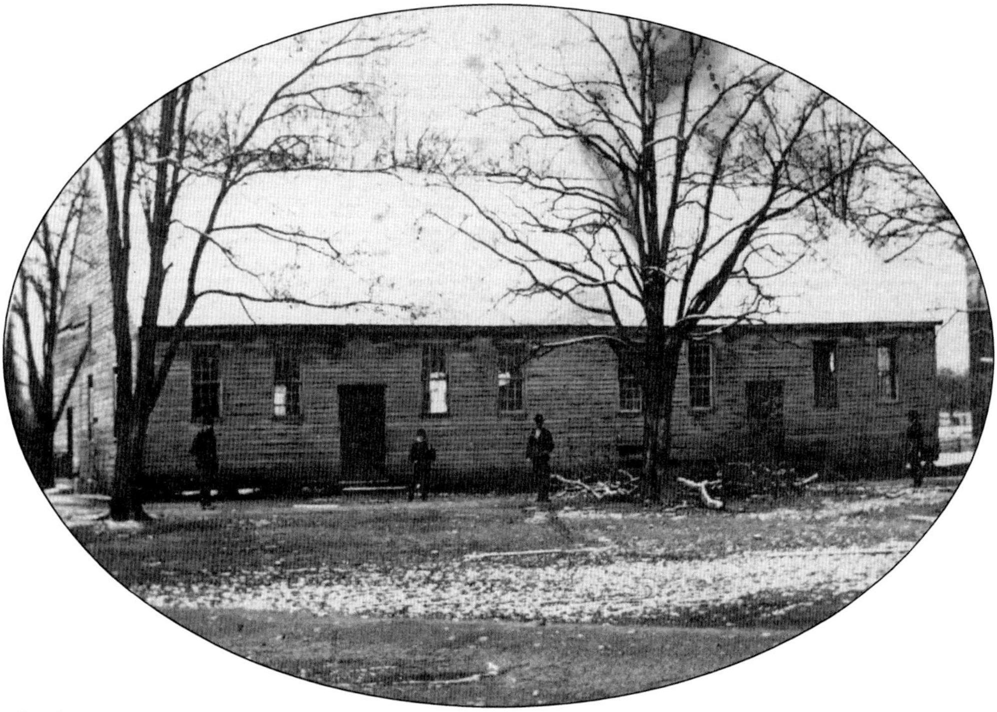

The first recorded Friends meetings held in Spiceland were in John Sheridan's (1775–1836) log barn in 1824. Later, Friends assembled under the trees for worship. In 1825, another log structure was used as a place of worship. A crude log building erected in 1828 served as the Friends meetinghouse for several years. The frame structure shown here was erected in 1833 and enlarged in 1839. Spiceland photographer Robert Gordon took this photograph.

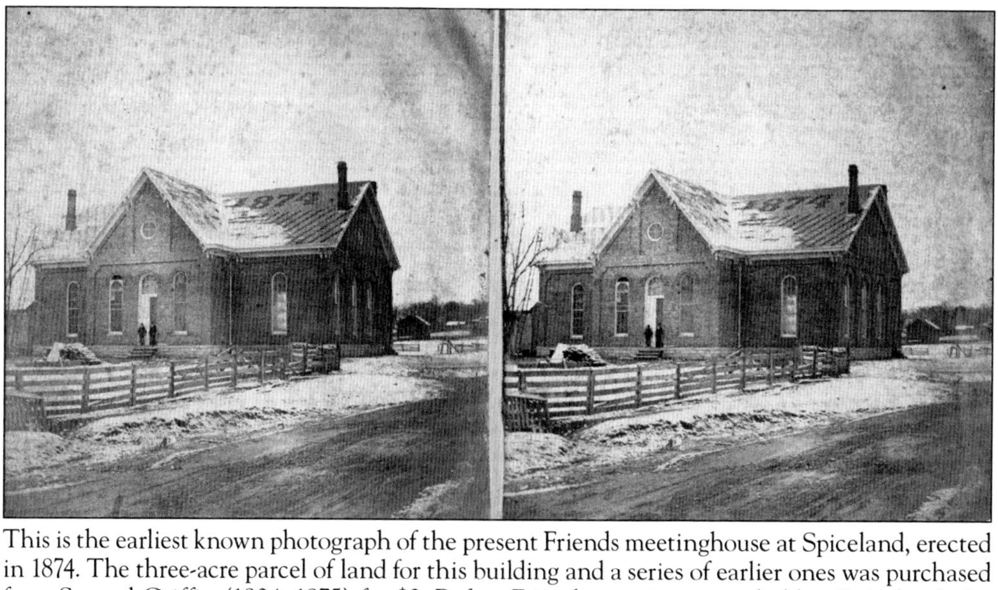

This is the earliest known photograph of the present Friends meetinghouse at Spiceland, erected in 1874. The three-acre parcel of land for this building and a series of earlier ones was purchased from Samuel Griffin (1804–1875) for $3. Before Friends meetings were held at Spiceland, the early pioneers had to walk or ride horseback to Greensboro, a distance of over three miles, and ford a sizable river.

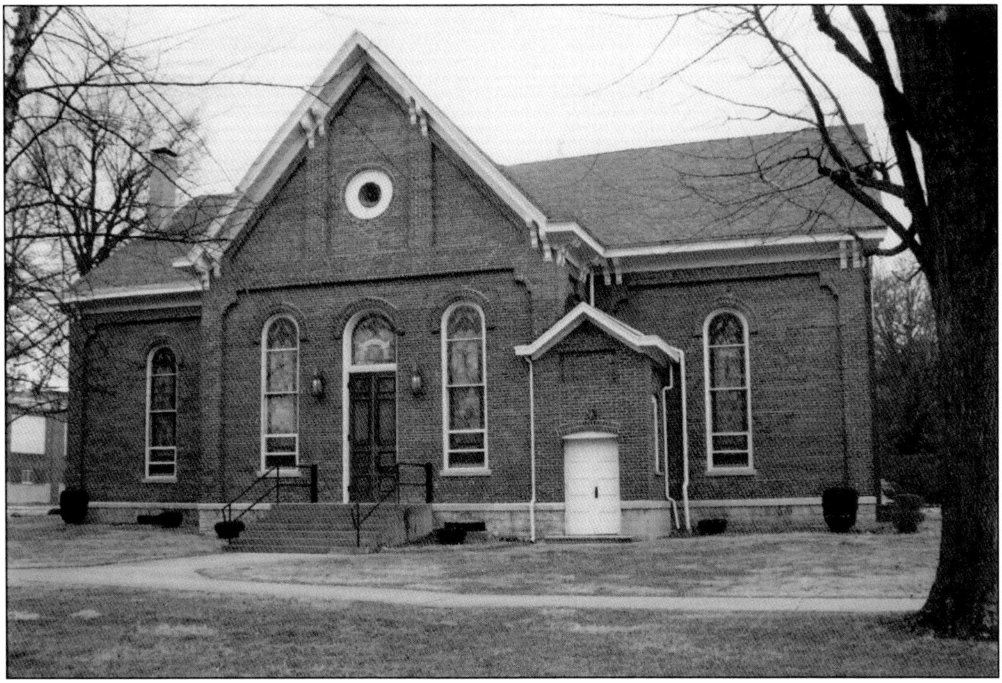

Erected in 1874, Spiceland Friends Meeting exhibits several Gothic and Victorian Italianate characteristics. Additions were made to the meetinghouse in 1929, 1968–1969, and 2005–2006, none of which are shown here.

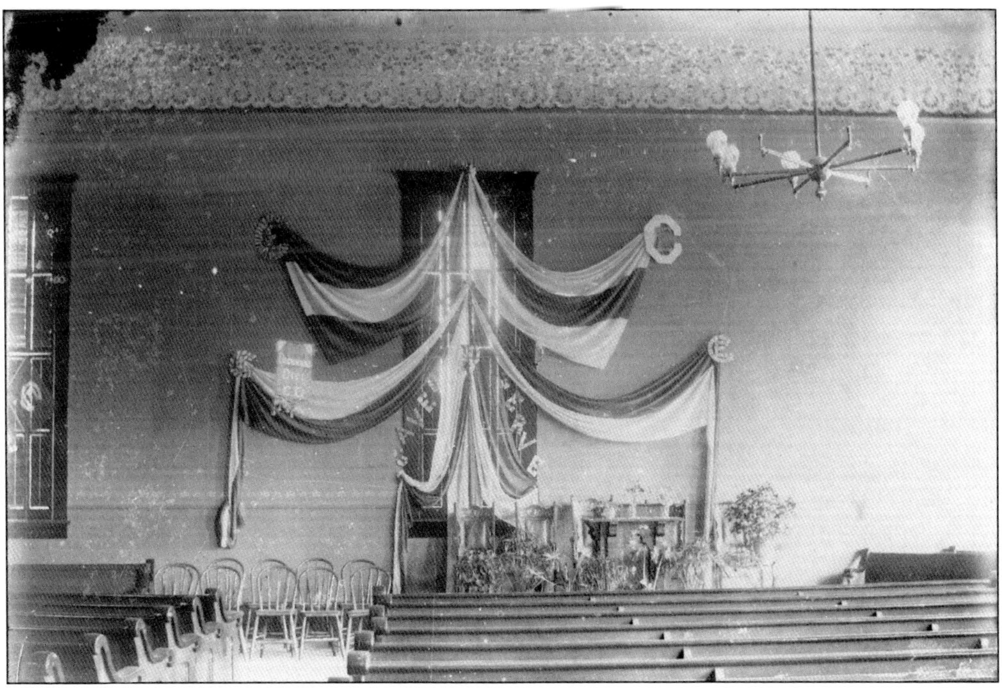

The interior of the meetinghouse is seen in this 1896 photograph. Note the wallpaper on the wall, the gaslight, and the pulpit furniture, which is still used today.

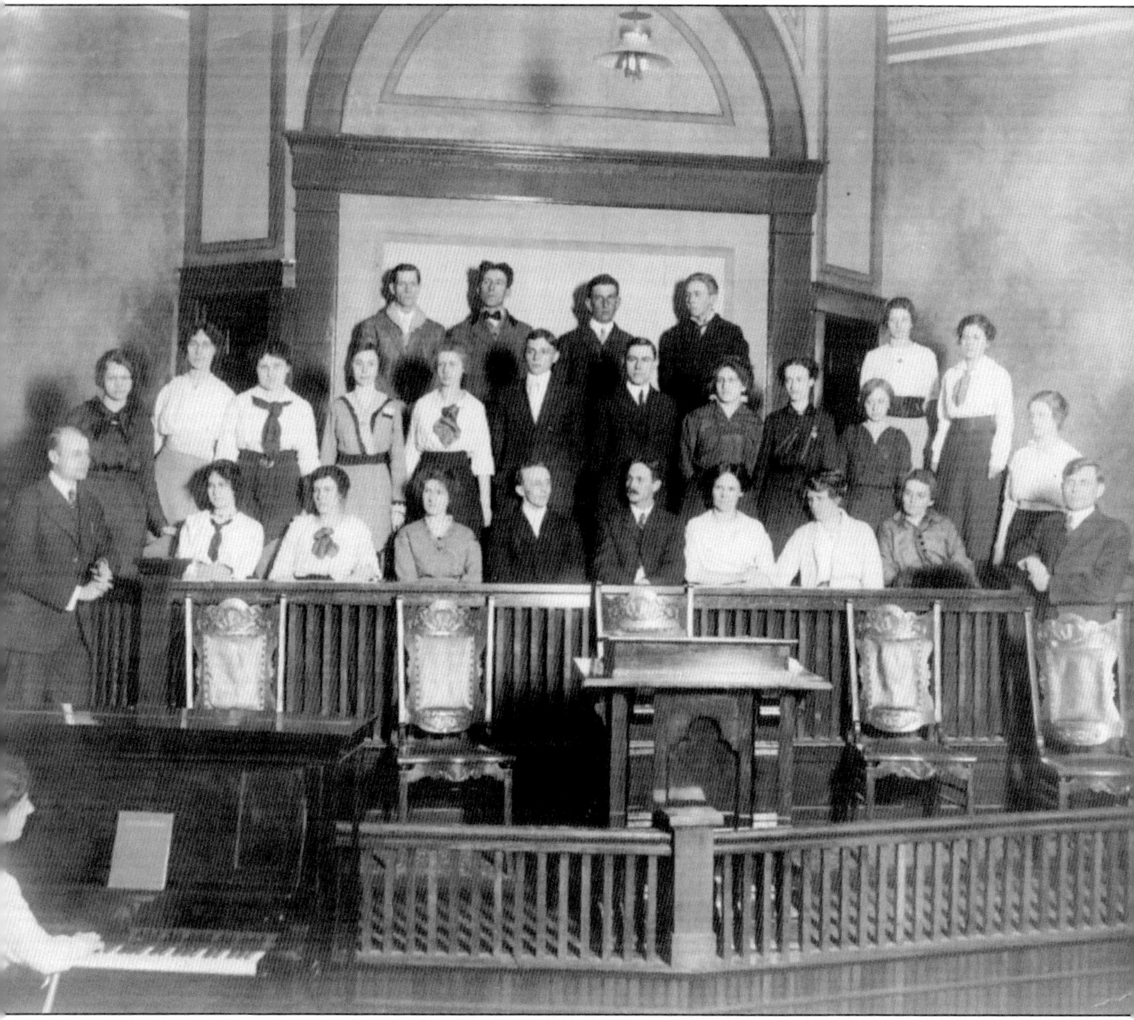

The 1911 choir at Spiceland Friends included, from left to right, (first row) unidentified, Juanita Hall, Irene Mercer, Margaret Cornell, Perry Wilson, Morris Coffin, Mary Cooper, Jessie Pierce, Pearl Coffin, and unidentified; (second row) Melissa Warrington, Gertrude Sutton, unidentified, Ruth Painter, Vernon Jarrett, Otis Coffin, Howard Basye, Ruth Harvey, Emma Kendall, Hazel Hoffman, Georgia Bowman, Mary Basye, and Mary Addison; (third row) Will Macy, Erbie Lee, unidentified, and Earl Antrim.

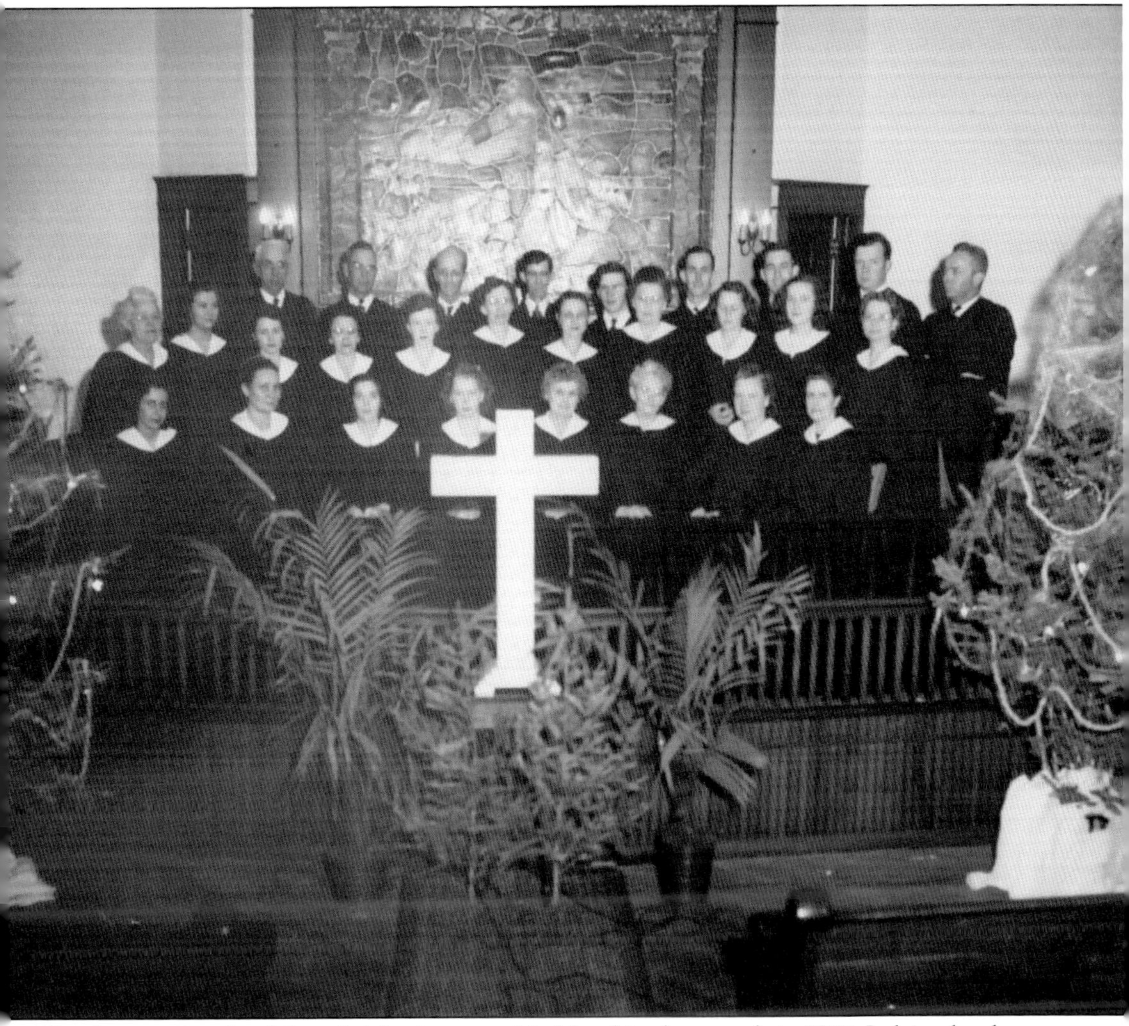

The choir at Spiceland Friends Meeting assembled for this photograph in 1948. Judging by the decorations, surely Christmas was approaching. From left to right are (first row) Anita Everhart, Mildred Baily, Jean Catt, JoAnn McCormack, Flossie Crum, Mollie Coffin, Esther Coffin, and Rua Trabue; (second row) Estella Coffin, Kathryn Pernett, Margaret Wake, Winifred Huff, Harriett Armstrong, Ruth Painter, Winifred Ratcliff, Clarice Kinkaid, Garnet Pea, Patricia Archibald, and Edna Burkett; (third row) Arthur Coffin, Verney Crum, George Coffin, Chester Cassidy (choir director), George Applegate, George Wilson, Charles Wilson, James Applegate, and Wilbur Coffin.

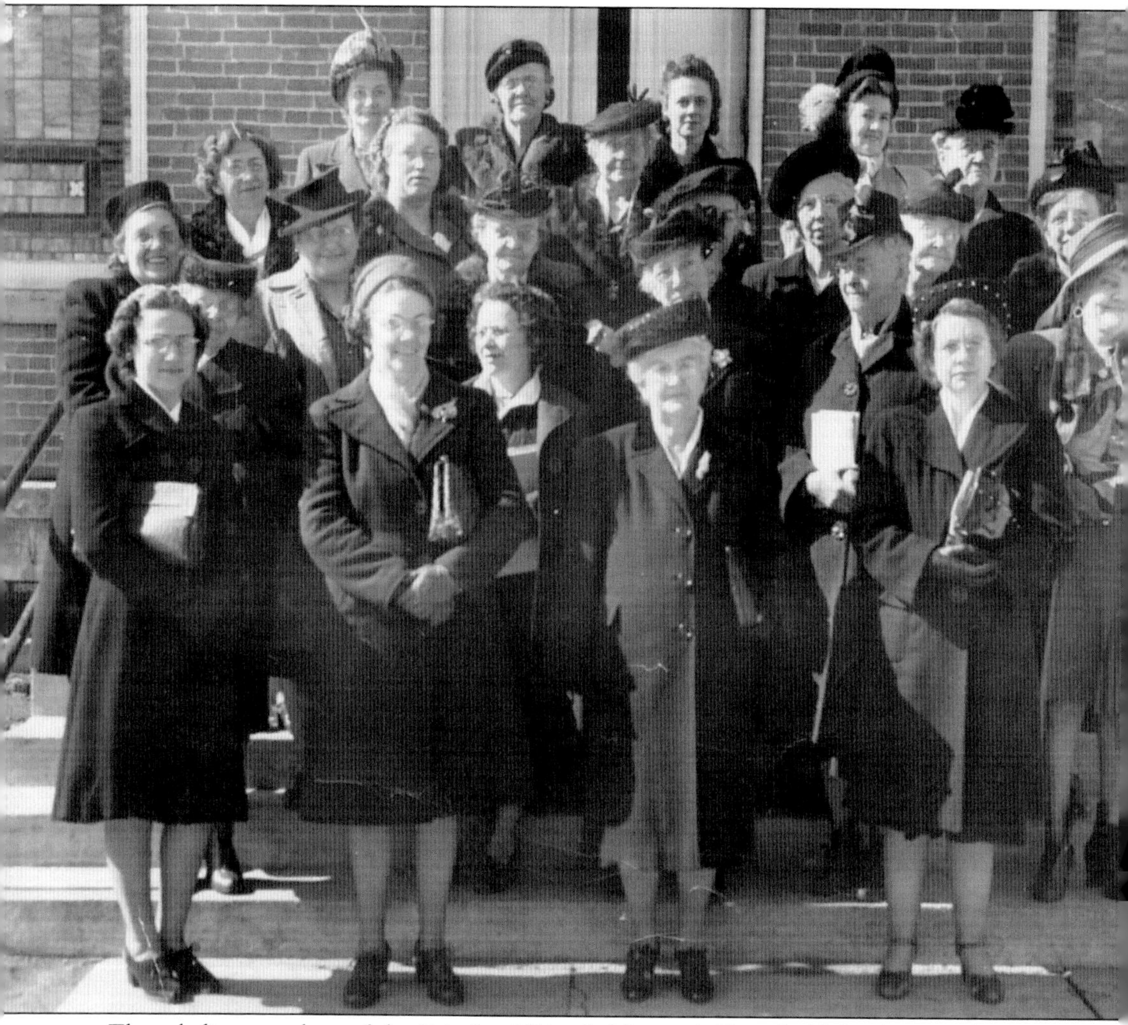

These ladies, members of the Spiceland Friends Meeting's Household Circle, assembled on the front steps of the church in 1948 for a group photograph. From left to right are (first row) Winifred Ratcliff, Goldie Bogue, Ethel Painter, and Edna Burkett; (second row) Emma Deem, Winifred Huff, Mayme Applegate, Lena Leighton, and Pearl Rifner; (third row) Marie Jarrett, Erma Pickering, Anna Odgers, Eva Griffin (partially hidden), Mary Wilson, Irene Allen, and Anna Applegate; (fourth row) Ruth Painter, Jeanette Coffin, Louisa Coffin, and Elma Lawrence; (fifth row) Ruth Bogue, Flossie Coffin, Eloise Reece, and Helen Barlow.

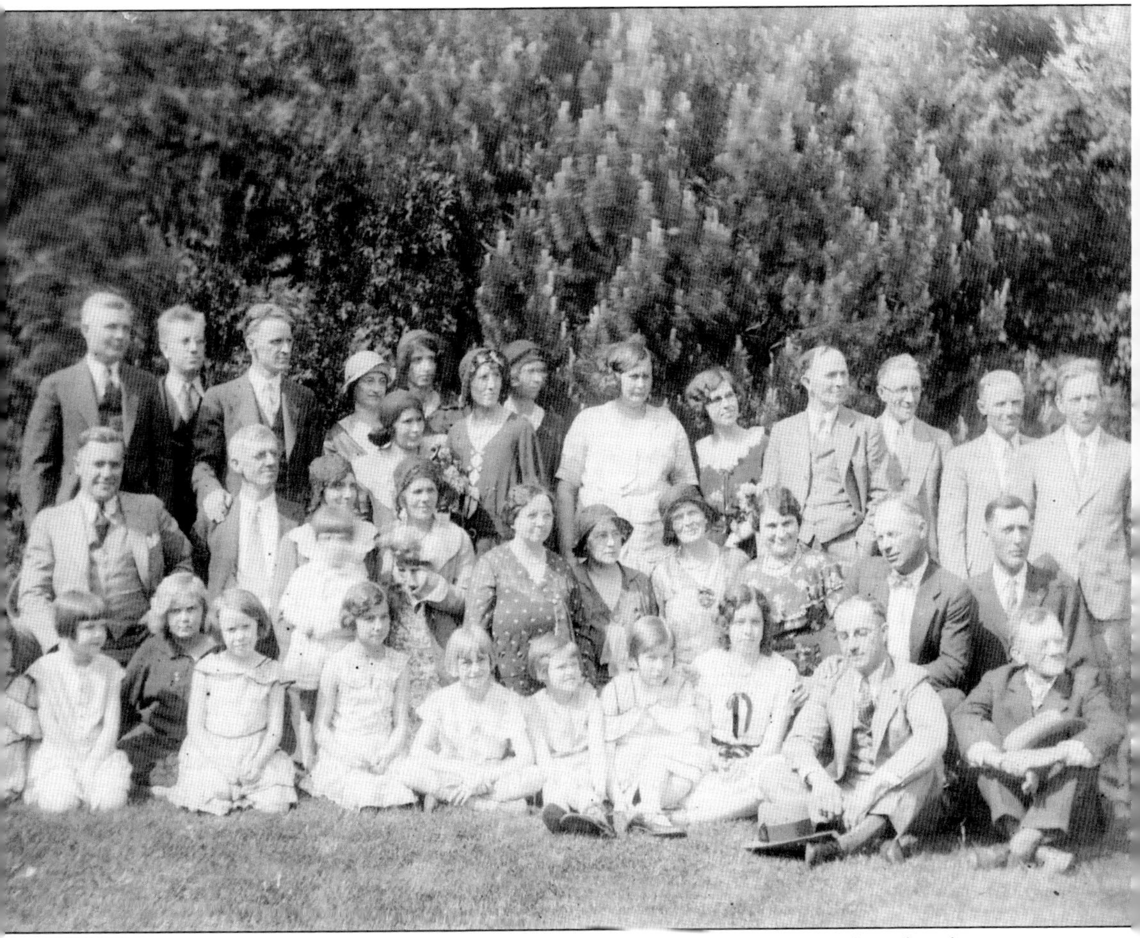

Members of the Whittier Sunday school class at Spiceland Friends Meeting gathered with some of their children for this 1931 photograph. From left to right are (first row) Margaret Huff, Janet Mercer, Catherine Cassity, Harriett Huff, Miriam Hoover, Lola Brown, Susanna Brown, Helen Huff, Reola Symons, Wayne Myer, and Will Brown; (second row) Clyde Mercer, Wade Kerr, Irene Mercer (holding Jean Mercer), Bertha Brown, Mary Brooks, Mary Smith, Jennie Kerr, Erma Pickering, Clifford Hoover, and Clarence Cassity; (third row) William G. Smith, Ray Brooks, Loring A. Eilar (class teacher), Clara Symons, Winifred Huff, Grace Hoover, Berniece Eilar, Mary Wilson, Maud Cassity, Mabel Myer, Kerney Wilson, Ralph Pickering, Lloyd Huff, and Albert Symons.

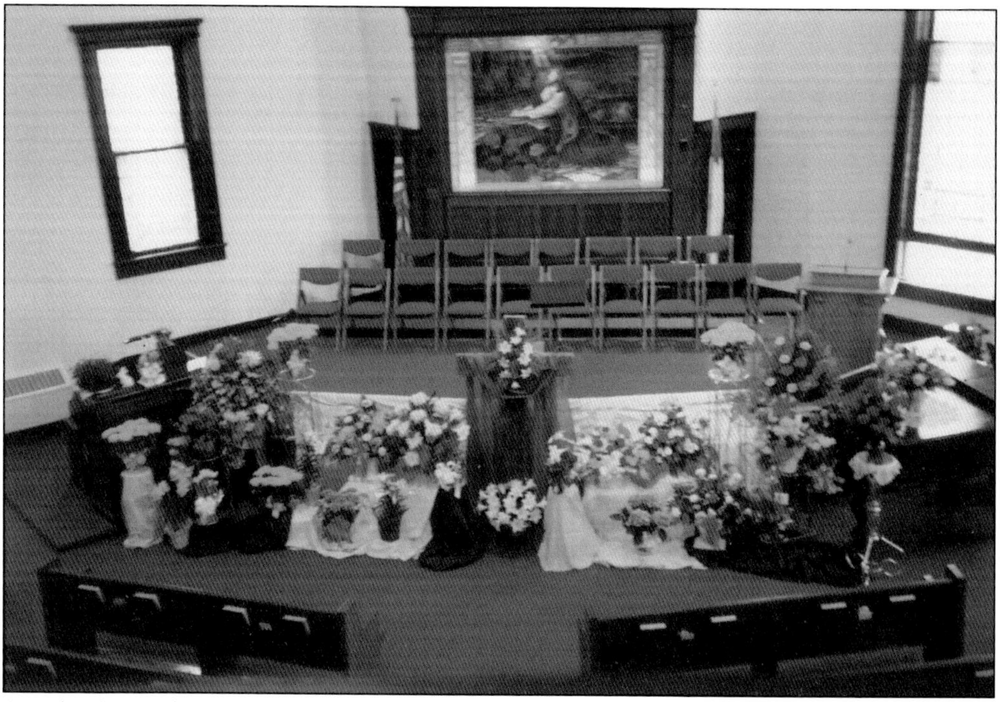

Spiceland Friends Meeting was preparing for Easter Sunday when this photograph was taken in 1992. The meetinghouse is noted for its beautiful stained-glass windows.

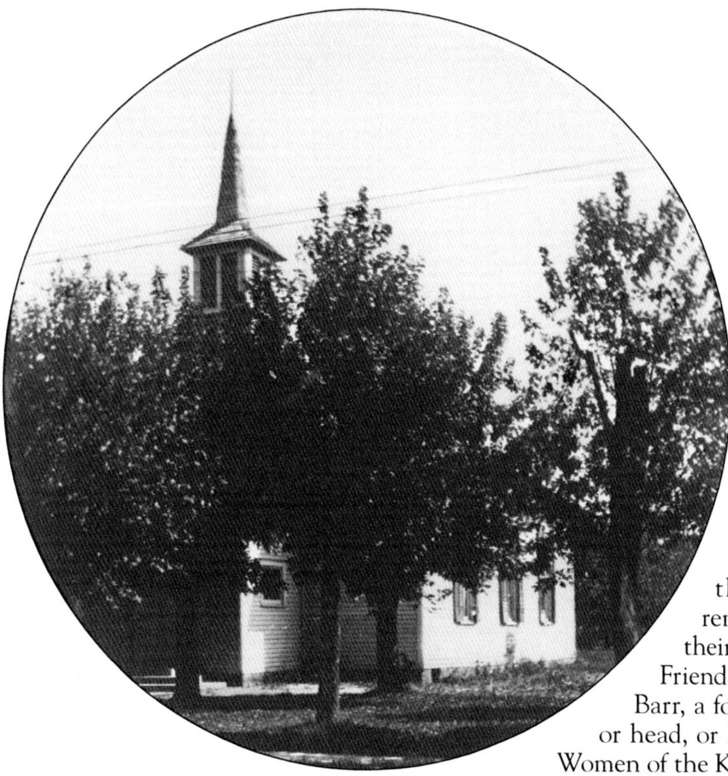

Quakers at Dunreith organized a meeting in 1867. After the church closed in 1931, the building was sold the next year, and the remaining members moved their membership to Spiceland Friends. In 1923, Daisy Douglas Barr, a former pastor, became the or head, or Imperial Empress, of the Women of the Ku Klux Klan in Indiana.

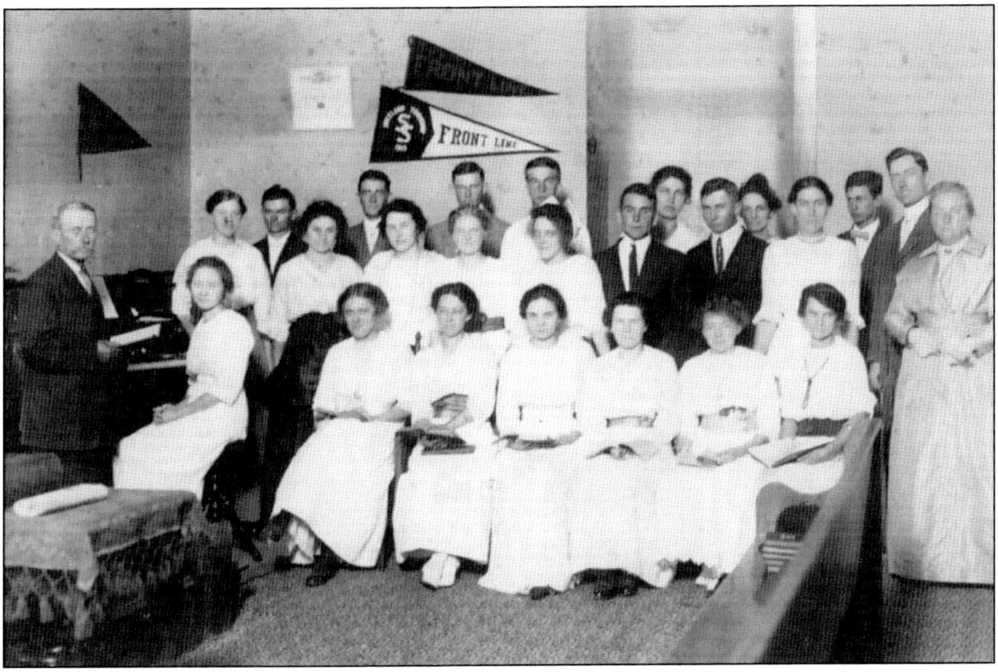

In this 1914 photograph, a group of young people at the Dunreith Friends Meeting pose for the camera, perhaps with their adult leaders. It is believed that Howard Henshaw, Edith C. Moffitt, and Flossie Crum may be among those pictured.

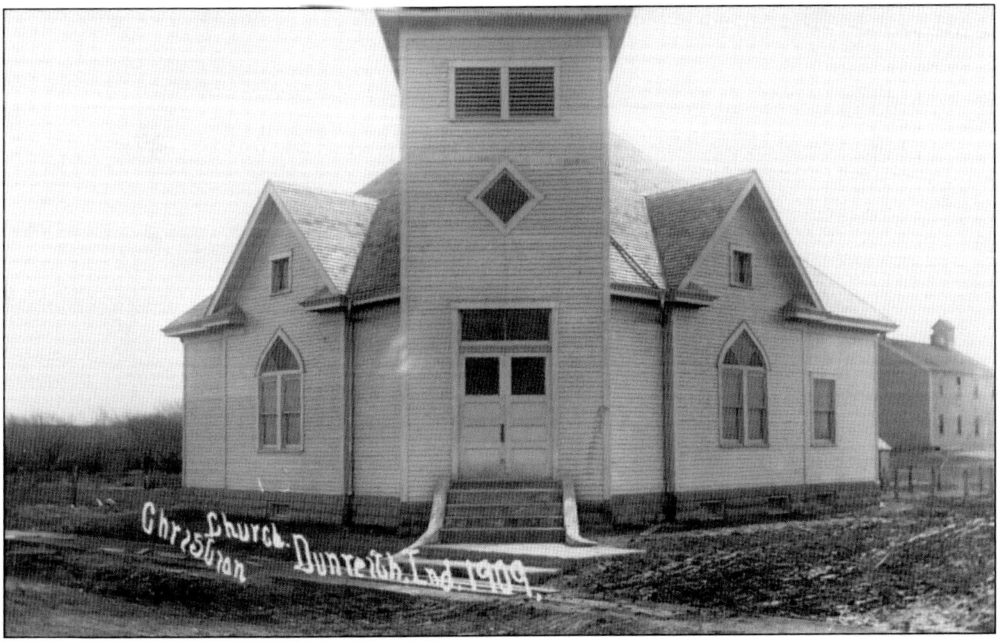

This postcard of the Dunreith Christian Church was taken shortly after the church was dedicated in January 1909. There has been a Christian church in Dunreith since 1838. In that year, Campbellites erected a log church to house their members. This old church was originally called the Buck Creek Christian Church, named for the nearby stream, and was south of the Pennsylvania Railroad and the Dunreith Cemetery.

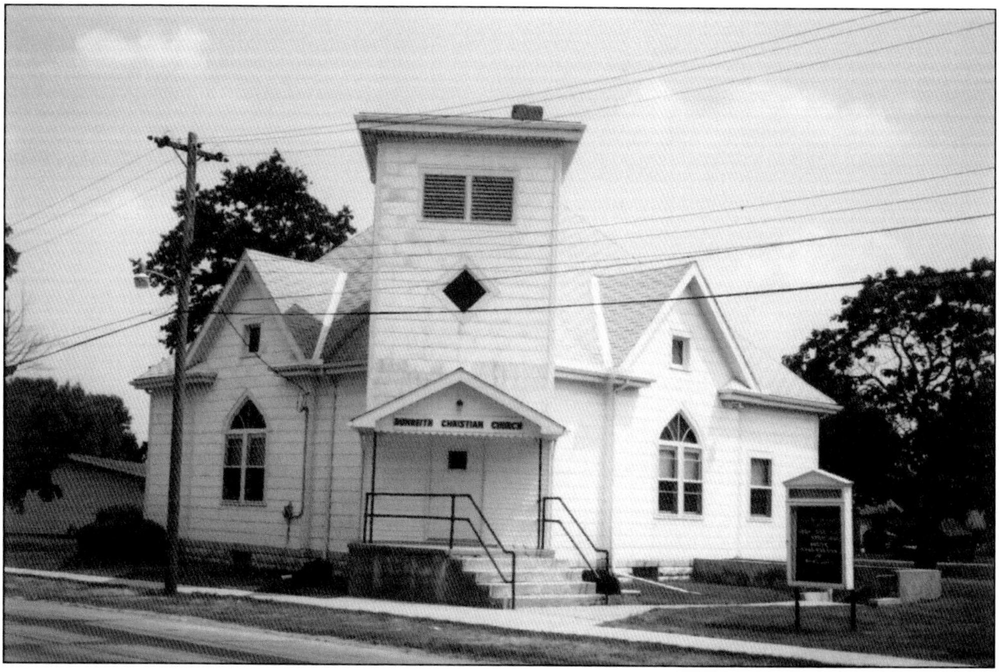

In 1875, the name Buck Creek Christian Church was dropped, and the church reorganized and was renamed the Dunreith Christian Church. Located on State Road 3, the church was frequently host to travelers who would stop for Sunday services. Other than the addition of a porch and different front steps, the outward appearance of the church has changed little over the years.

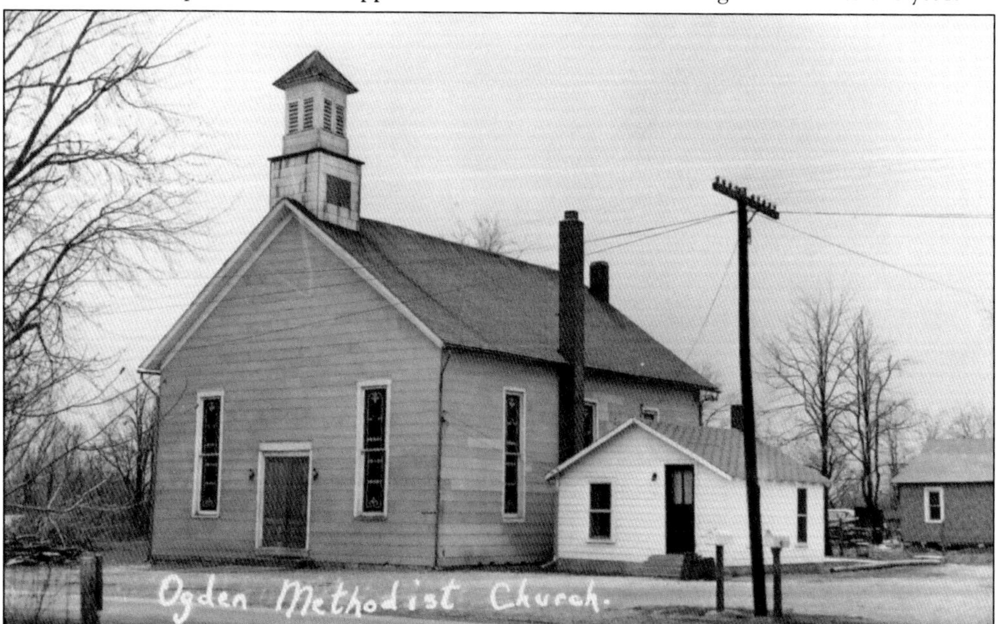

The Ogden Methodist Church came into being during the Civil War. During the formative years of the church, members met in various homes and in the town hall until the church pictured here was completed around 1874. This photograph was taken in 1963. The church closed on July 1, 2012.

Shown here is the first Methodist church to serve the Spiceland community. Erected in 1877, the church was located on East Maple Street. When a new church was built in 1905, this building was sold to blacksmith John J. Grau and moved to East Main Street. Later, the building was purchased by Lemuel Rifner and used as a fruit storage facility.

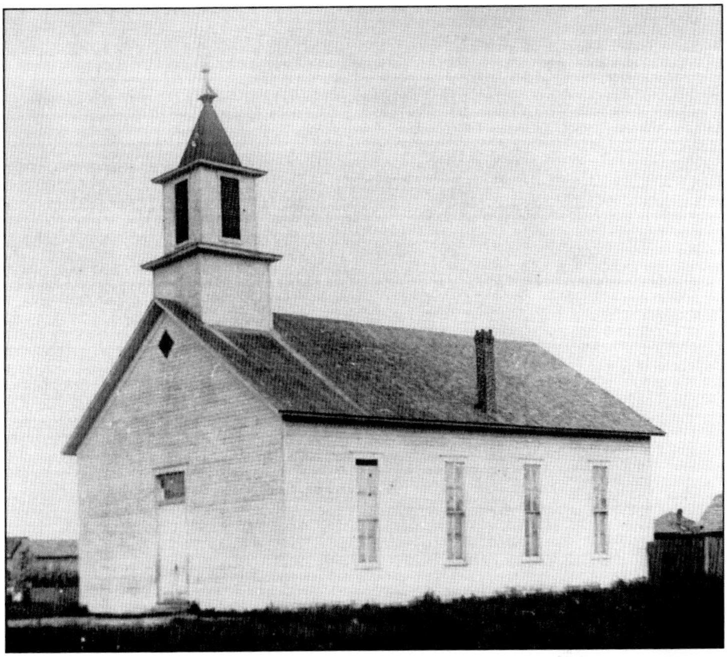

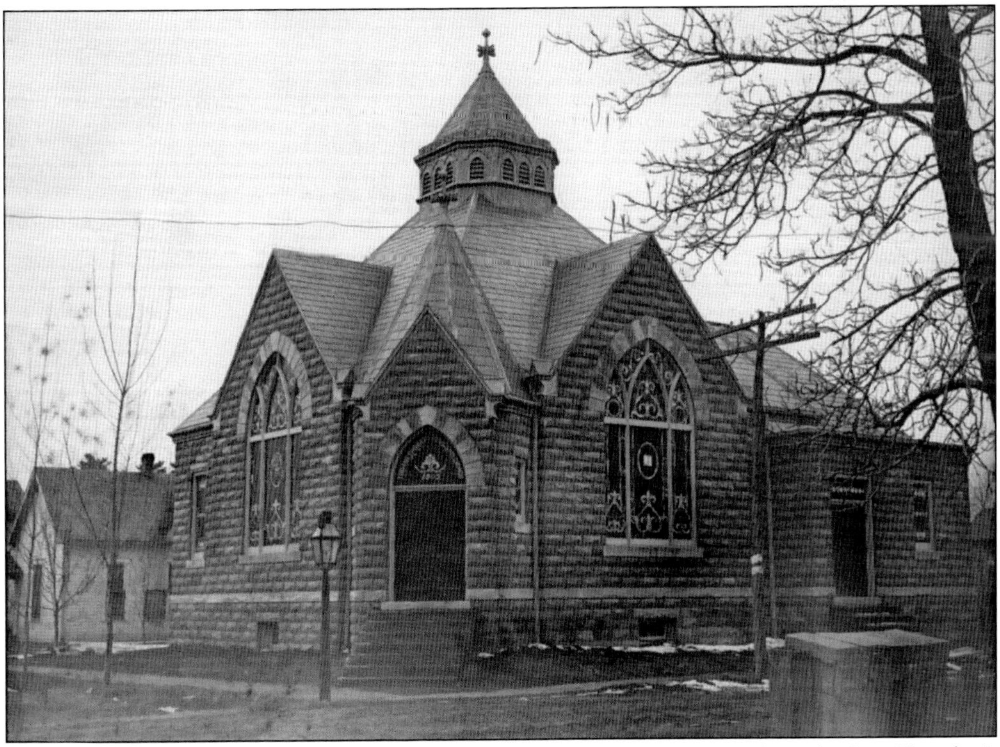

This is the earliest known photograph of the present Spiceland United Methodist Church. It was erected in 1905 at a cost of $5,000 and dedicated on February 25, 1906. The architect, a gentleman from Richmond, Indiana, charged $80 for his services. Pews for the new church cost $131.76, and the stained-glass windows were purchased for $308.45. Of note in this photograph is the gas streetlight.

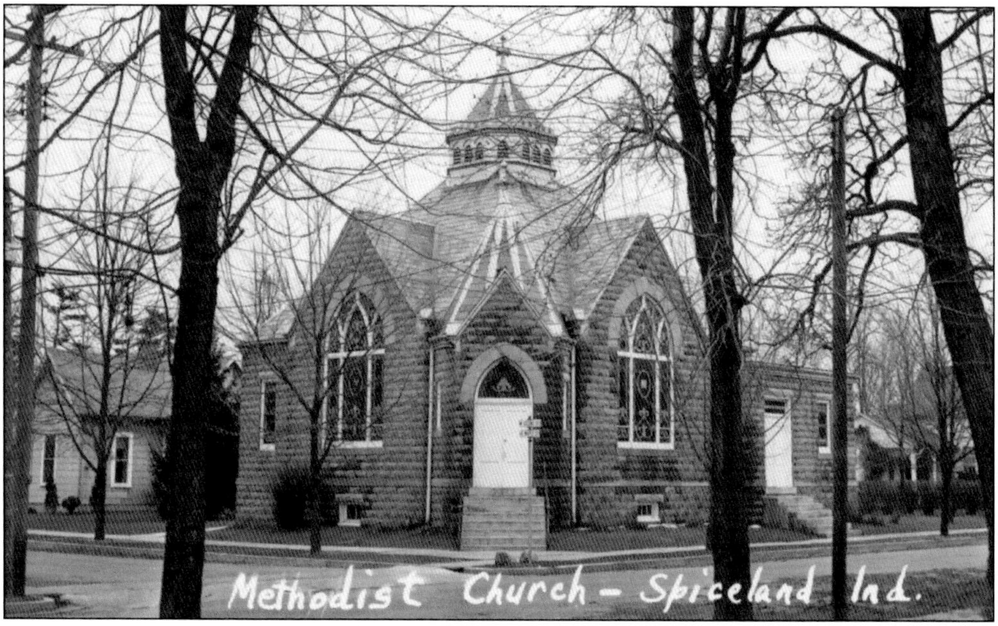

The outward appearance of the Spiceland United Methodist Church has not changed much since the building was dedicated. In this 1963 photograph, the church parsonage can be seen on the left.

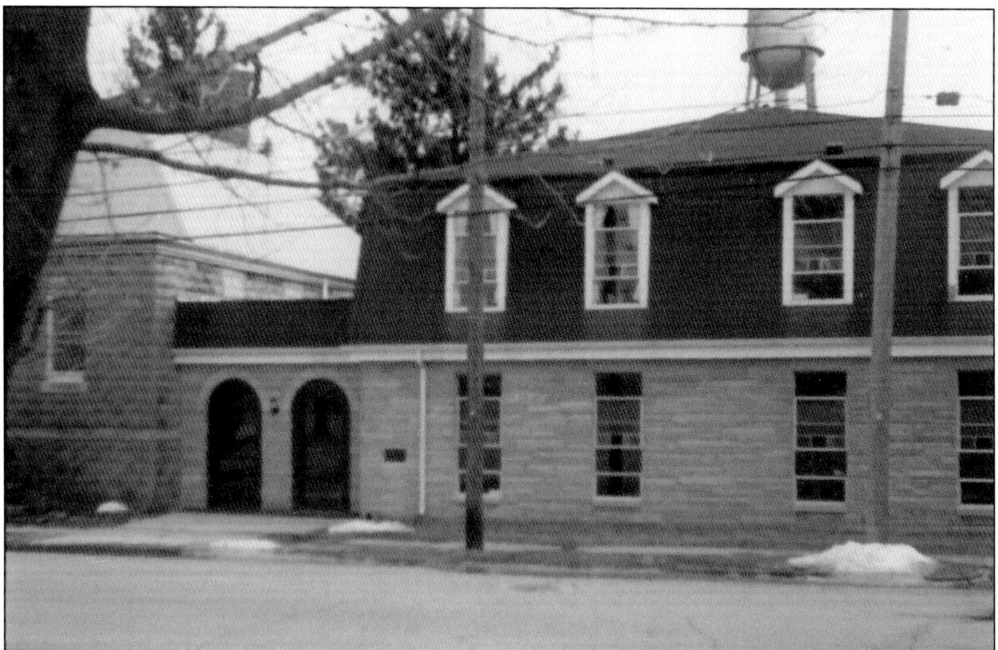
Sunday-school work has always been faithfully carried out by the Spiceland Methodist congregation. S.E. Pickering, a teacher in the Spiceland grade school, served as Sunday school superintendent for 41 years. A ground-breaking service for a new educational wing (shown here) was held on June 5, 1966.

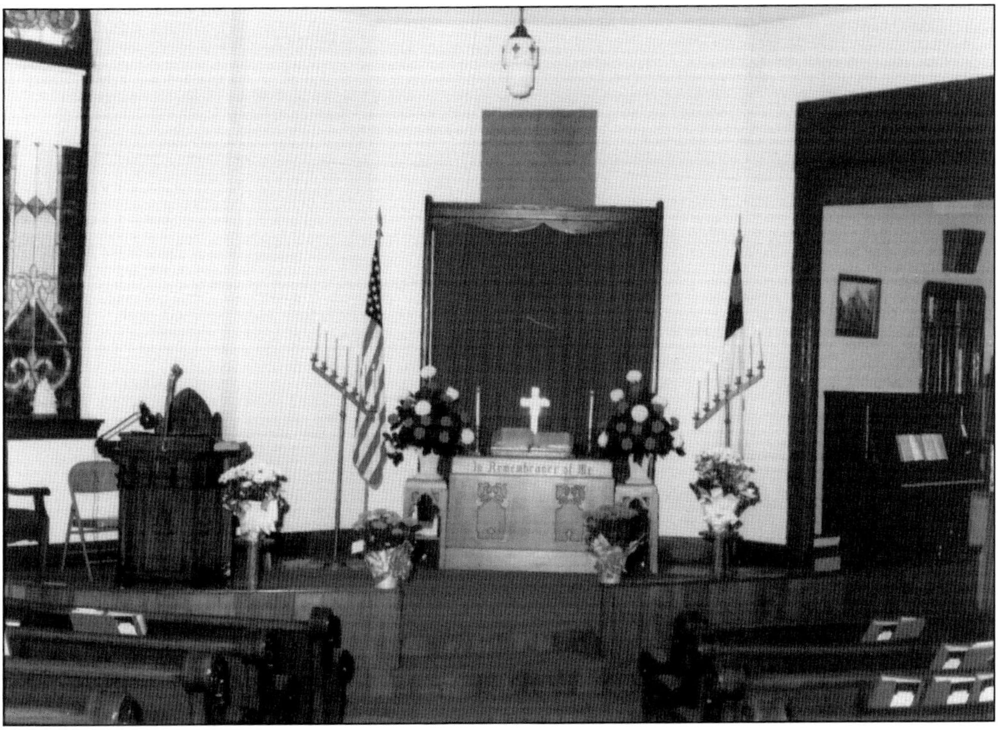

The interior of the Spiceland United Methodist Church is seen in this photograph, taken in the fall of 1977.

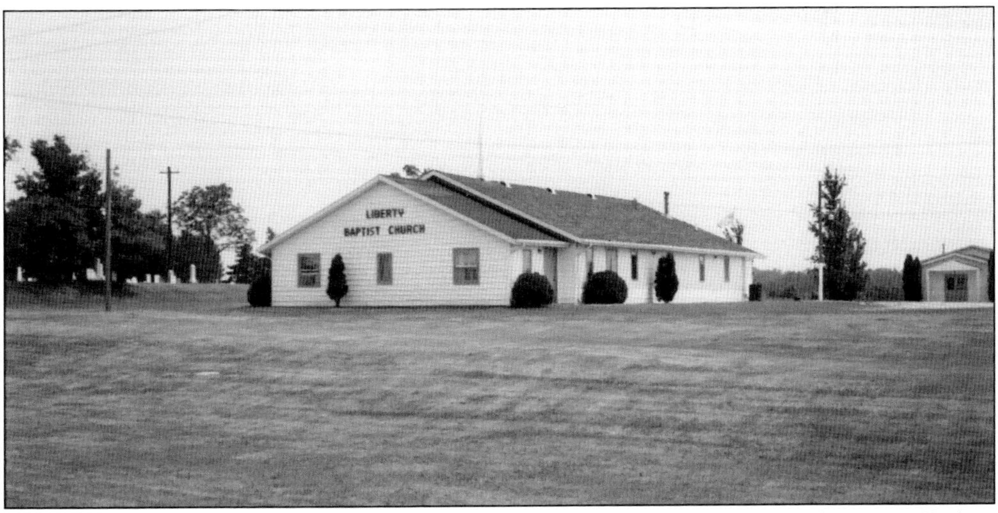

The Liberty Baptist Church at Dunreith was founded in 1982 by Rev. Leonard R. Dice. Earlier, in the 1960s, Dice had started a Baptist church in Spiceland, but it closed.

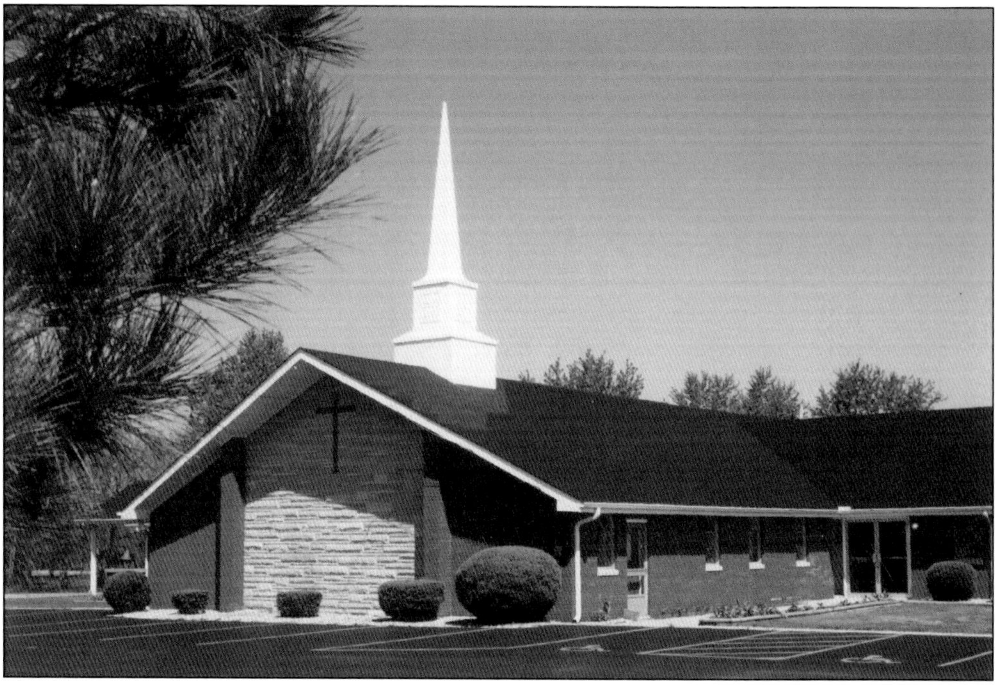

The Spiceland Church of the Nazarene was founded in 1963 by Rev. Bill Selvidge. Located on State Road 3 in Spiceland, it remains very active in ministry to the community and surrounding areas. In 2013, the church celebrated its 50th anniversary. (Courtesy of Mark Herbkersman.)

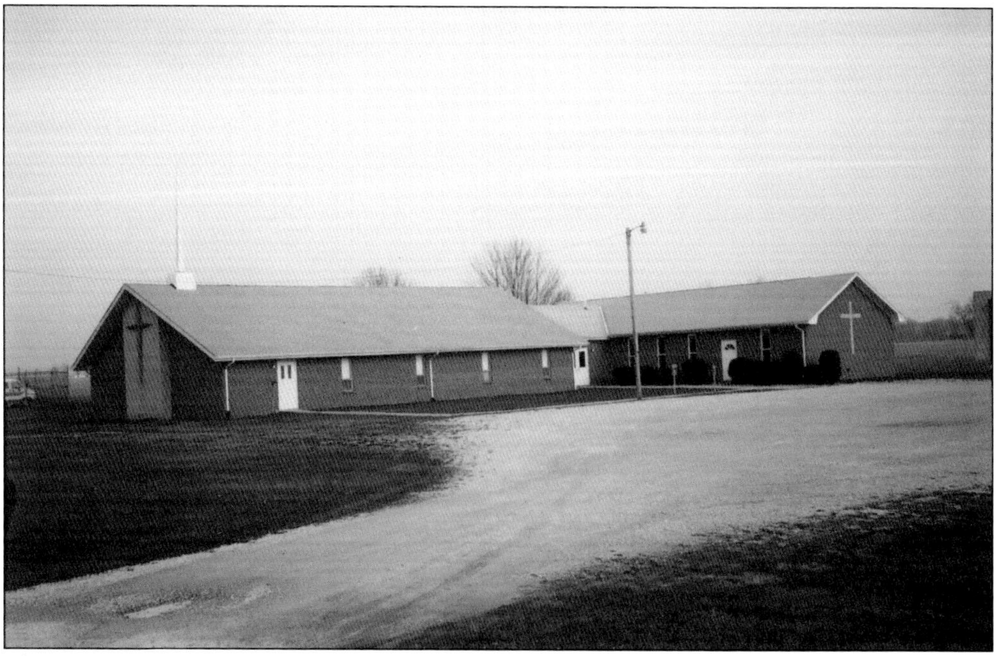

The Smyrna Baptist Church, sometimes referred to as the Smyrna Missionary Baptist Church, was organized on October 2, 1968. The first portion of the present church was dedicated on October 18, 1970, and ground was broken on April 10, 1977, for the addition of a larger auditorium. The church is located at the southeastern edge of Spiceland. (Courtesy of Larry Delon.)

Three

BE IT EVER SO HUMBLE

A variety of different types of older homes can be found today in Spiceland Township, from simple cottages to grand Victorian Italianate edifices. Thomas (1782–1867) and Mary Greenstreet (1787–1870)—who, on March 2, 1822, became the fourth family to move to this unbroken wilderness—found the forest full of Indians, bears, and deer. Wolves made nightmares of the nights with their doleful howls. Their first home was a crude structure made of forked poles, with saplings and brush spread over the poles for a roof.

The pioneers who inhabited the earliest of the homes shown were poor and dependent upon each other in many respects, but these men and women were otherwise nearly self-supporting. Besides their provisions, they raised flax and wool and made nearly all of their own wearing apparel and bedding.

The diet in the early pioneer township homes was simple and not very nutritious. Corn bread and wild game, such as squirrel, venison, and wild turkey, were plentiful. Very few vegetables were available. Milk and butter were usually available, but coffee, tea, and fruit were considered luxuries for special occasions. These things mainly constituted the bill of fare in the homes of the early pioneers.

Three of the homes pictured in this section date back to the 1830s. Blueprints for another home came from New York City, with a local carpenter in charge of the house's construction. In the late 1920s, Sears, Roebuck & Co. shipped a complete home to Spiceland by rail. Of course, assembly was required locally. One of the Victorian homes pictured is so large that two furnaces are required to heat it.

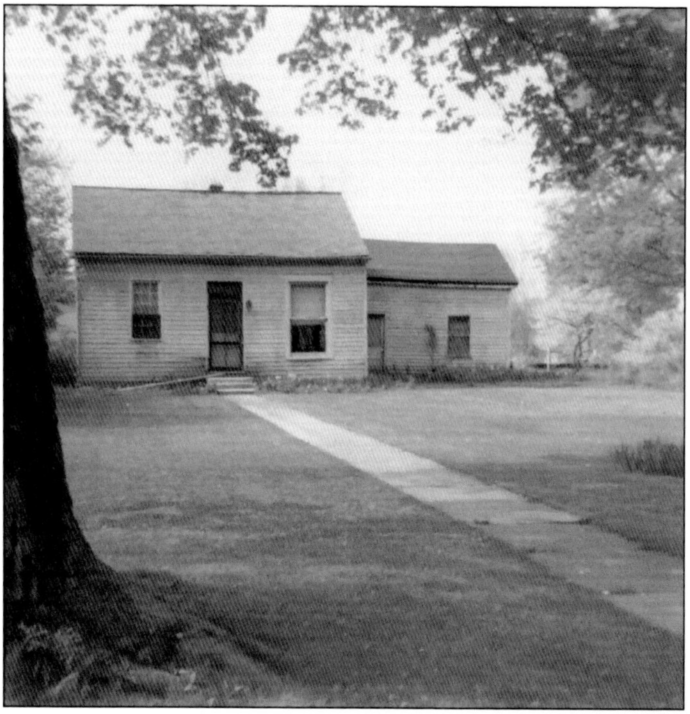

This was originally the Spiceland home of Charles Boone, his sisters Dorcas and Betsy, and their mother, also named Dorcas Boone. The next owners were Dr. Henry T. Jones (1845–1922) and his wife, Carrie (1856–1918). Dr. Jones used the wing on the right for his office. The home was eventually razed.

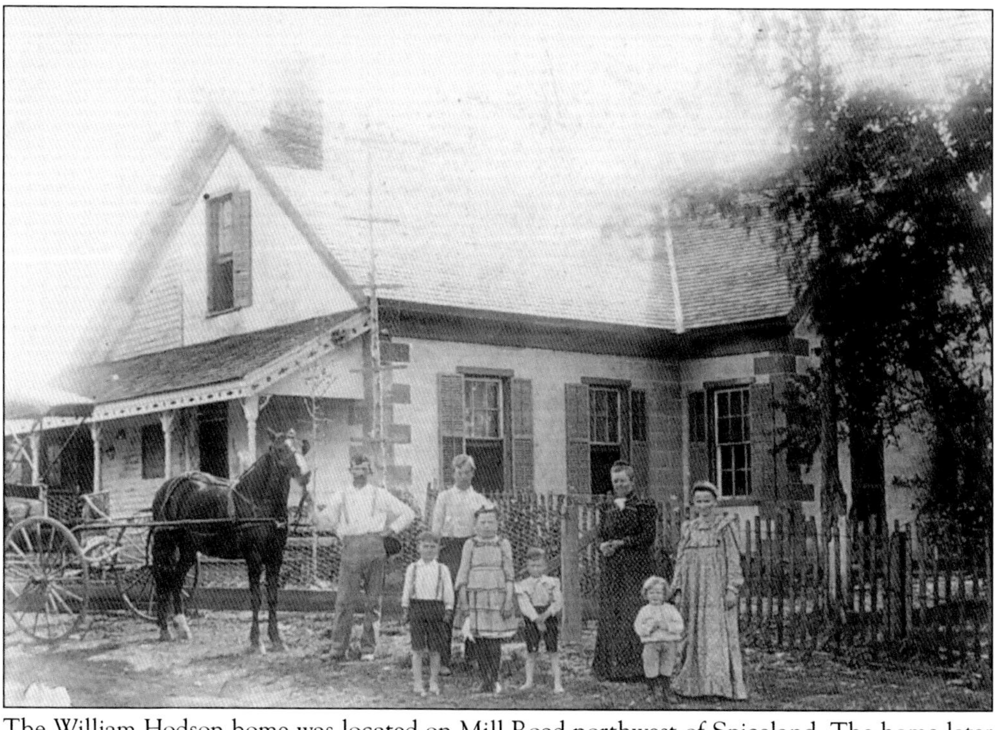

The William Hodson home was located on Mill Road northwest of Spiceland. The home later burned down. Standing in the yard in this April 1902 photograph are, from left to right, (first row) Jesse Jackson, Georgia Hodson, Guy Jackson, and Cassell Jackson; (second row) Clarence Jackson, Omar "Ben" Hodson, Sarah Jane Hodson, and Belle Jackson. (Courtesy of Martha Resler.)

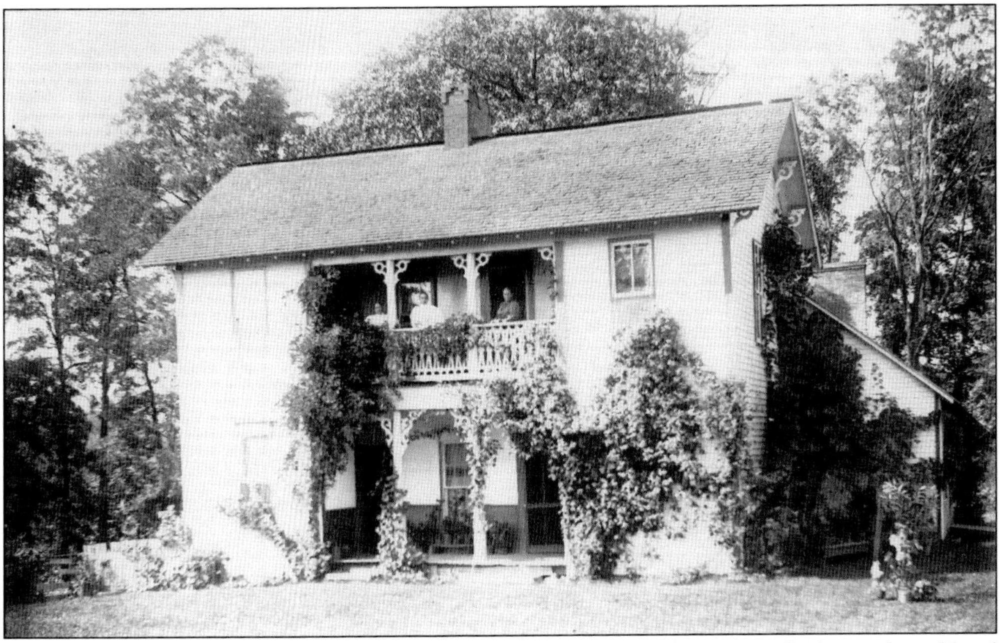

Isaac Hodson (1795–1890) arrived in Spiceland from North Carolina in 1825. He purchased land and then built a pole log cabin, where the first school in the community was held. As the years passed, he added to his cabin and covered it with siding. Hodson married Welmet Elliott in 1829. Albert Hodson, the youngest of their five children, remained with his parents and married Mary Emily Hiatt in 1875. He then added the two stories seen here to the house his father had built. By 1985, the home was in deplorable condition and was burned down by the owner.

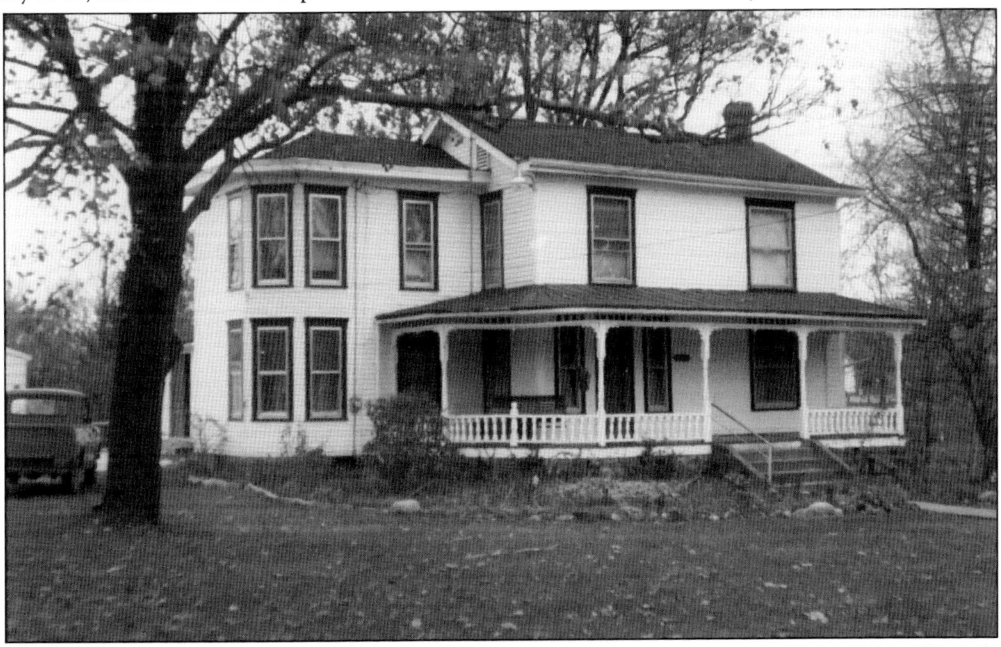

Erected in the 1860s, this Spiceland home was the residence of Nathan (1821–1895) and Sarah Scovell (1824–1870). The home has beautiful parquet floors and pink fireplaces in the front living rooms.

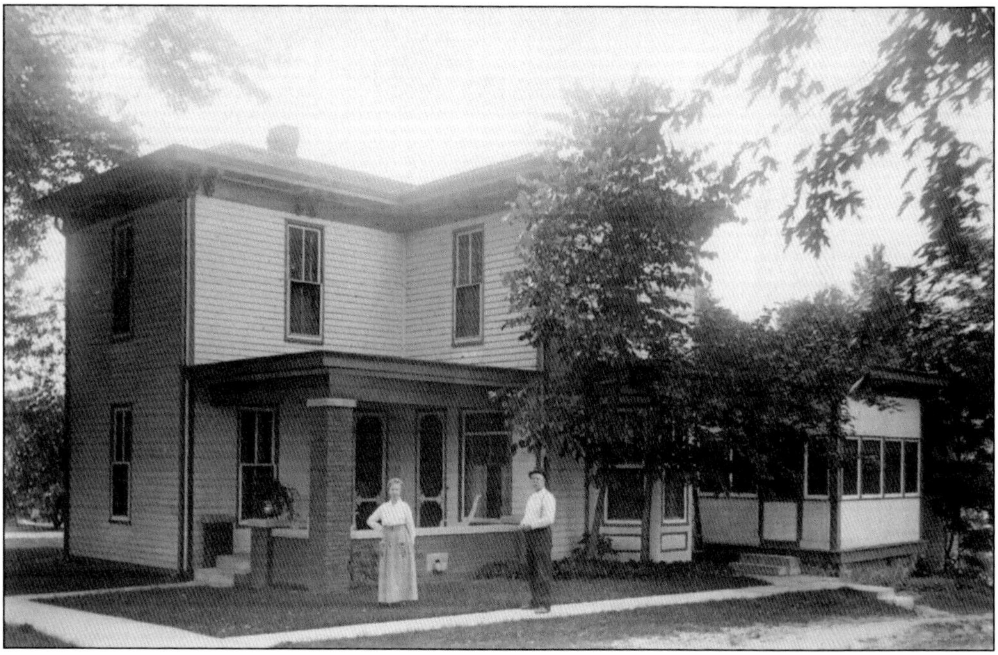

Oliver C. and Edna Steele are seen here around 1915 in front of their home on West Broad Street in Spiceland. Steele was the founder and owner of the Oliver C. Steele Manufacturing Company.

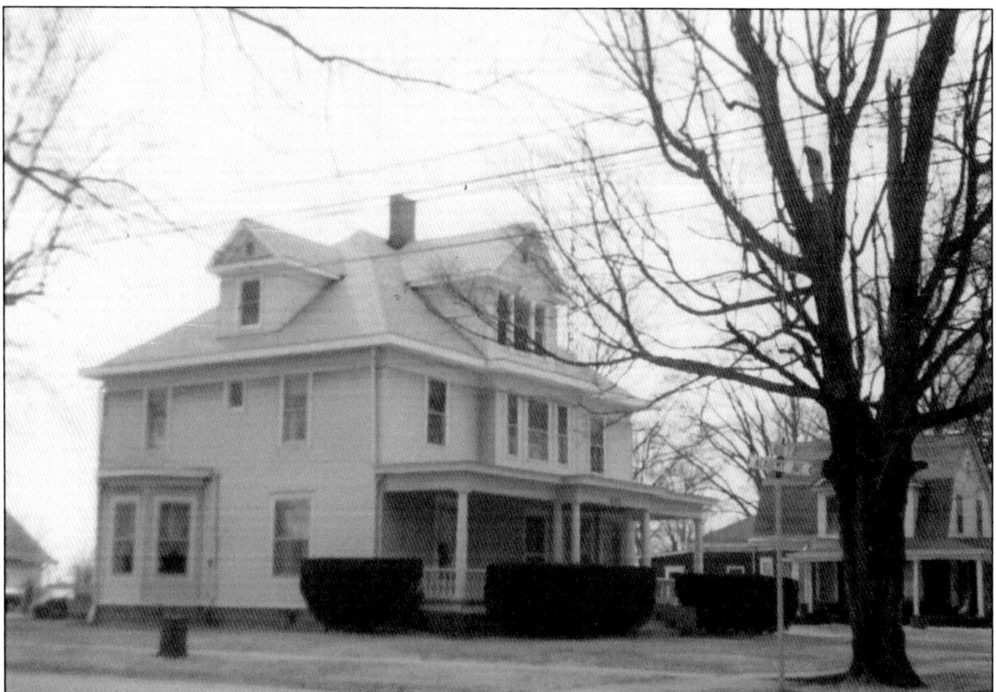

Spiceland merchant John S. Griffin and his wife, Ruth, had this beautiful West Broad Street home built in 1898. The home has three stories, an open staircase, and beautiful woodwork.

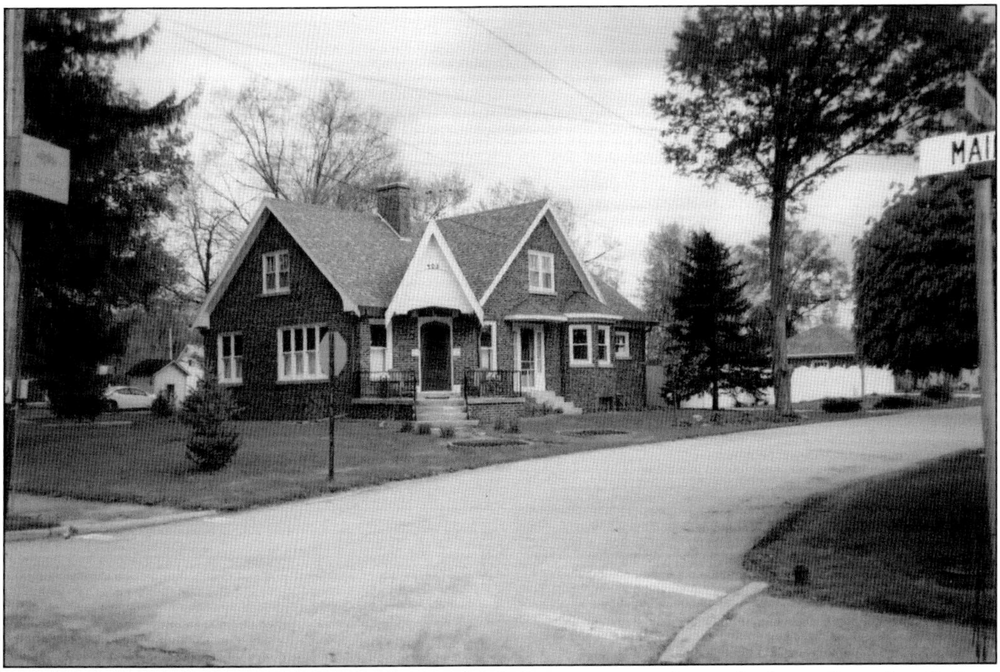

Charles L. Stubbs and his wife, Parthenia, had this attractive home built on Spiceland's East Main Street in 1935. An earlier home had occupied the spot, but it was moved to East Maple Street so this one could be built.

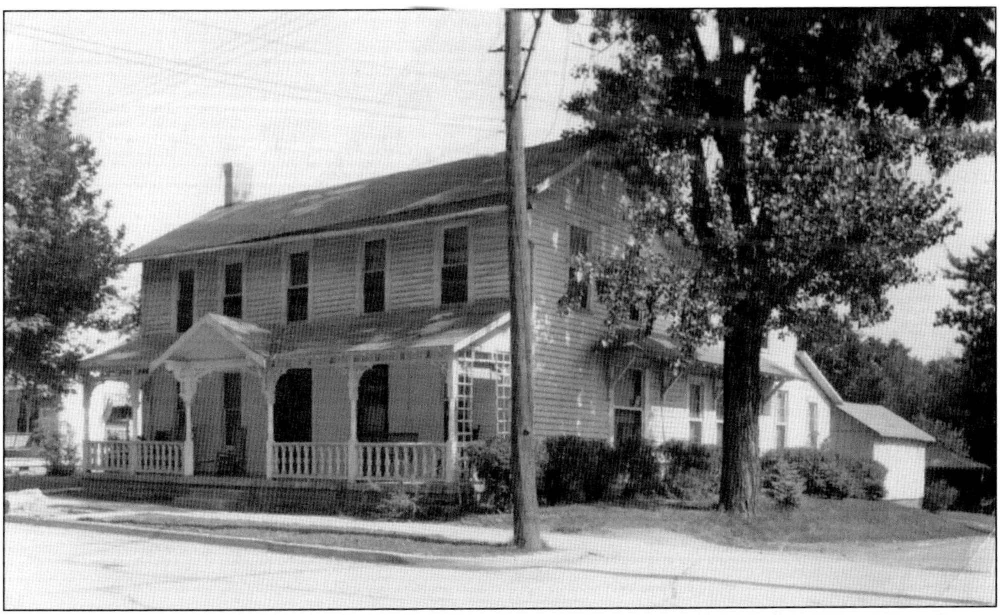

Pictured here in 1938 is the home known for years as "the Beehive," located on West Main Street in Spiceland. The name comes from the fact that it has been the center of activity, or beehive, for years. Erected prior to 1838, the home served as Spiceland's first post office. The Federal-style home, whose Victorian porch was added at a later date, was a depot on the Underground Railroad in the pre–Civil War days. Slaves were hidden in a concealed cupboard. In the early 1900s, it operated as a hotel known as the Haisley House.

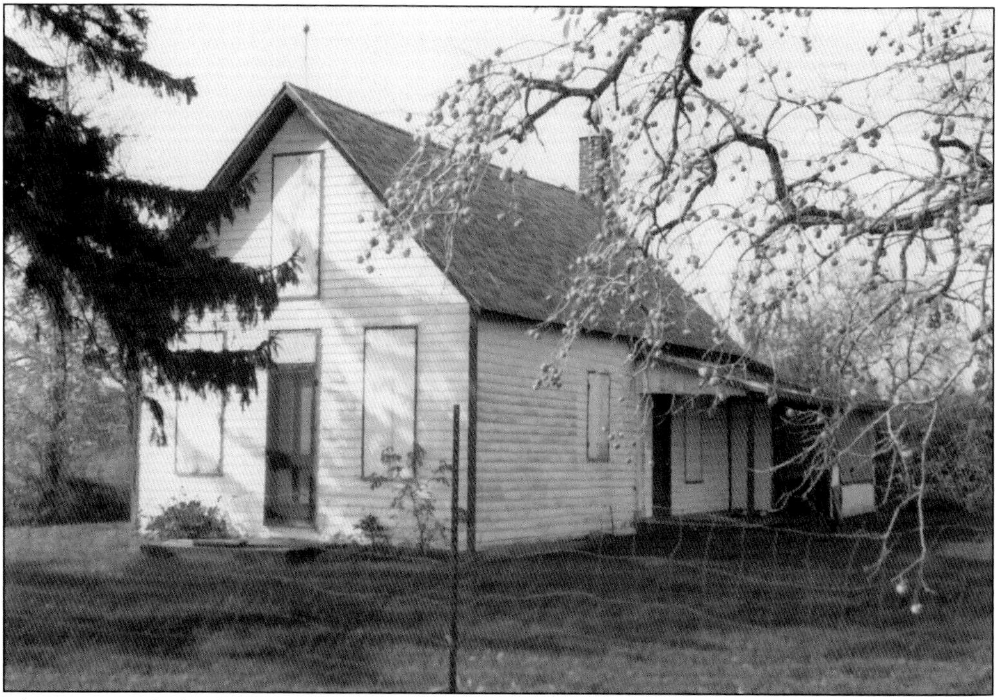

The cottage of Charles and Bertha Elliott stood northeast of Spiceland and was razed in 1979. Seen in this photograph are branches of a large persimmon tree loaded with fruit. At one time, 32 such trees were located on the property; they were planted from seeds brought back from Kansas following a 1904 trip that included a stop at the St. Louis World's Fair. People came from miles around every fall for persimmons, and they were sold for 10¢ a quart.

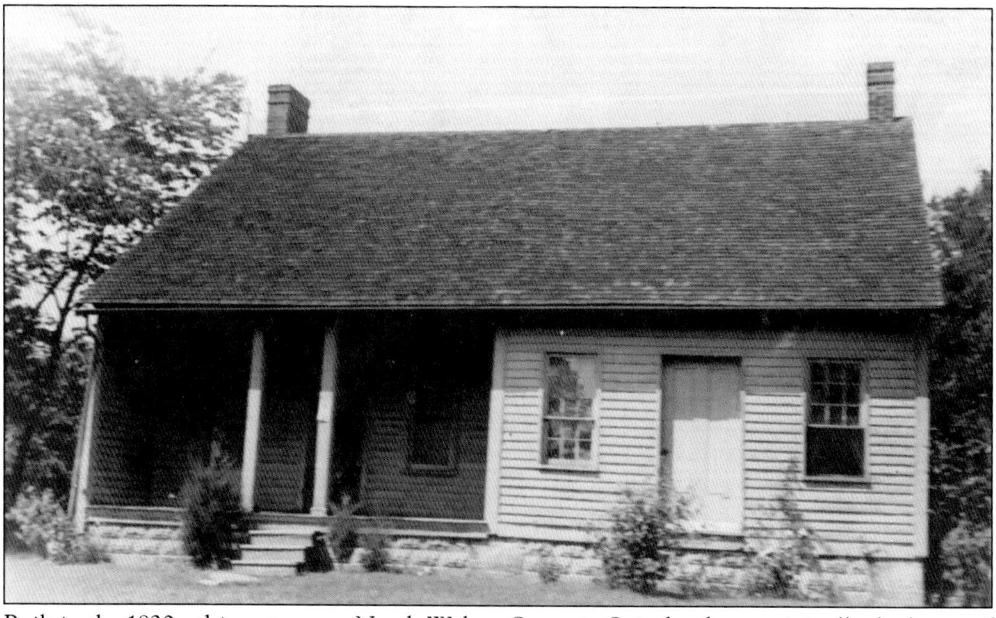

Built in the 1830s, this cottage on North Walnut Street in Spiceland was originally the home of George and Mary Evans. Later owners were Alfred (1808–1871) and Charity Bogue (1817–1910). Pictured in 1938, the home still serves as a residence today.

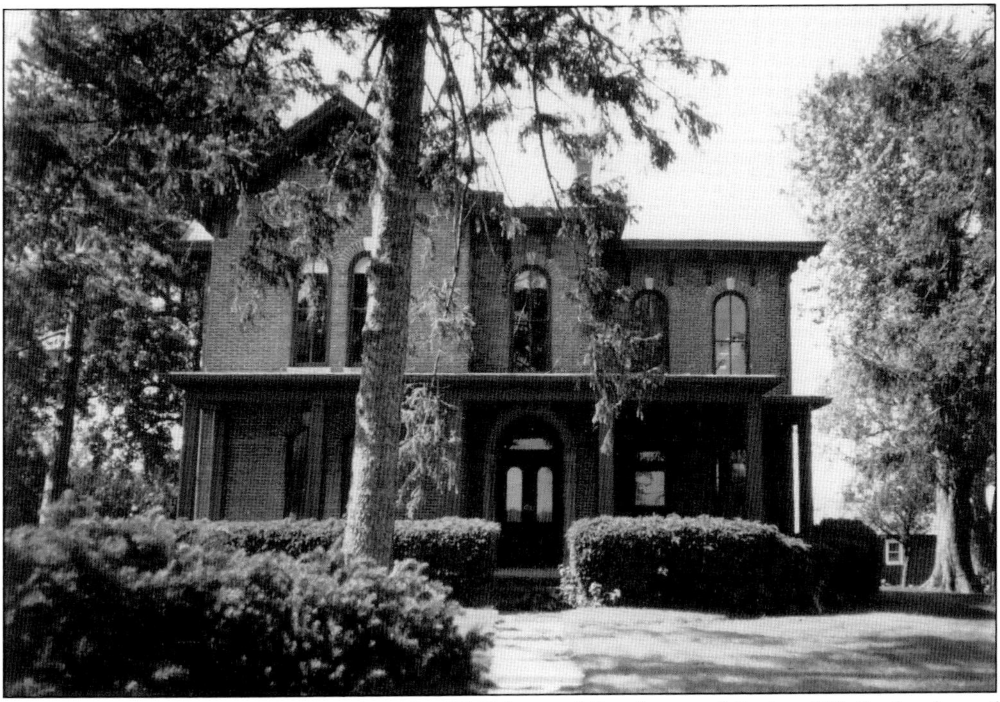

The Eli F. Hodson home is located on the Old National Road west of Ogden. While the date of its construction is unknown, it is Italianate in design, has double front doors, and is heated by two furnaces. Hodson, a merchant first in Spiceland and then in Knightstown, died in 1887.

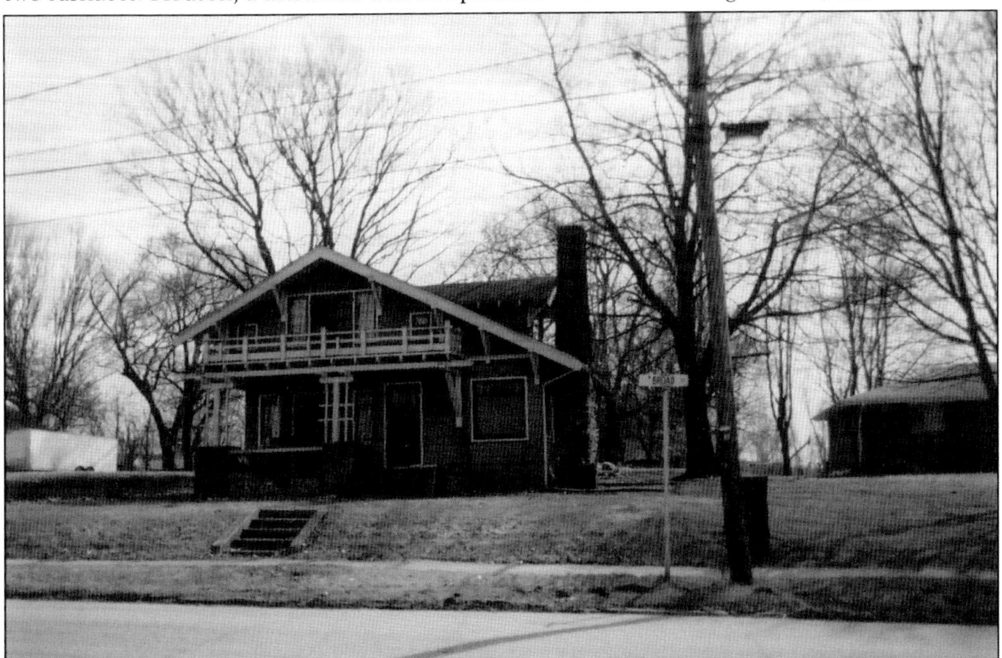

New Castle and Spiceland mortician V.T. Davis and his wife, Blanche, had this home built in the 1920s. Plans for the home were found in a Sears, Roebuck & Co. catalog. Material for the home was purchased, sent to Spiceland by rail, and then assembled by local contractors.

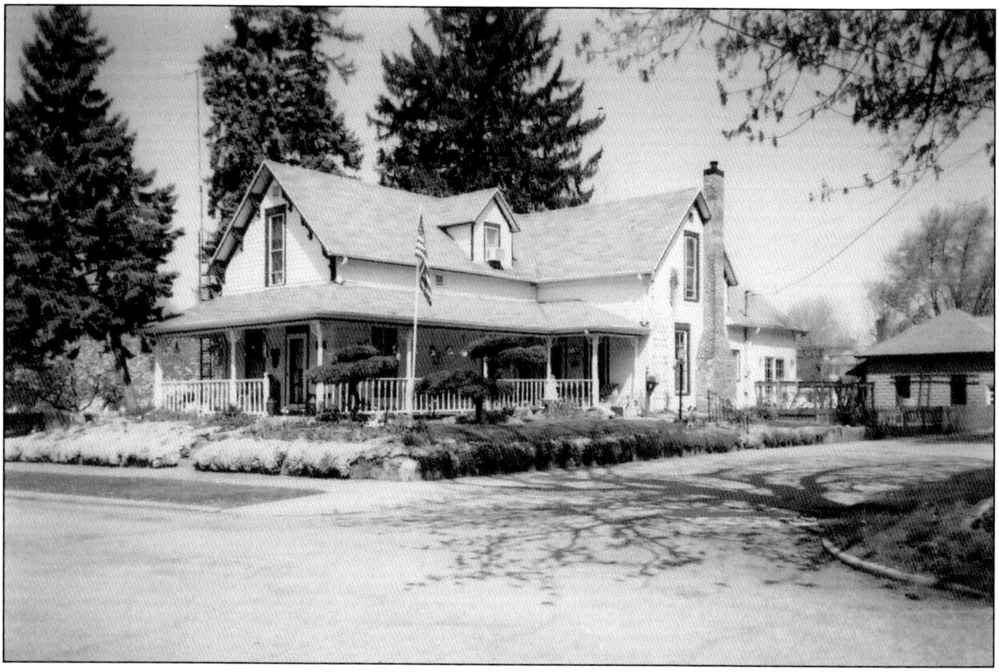

It is not known when Luther O. and Emma Draper acquired this East Broad Street home in Spiceland. While the Drapers lived there, it was known for its extensive gardens, complete with trelliswork, benches, seasonal flowers, stone walkways, and a fishpond. The fishpond remains to this day, nearly 70 years after the death of Emma Draper.

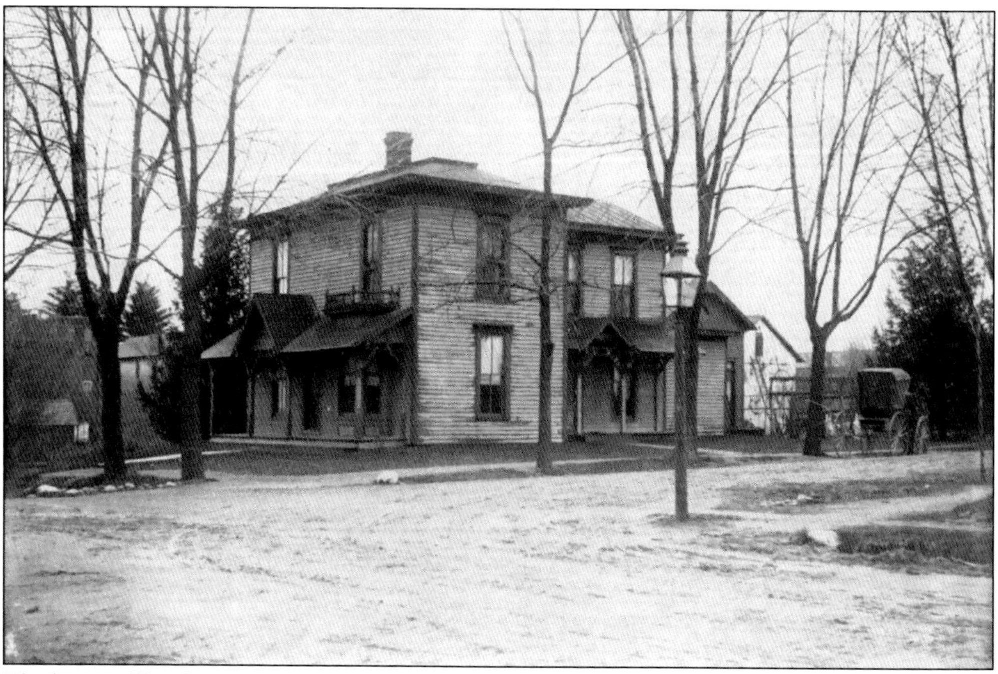

The home of Dr. George D. Baily, founder of the Spiceland Sanitarium, was located at the corner of Broad and South Pearl Streets in Spiceland. Later occupants were Dr. Jehu Stuart and then Dr. Hockett. Shown here in 1896, the residence was razed in the 1950s.

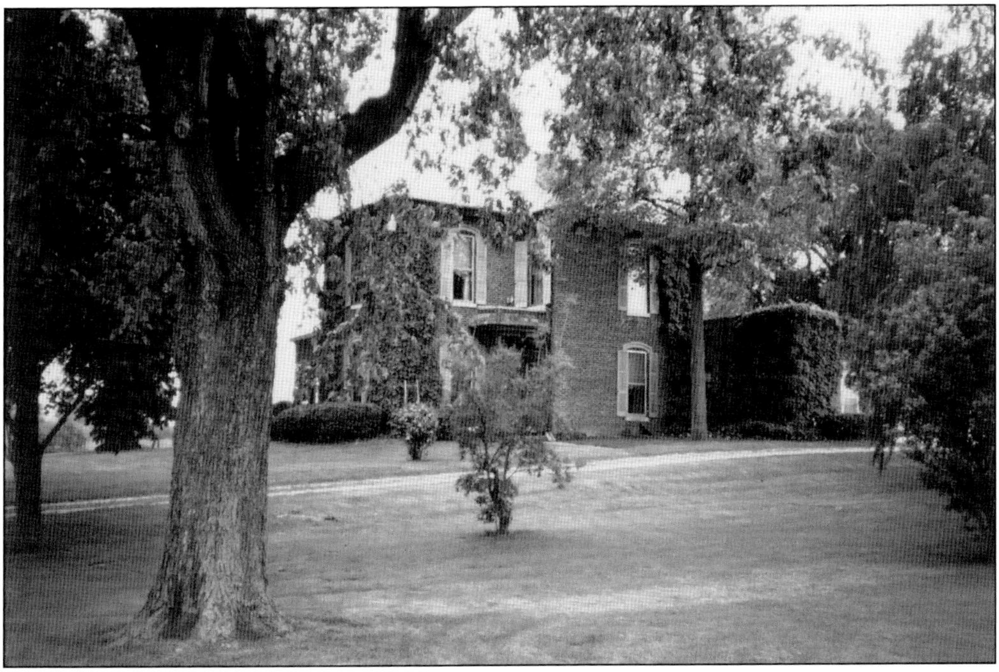

Located on the Spiceland Pike north of Dunreith is this home, built by William (1827–1904) and Caroline Edgerton (1831–1917). Active abolitionists and prohibitionists, one unique feature of the home is the ruby-red glass front door, which enables a person to look outside from the inside of the home but prevents the person on the outside from being able to view the home's interior. Edgerton's tombstone in Circle Grove Cemetery reads, "Always faithful to his convictions of right, regardless alike of the praise or blame of his fellow man."

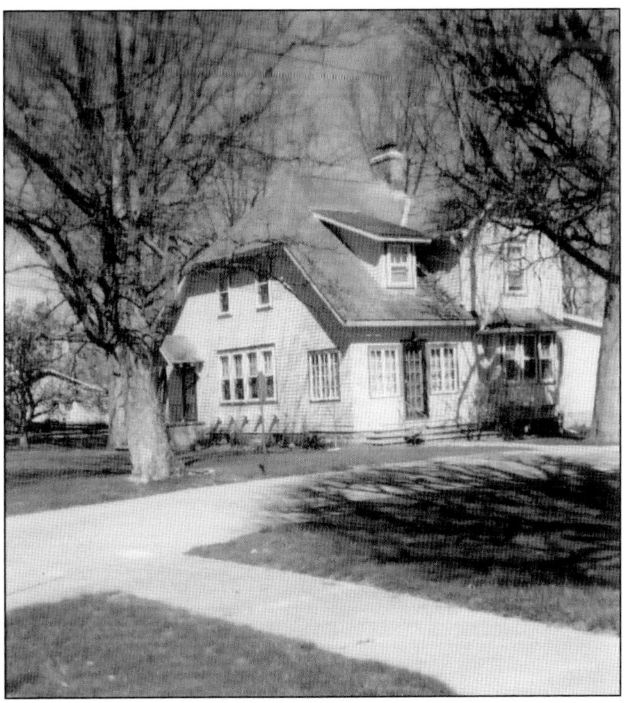

A.J. Simberg, a resident of New York City and an architect with the firm Building Age, drew the plans for the Spiceland home of Elmer F. and Jessie Pidgeon in 1921. The home was built in 1922 by Sylvester "Ves" Lykins, a local contractor.

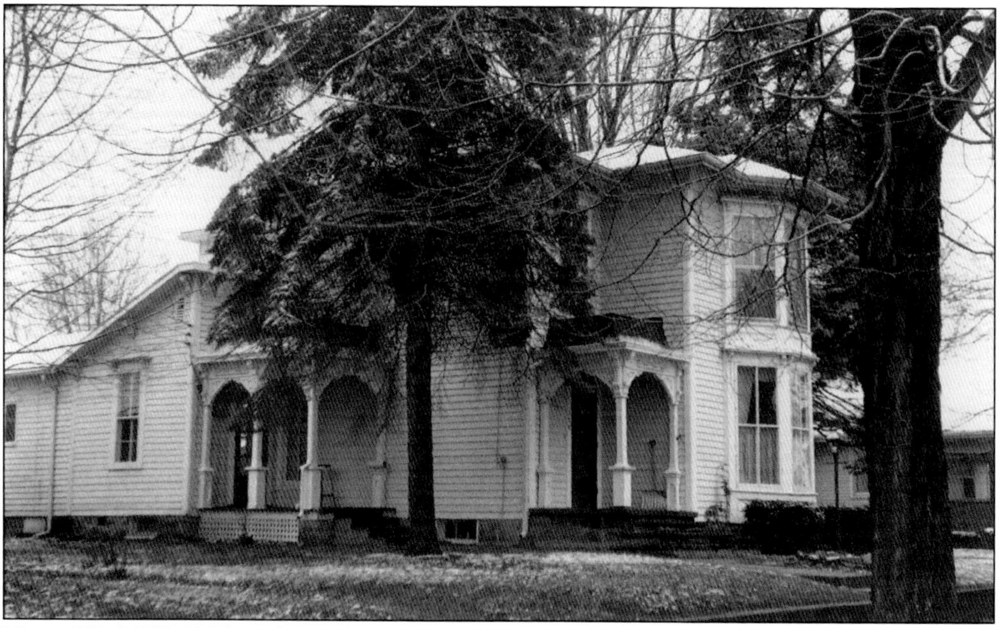

Henry W. (1837–1920) and Martha E. Charles (1847–1923) had this home built on Spiceland's South Pearl Street in the 1880s.

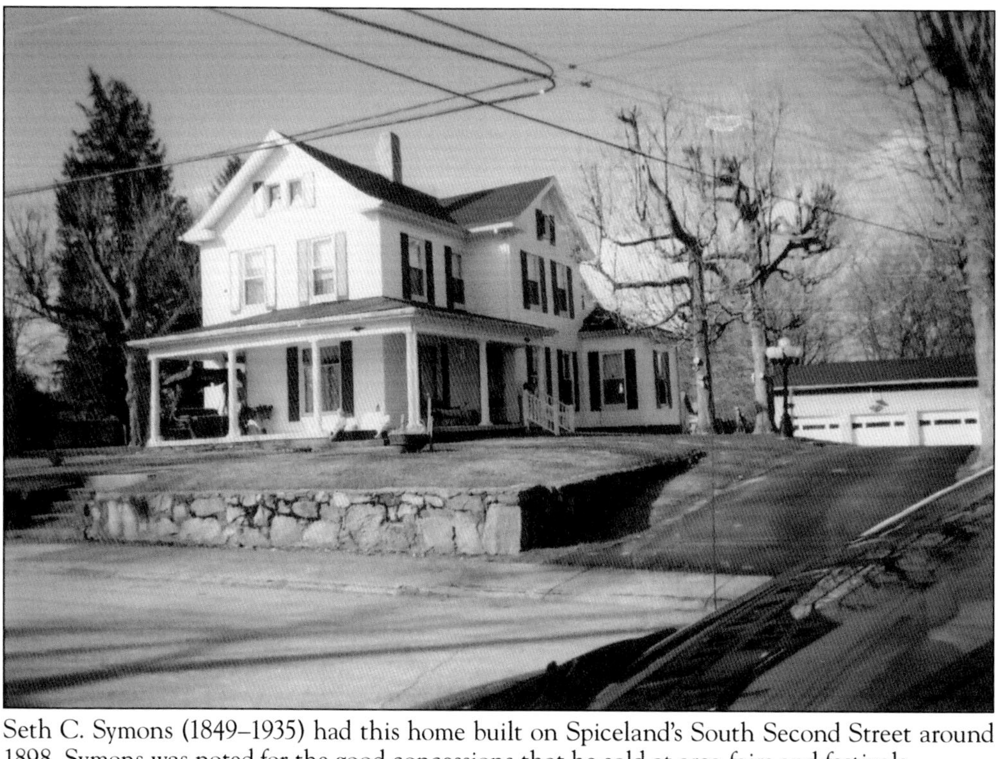

Seth C. Symons (1849–1935) had this home built on Spiceland's South Second Street around 1898. Symons was noted for the good concessions that he sold at area fairs and festivals.

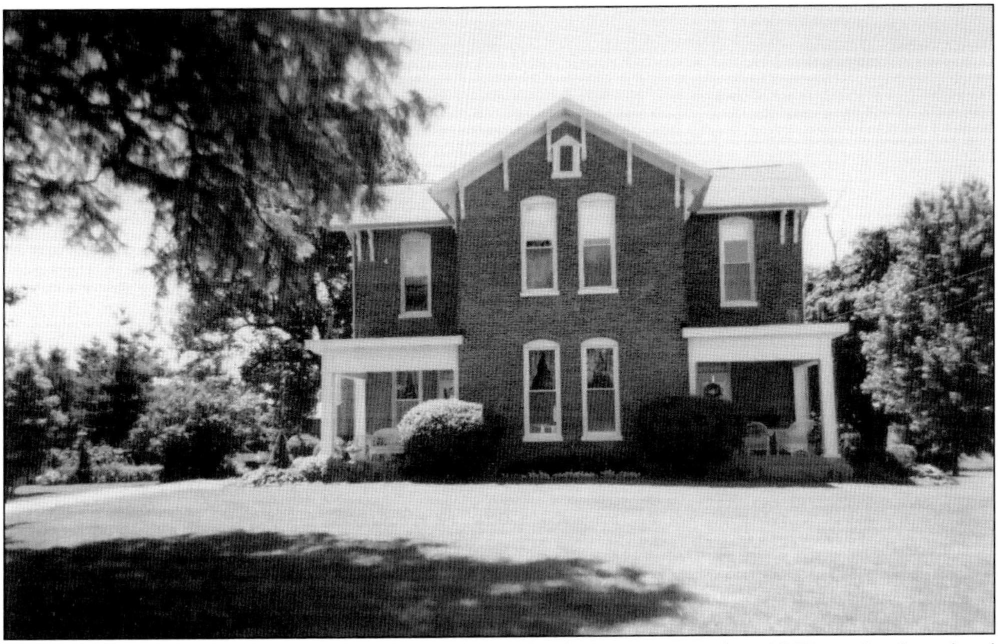

Italianate in design, the home of Elwood and Sarah Pleas was erected in 1867 on the Spiceland Pike between Dunreith and Spiceland. Elwood Pleas, a Civil War veteran, was once the editor of the *New Castle Courier*. Sarah Pleas was a peony grower, and the remains of some of her peony gardens are still visible in front of the home.

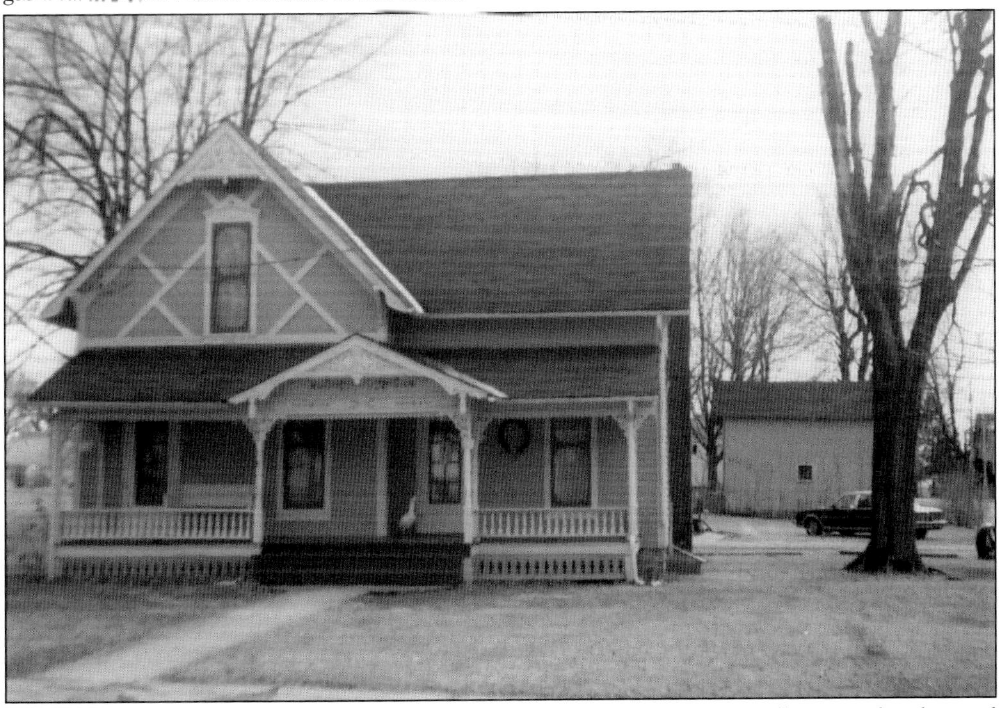

The John Stigleman home in Spiceland was erected around 1892. An excellent woodworker and the owner of a furniture factory, he made certain the trim in each room was made from a different wood, such as walnut, oak, and cherry.

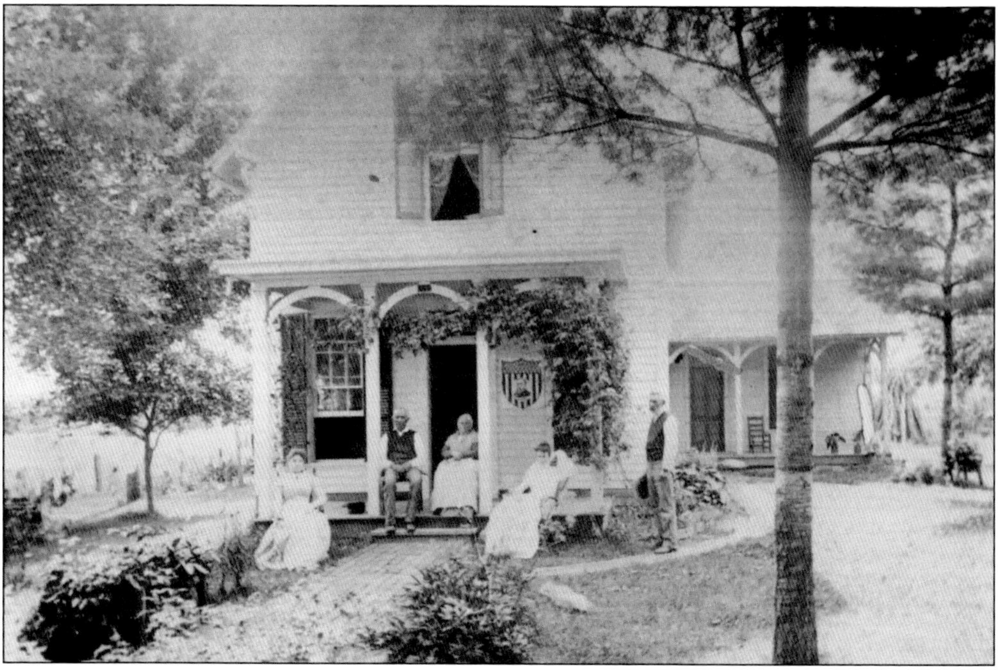

The home of John (1804–1893) and Rebecca Hiatt (1806–1897) was built in 1843 and is located on South Pearl Street in Spiceland. The Hiatts can be seen sitting on their front porch. As evidenced by the photograph of Benjamin Harrison visible on the porch wall, this image dates from either 1888, the year Harrison won the presidency, or 1892, the year he lost his bid for reelection.

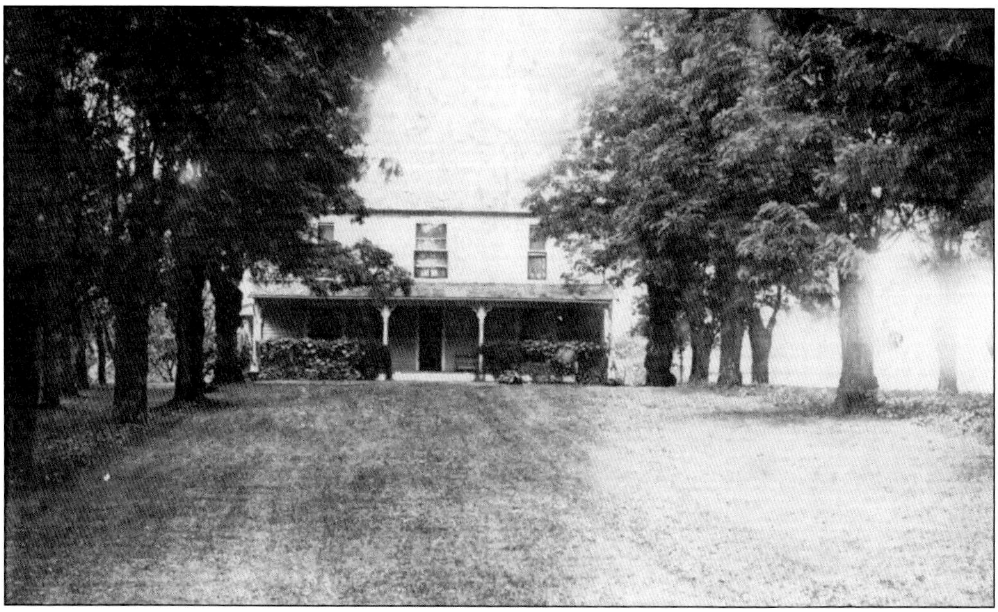

The Griffin-Moffitt home in Ogden is the subject of this 1913 photograph. Samuel Griffin (1804–1875) and his wife, Lydia (1804–1886), had the home built in 1850, the year they moved from Spiceland. The next occupants were Sarah Catherine (1850–1922), the youngest of the Griffins' 12 children, and her husband, James Moffitt (1842–1909). The home is still standing today but is in deplorable condition.

Four

Dear Old Golden Rule Days

Education has always been a top priority for residents of Spiceland Township. Isaac Hodson (1795–1890) conducted the first school in the township in 1826, using his log cabin for instructional purposes. Quakers soon took up the matter of educating their children, and, by 1851, a frame school had been constructed. In 1861, another frame building was built, and the school began to come into prominence.

The year 1863 marked a new period in the history of the Spiceland school, with the employment of Clarkson and Hannah Davis. This husband-and-wife team was keenly aware of the opportunities for further development of the school. Because of their influence, the school was incorporated in 1870. With that act, Spiceland Academy had its beginning.

Although a brick building was erected in 1872, a new building was needed by 1912. The old building was razed, and a new brick one was constructed. Until this time, the expenses of the school had been met by the tuition paid by the students and by an endowment that had been established by members of the Spiceland Friends Meeting, with other people interested in the welfare of the school also donating. Later, arrangements were made whereby public school corporations could pay the tuition of students. The academy then served as the high school for Spiceland Township, and many students came from adjoining townships and nearby states.

However, this all changed in 1917 when the attorney general of Indiana handed down the opinion that private and parochial schools were not intended to be included in the interpretation of an earlier law as being schools to which public school trustees might transfer high school students and pay their tuition. This was a death blow to the academy. Even though a valiant effort was launched by the Friends meeting to save the school, it was not to be.

The academy's last graduating class was in 1921. In 1922, the entire facility was sold to the township, and the former academy became a public high school. From that date until the school closed in 1969, Spiceland Township students attended Spiceland High School, using the same building that had once been known as Spiceland Academy. The school was the next-to-last Friends academy closed in Indiana.

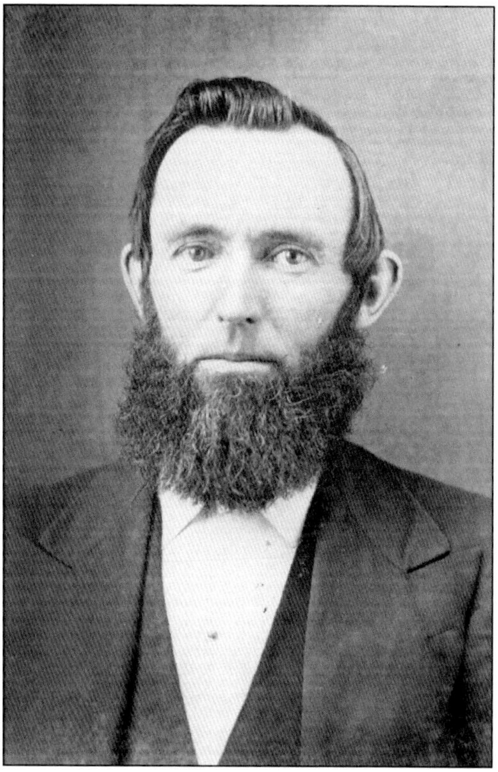

Clarkson Davis (1833–1883) and his wife, Hannah E. Davis (1841–1898), came to Spiceland to teach in 1863. This husband-and-wife team is credited with founding Spiceland Academy. Even though Clarkson Davis was never in robust health, he and his wife devoted all of their energy to the school. He served as superintendent from 1863 to 1867, 1868 to 1874, and 1876 to 1882. Poor health forced him to leave the school on three occasions to regain his strength. On one of those occasions, he and his wife traveled to Europe. Following the death of her husband, Hannah Davis spent time studying in Italy and Germany. In 1892, she accepted a position at the University of North Dakota, where she remained for the rest of her life. Following her death on March 24, 1898, her body was brought back to Spiceland for burial. Her funeral, attended by over 2,000 people, was the largest ever held in Spiceland.

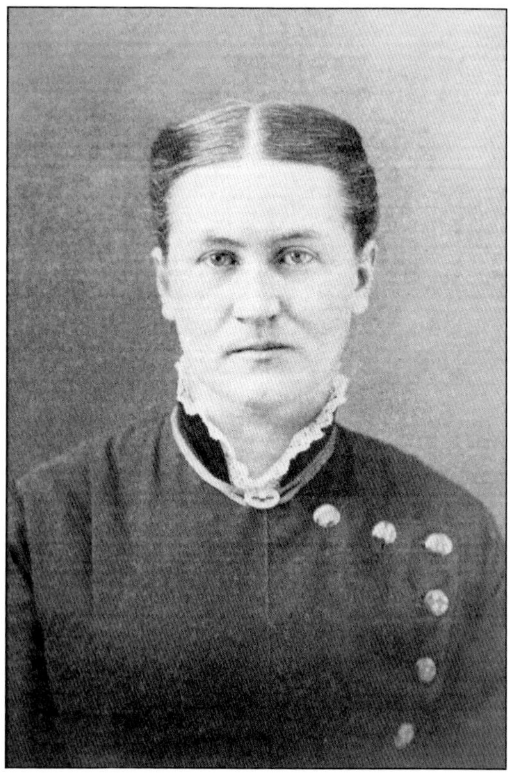

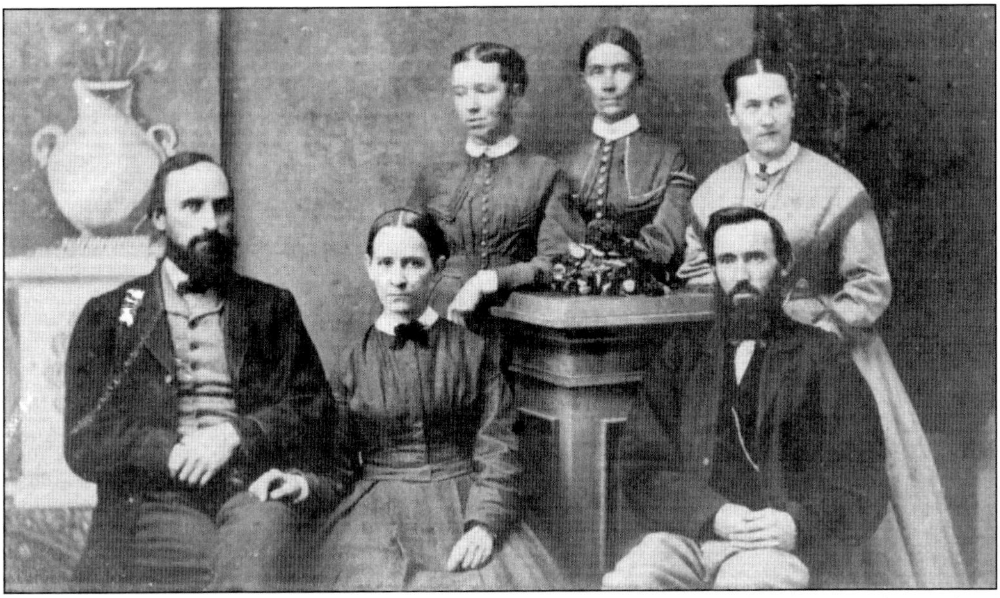

Teachers at Spiceland Academy for the 1870–1871 school year posed for photographer Robert Gordon. From left to right are (first row) William B. Morgan, Sarah Morgan, and Clarkson Davis (superintendent); (second row) Luzena Thornburg, Martha Ann Macy, and Hannah Davis.

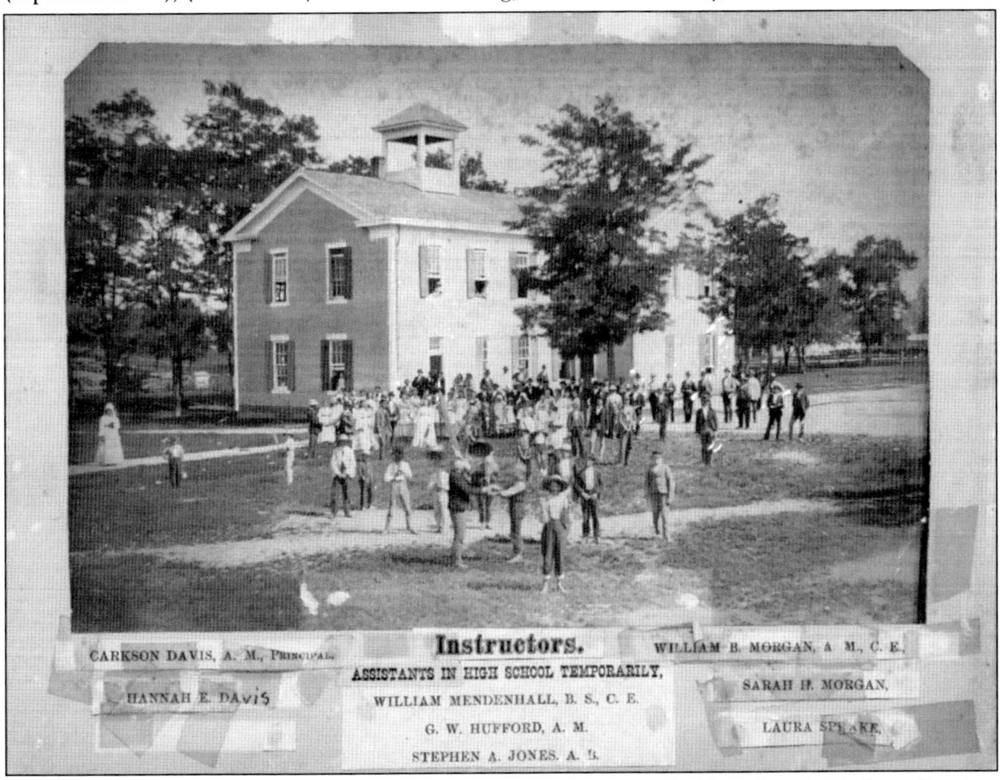

This photograph of the 1861 frame academy building was probably taken by Robert Gordon sometime in the 1870s. Note the long dresses, straw hats, and bonnets worn by the students. Some of the boys appear to be barefoot.

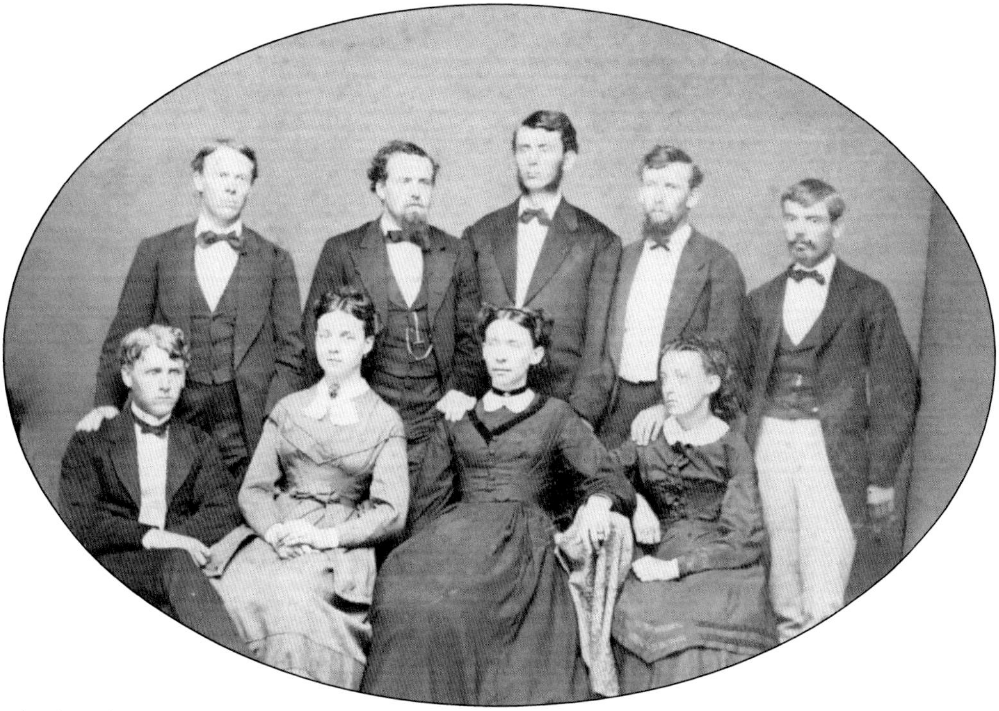

The first class to graduate from Spiceland Academy was in 1870. Shown here is the second class, in 1871. From left to right are (first row) Richard Gause Boone, Mary Ballenger, Lida Edwards, and Louisa Wickersham; (second row) Walter Jones, Alvin H. Jenkins, Macy I. Good, Cyrus R. Dixon, and Dallas Sisson.

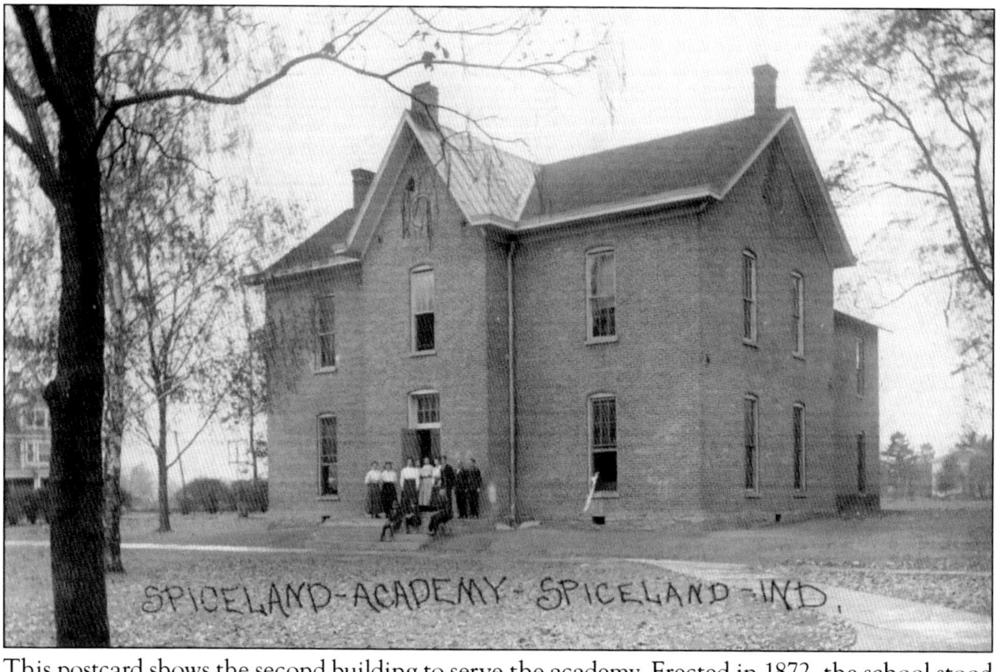

This postcard shows the second building to serve the academy. Erected in 1872, the school stood south of the Friends meetinghouse and was enlarged in 1879. This building was razed in 1914.

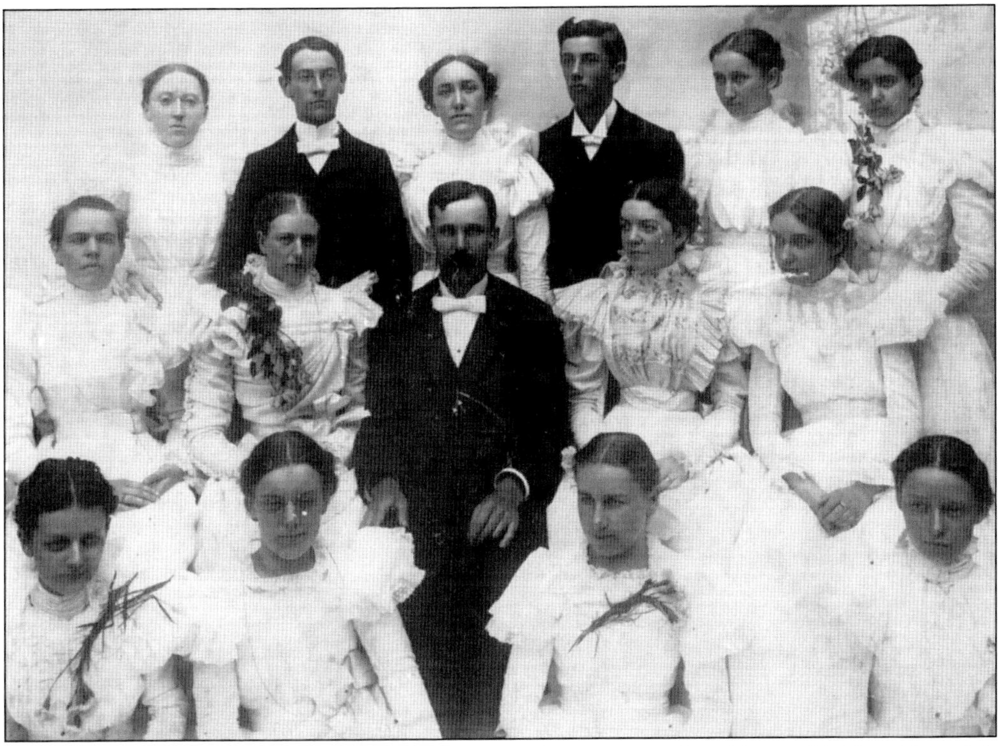

Members of the academy class of 1897 are shown with superintendent George W. Neet. From left to right are (first row) Fanny Hayes, Clyde Sisson, Elva Hodson, and Ethel Rifner; (second row) Jessie Leakey, Minnie Strattan, Neet, Pearl Millikan, and Lois Henley; (third row) Josie Harland, Charles Harper Smith, Mayme Stafford, Irving White, Floy Huddleston, and Leoti Applegate.

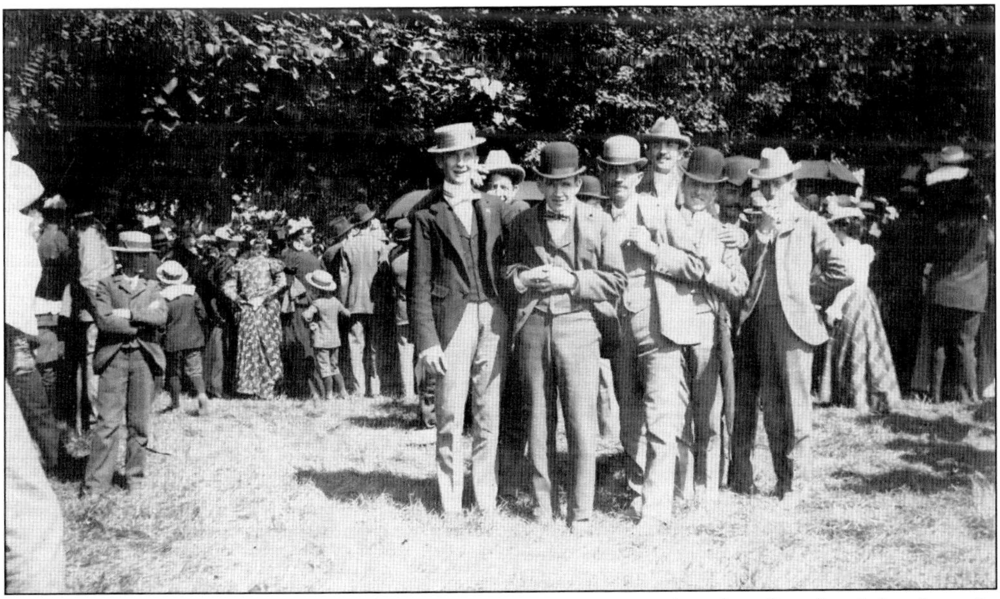

Field Day, a day devoted to fun and sports activities, was introduced at Spiceland Academy in 1891. The yearly event continued until Spiceland High School closed in 1969. These gents were all dressed up and ready for the day in this 1898 photograph.

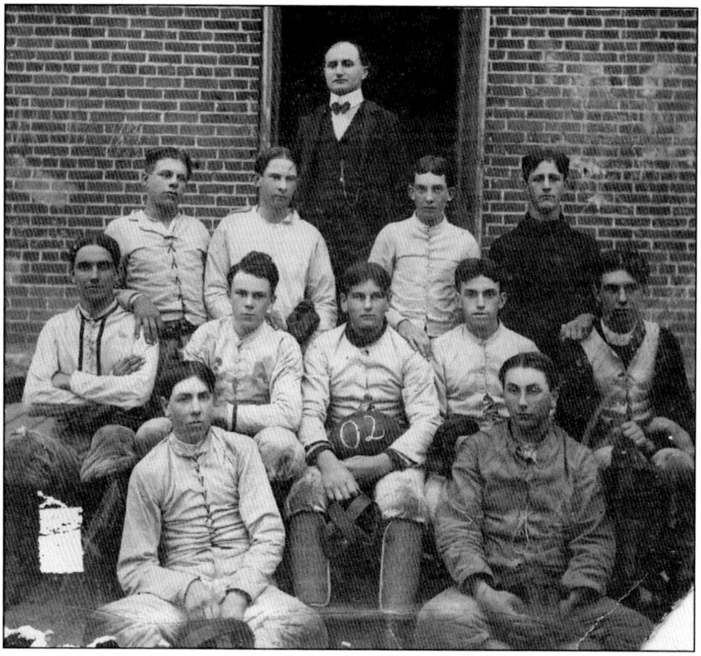

This is believed to be the oldest photograph in existence of a Henry County football team. A fatal accident early in the 20th century caused Spiceland Academy to discontinue the sport. This 1902 team included, from left to right, (first row) Warren Edwards and George Coffin; (second row) Ernest Coffin, Harold Wright, Wendell Pitts, Rupert Redic, and Ralph Stubbs; (third row) Clifford Hoover, Carl Newby, Charles Arden Stubbs, and Walter Wright. Standing is academy superintendent Homer H. Cooper.

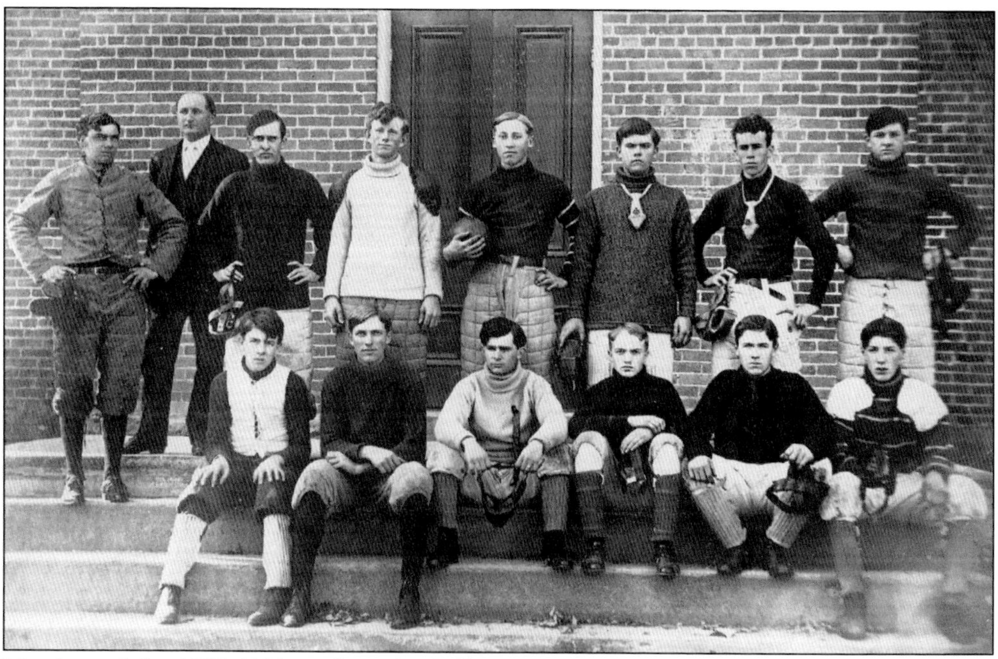

Members of the 1907–1908 academy football team are not wearing matching gear, which was evidently not a requirement at this early date. Or, they may be wearing their practice attire. The team members are, from left to right, (first row) Andrew Markle, Everett Kennard, Glen Kirkham, Arthur Hall, Ralph Test, and Elgar Pennington; (second row) James McGrady, Homer H. Cooper (academy superintendent), Griffin Moffitt, Walter Hays, Ross Williams, Hoyt Reece, Charles Reece, and Howard Harvey.

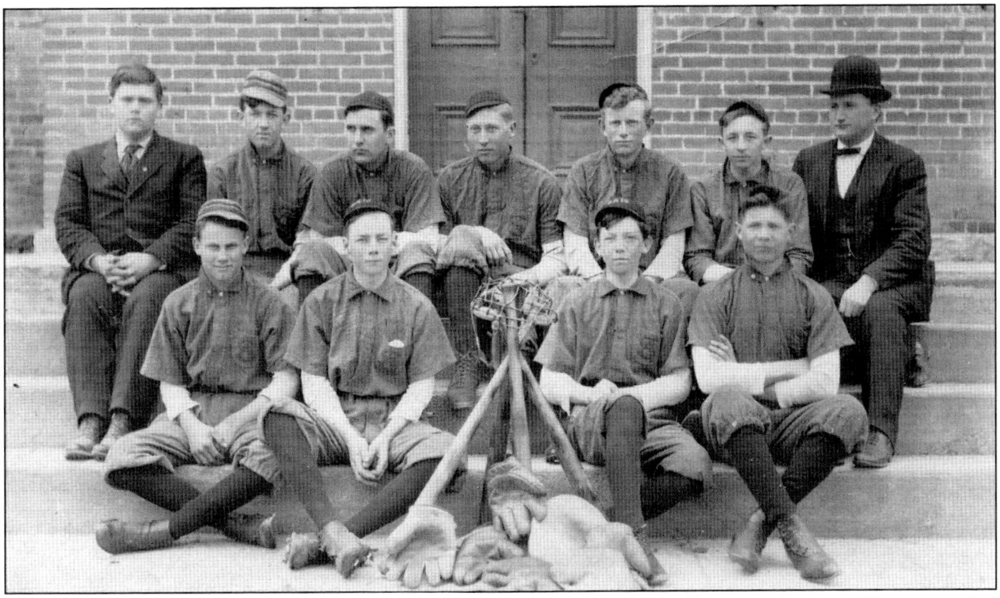

The academy was noted for its outstanding baseball and basketball teams. Pictured here are the baseball boys of 1909. From left to right are (first row) Elmer Grimm, Castle Wilson, Alvin Hardin, and W.G. Smith; (second row) Hoyt Reece, Howard Harvey, Griffin Moffitt, Ross Williams, Walter Hays, Perry Wilson, and Homer H. Cooper (academy superintendent).

In the heyday of Spiceland Academy, the idol of the fans was John "Snowball" Merida. He was about six feet tall, had extra big hands, and could play any position on the field, although he usually served as catcher. Whether he was ever in school or not is left up to conjecture, as there were no stringent rules in those days. His career at Spiceland lasted from about 1895 to 1903. He could have played in the Major Leagues had it not been for the color barrier of those days. There was, however, no integration problem at the academy. He later played for New Castle's Krell-French Piano Company baseball team, as well as for the Indianapolis ABCs and the Kansas City, Missouri, Monarchs, both African American clubs. He died on May 11, 1911, in Kansas City, and his remains were brought to Spiceland for burial.

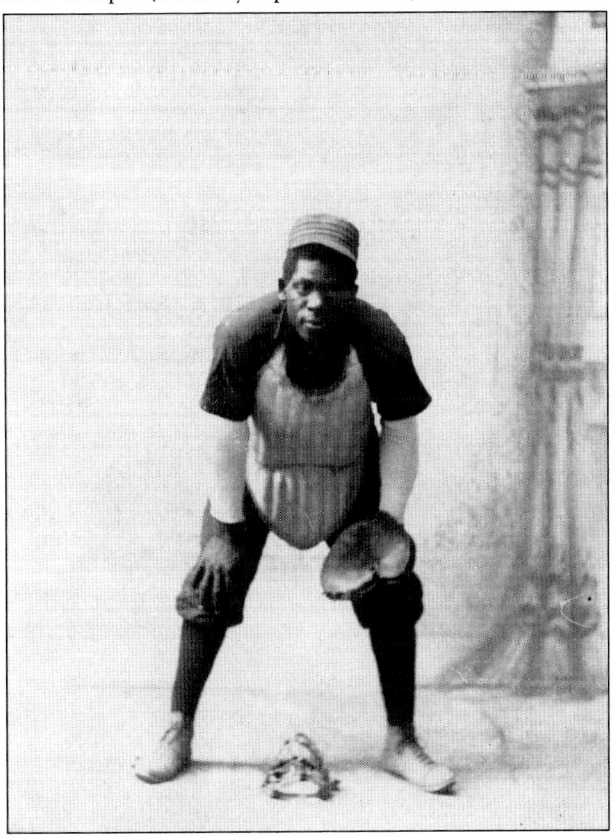

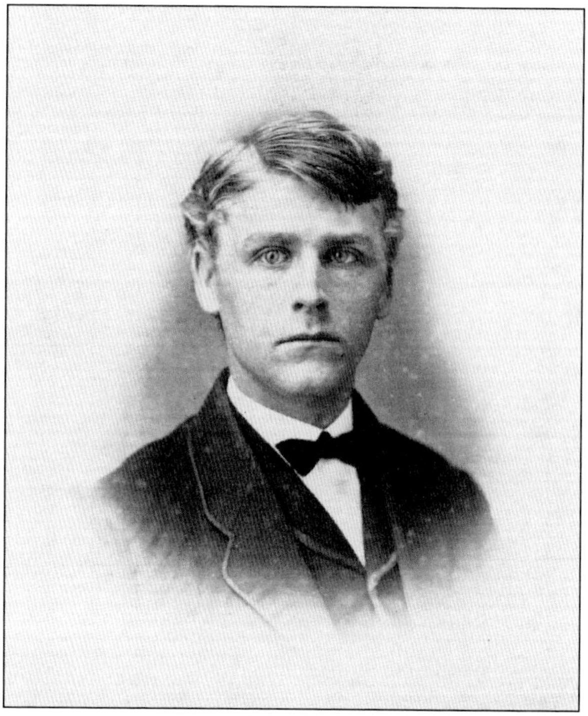

An 1871 graduate of Spiceland Academy, Richard Gause Boone became a noted author and professor. In 1898, he was made president of Michigan State University. From 1899 to 1905, he served as superintendent of schools in Cincinnati. For a time, he was also a professor at both Indiana University and the University of California.

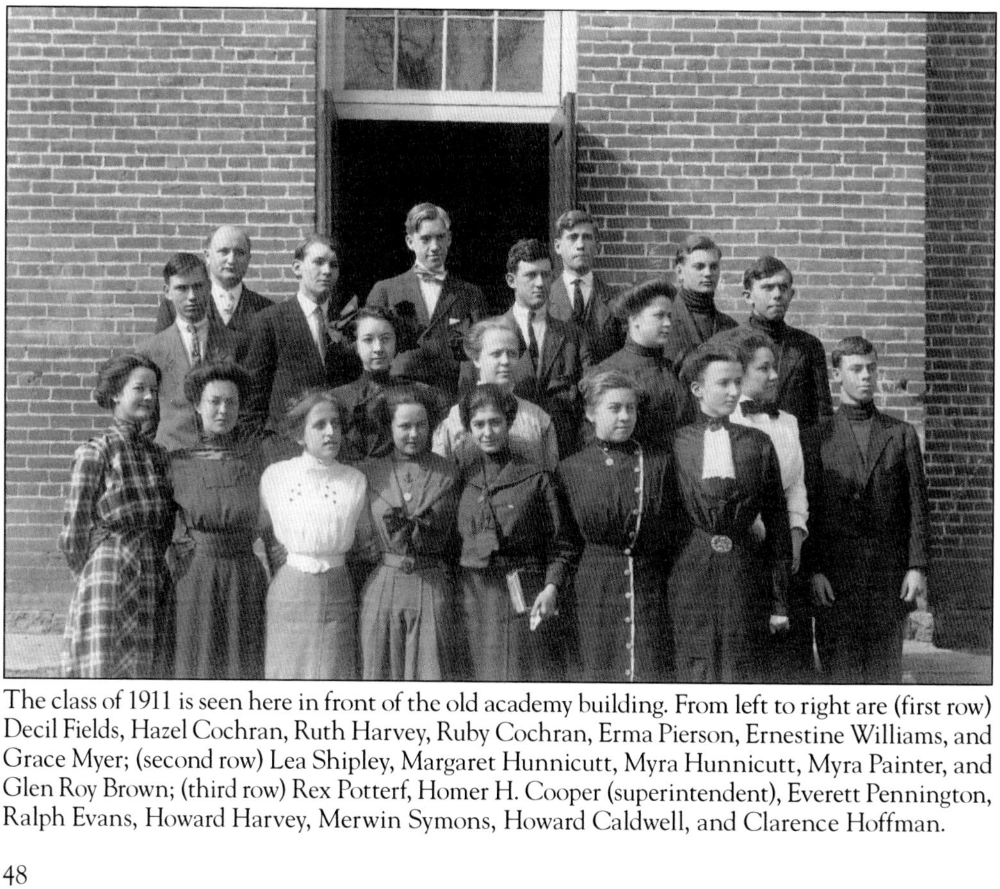

The class of 1911 is seen here in front of the old academy building. From left to right are (first row) Decil Fields, Hazel Cochran, Ruth Harvey, Ruby Cochran, Erma Pierson, Ernestine Williams, and Grace Myer; (second row) Lea Shipley, Margaret Hunnicutt, Myra Hunnicutt, Myra Painter, and Glen Roy Brown; (third row) Rex Potterf, Homer H. Cooper (superintendent), Everett Pennington, Ralph Evans, Howard Harvey, Merwin Symons, Howard Caldwell, and Clarence Hoffman.

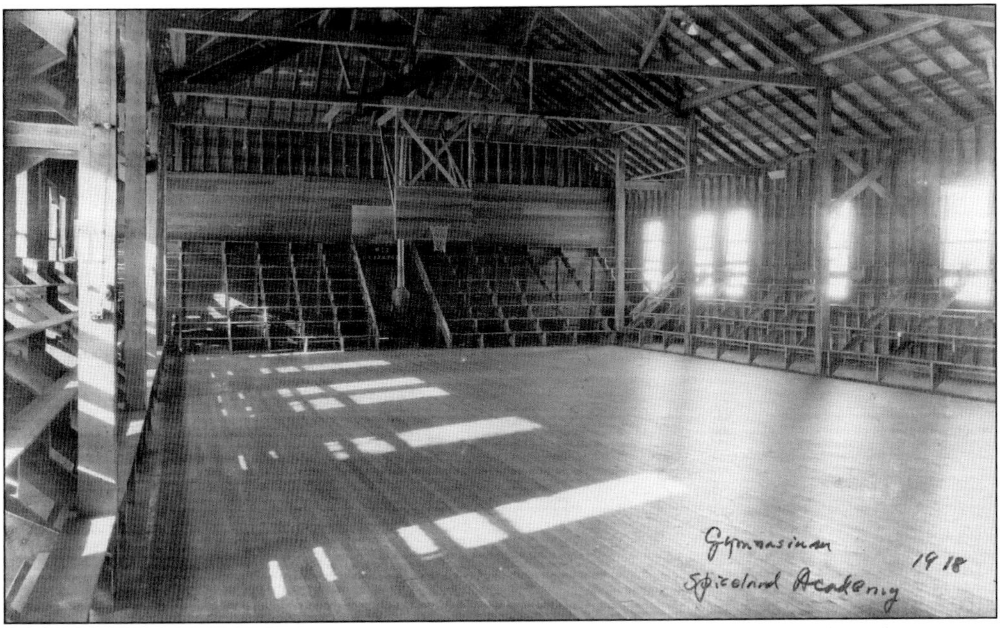

The frame gymnasium at the academy was erected in 1918 and served the school until a new one was built in 1937. Upon careful examination of this photograph, a stove can be seen behind the basketball hoop. Hopefully, no student ran into the stove when attempting a basket.

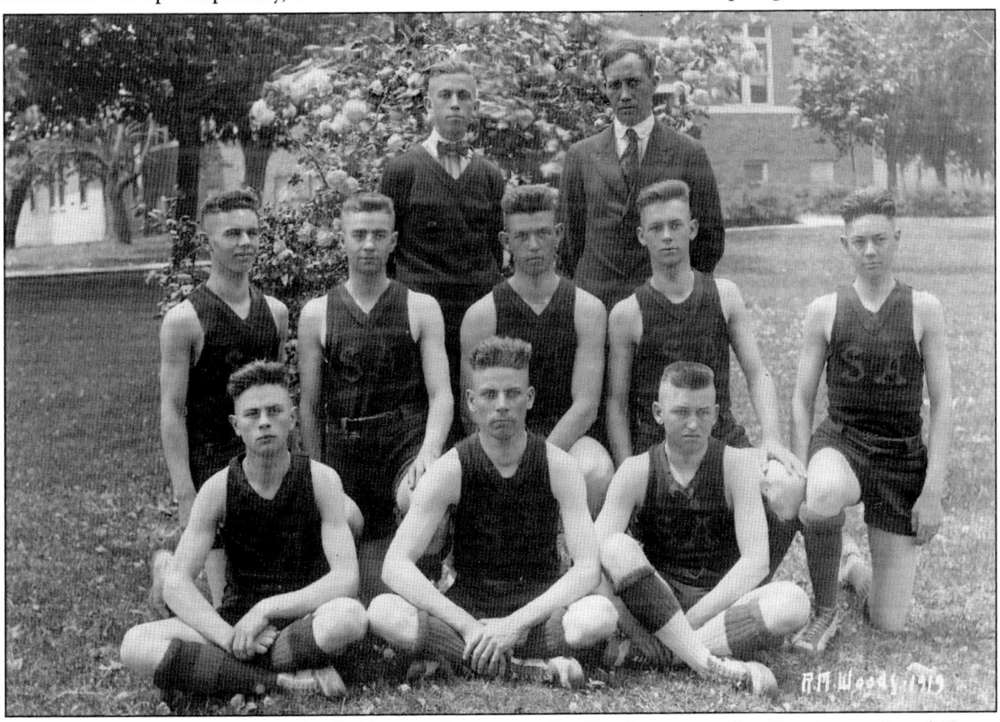

The academy's 1919–1920 basketball team, known as the Quakers, won the district sectional. From left to right are (first row) William "Bill" Coffin, Dwight "Pete" Shepherd, and Charles Ratcliff; (second row) Don Chew, Robert Myer, Russell "Pete" Reece, Roger Pierson, and Earl McNew; (third row) Ralph Leigh (manager) and Chester Reagan (coach).

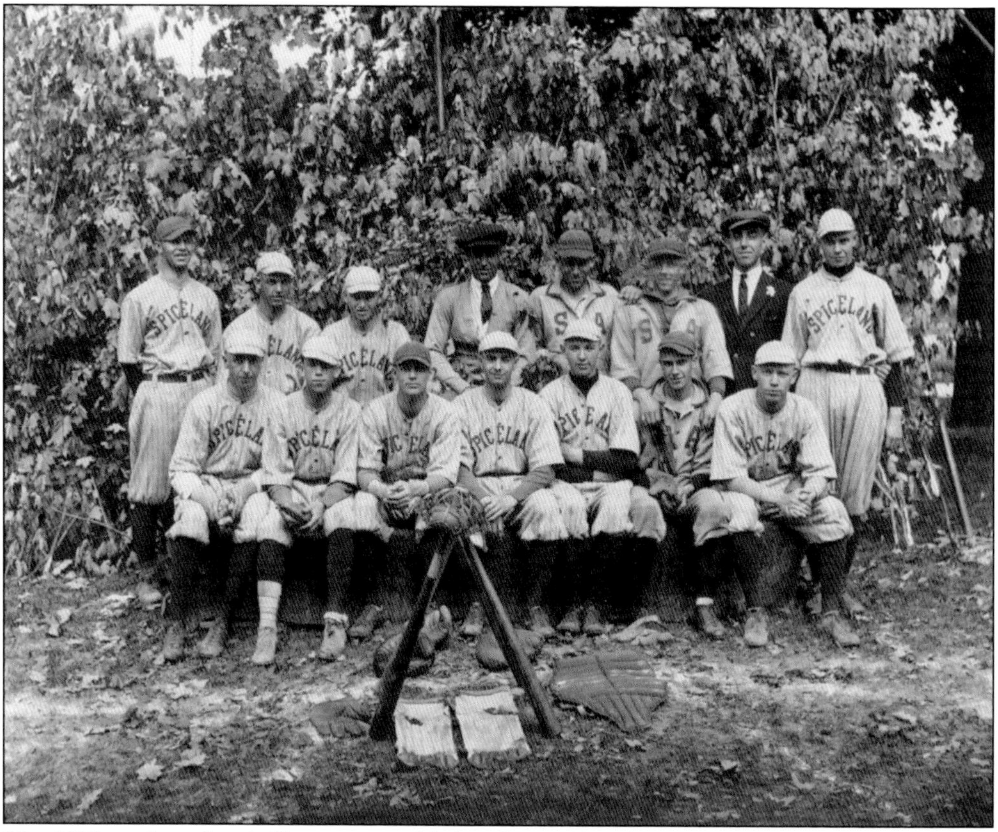

The 1920 academy baseball team assembled in front of brush that had been cut and used for a backdrop. From left to right are (first row) Lowell "Benny" Stafford, Ralph Leigh, Roger Pierson, Robert Myer, Wayman Casey, Walter "Punkin" Starbuck, and Wilbur "Toddy" Carr; (second row) Don Chew, Russell "Pete" Reece, Charles Ratcliff, Chester Reagan (principal and coach), Victor Reece, Rexford G. Wright, Clyde Rogers (teacher), and Elmer "Sheeney" Poer.

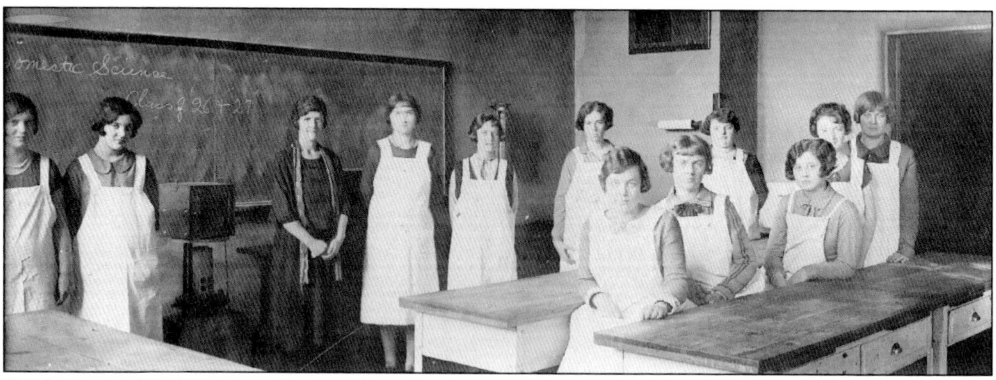

Students in the domestic science class at Spiceland High School pose for a photograph in 1926. The class members are, from left to right, (seated) Ruth Brewer, Doris Brown, and Pauline Stewart; (standing) Dorothy Jay, Sylvira Flanagan, Mabel Hodson (teacher), Evelyn Johnson, Emma May Copeland, Thelma Franklin, Ruth Griffin, Mamie Magee, and Anna Hopper.

In 1928, Helen Heffernan was crowned the queen of field day. From left to right are (first row) Harriett McShurley, Hefferman, and Myrtle Divilbiss; (second row) Virginia Wilson, Amy Gardner, and Maxine Groves.

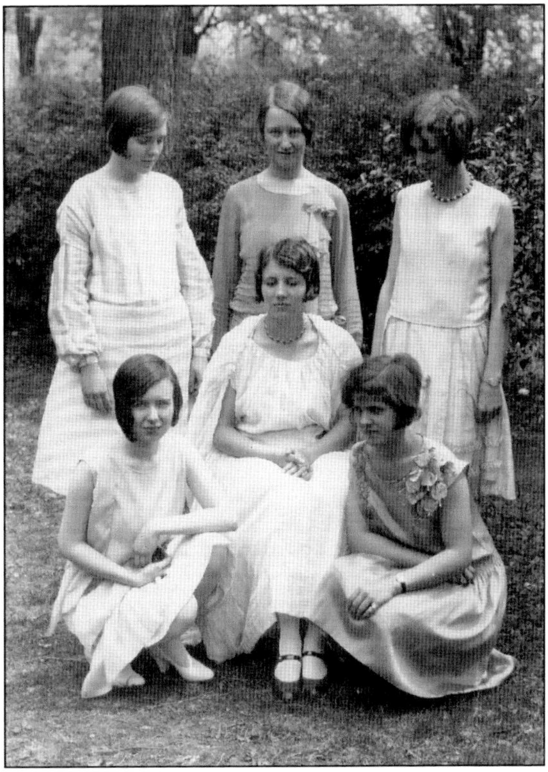

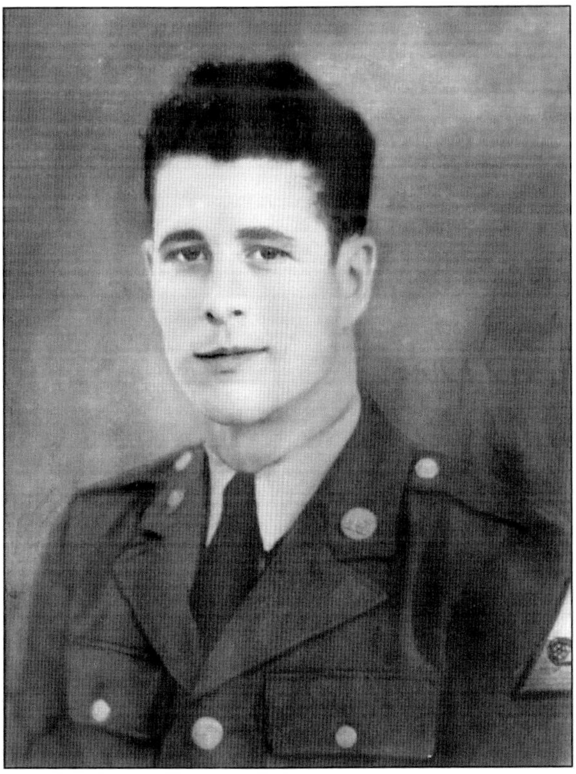

Charles O. Byrket, a member of the class of 1935, joined the Army on September 25, 1941, and left the United States for foreign service on May 31, 1942. While serving as a private in the Sixth Armored Infantry, Byrket was killed in action in Oran, Algeria, on November 8, 1942.

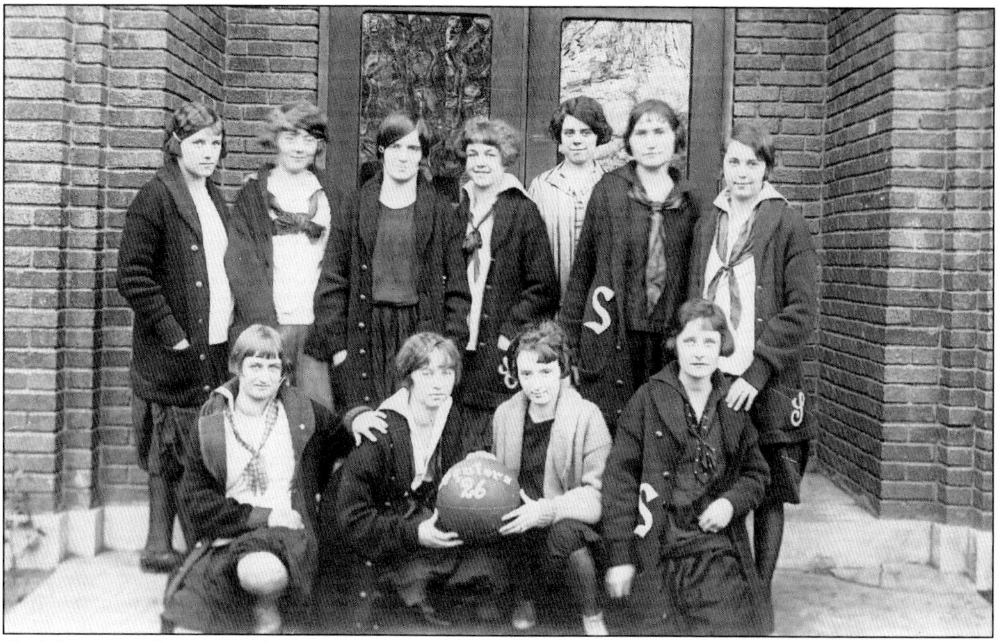

Girls basketball was popular at Spiceland High School in the 1920s and 1930s. Shown here is the 1926 Quaker team. From left to right are (first row) Phyllis Johnson, Louise Catt, Mamie Magee, and Emma Mae Copeland; (second row) Elizabeth "Bessie" Allen, Charlotte Deem, Dorothy Jay, Berniece Harrison, unidentified, Evelyn Johnson, and Lenore Harrison.

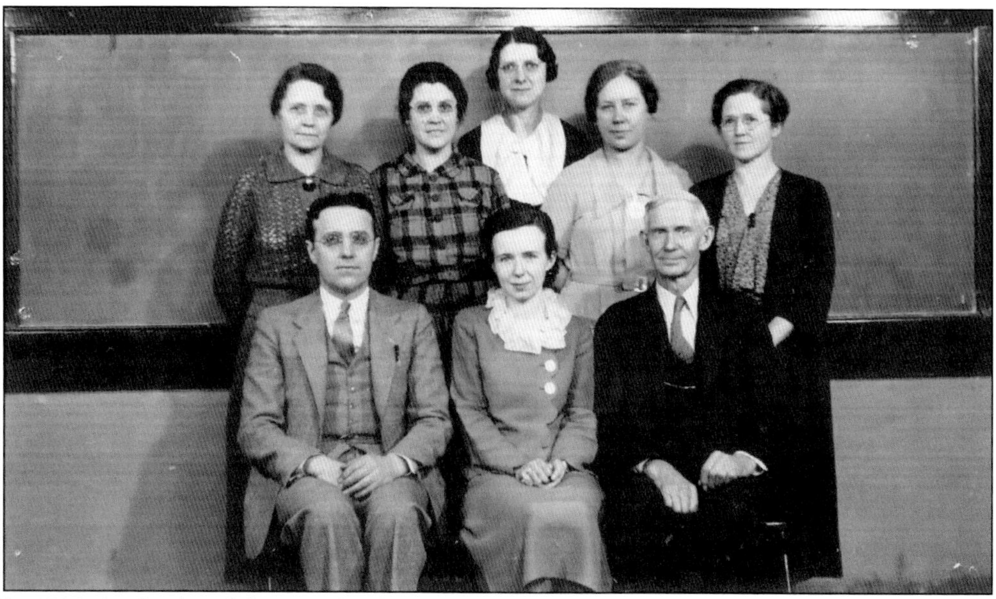

In 1936, the faculty of the Spiceland grade school assembled for a group photograph. From left to right are (first row) Walter M. Pitts, Harriett Evans, and S.E. Pickering; (second row) Laura Rubey, Martha Jane Wise, Edith Hoover, Nellie Addison, and Lena Holtsclaw.

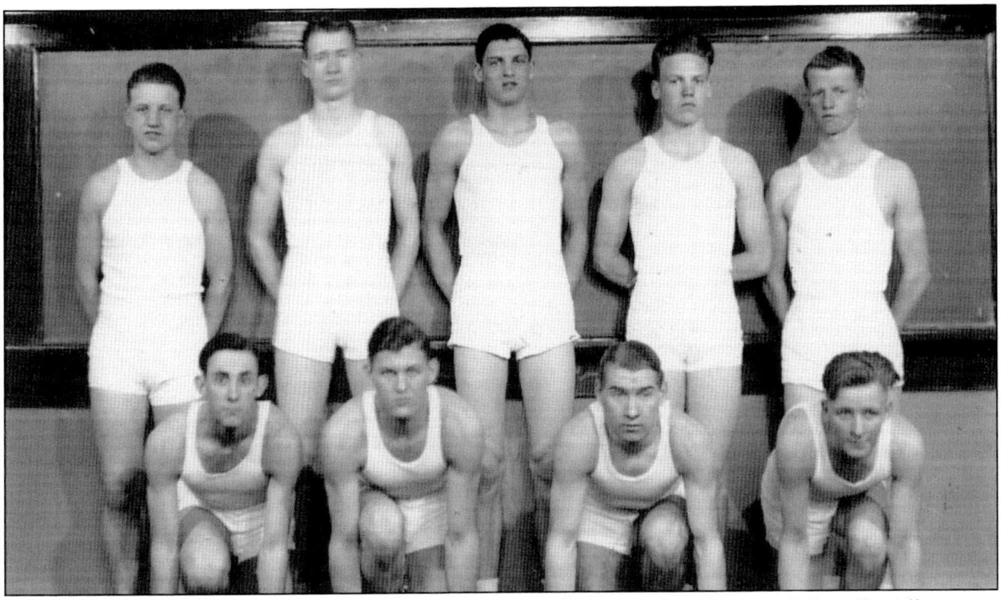

Spiceland High School's track stars of 1936 are, from left to right, (first row) Orville Albertson, Charles Livingston, Charles "Archie" Brown, and Don Helms; (second row) Bob Lockridge, Luther Pidgeon, James Livingston, John Mote, and Gerald Bowman Jr.

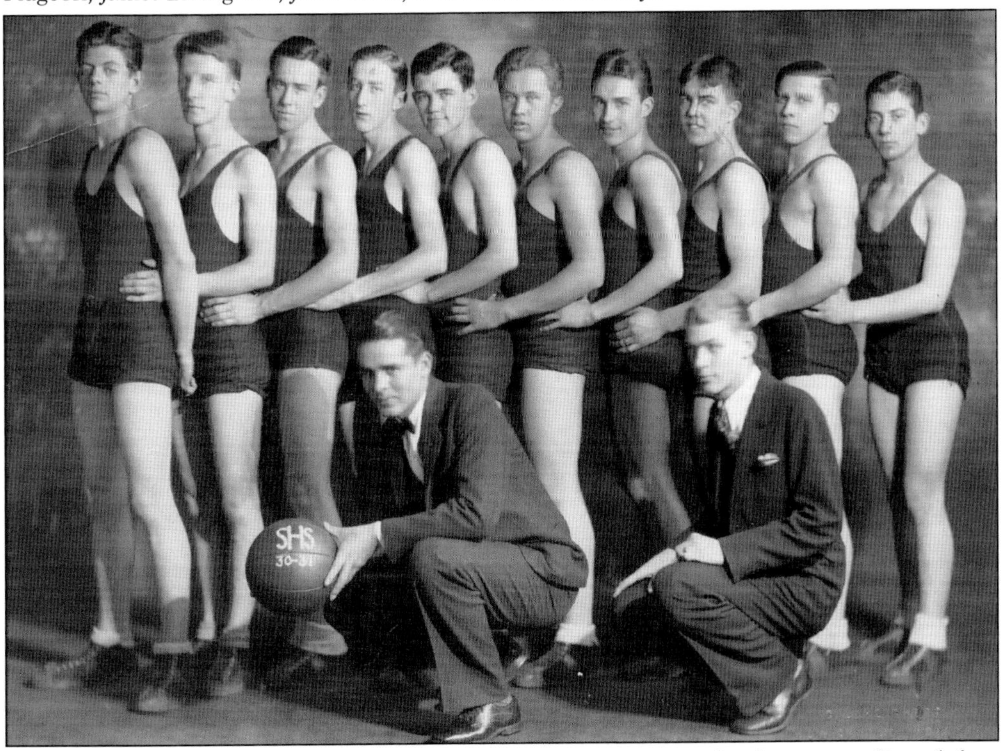

The 1930–1931 Spiceland Yellow Jackets struck an interesting pose for the camera. From left to right are (first row) Russell Hensley (coach) and Cosby Johnson (manager); (second row) Miles Curry, Francis Allen, Ellis Adams, Kerney Wilson Jr., Frederick Van Duyn, Horace Murphy, Myron Brown, Charles Applegate, Maurice Black, and Joseph Johnson.

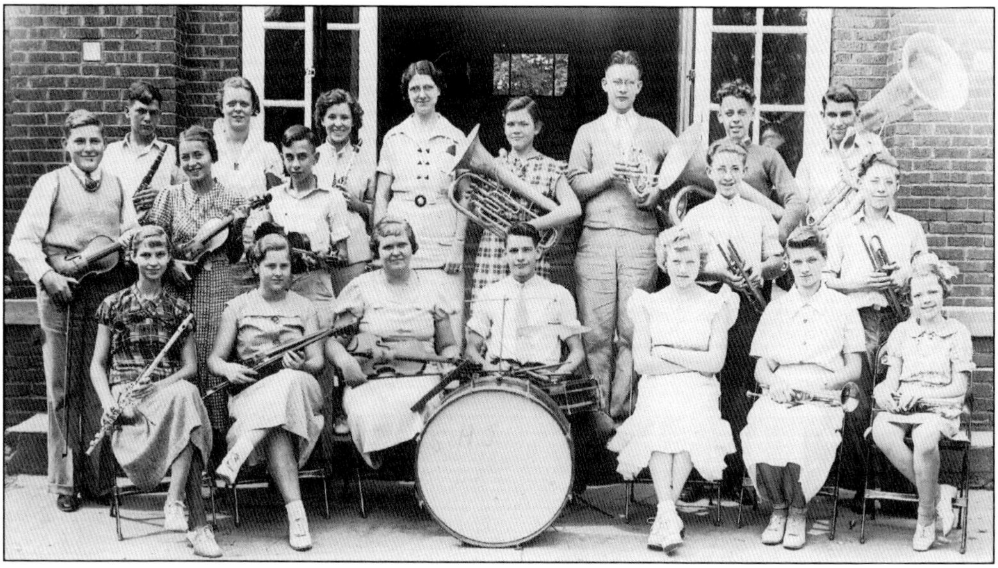

The Spiceland High School orchestra is seen in this 1935 photograph. From left to right are (first row) two unidentified, Catherine Cassity, unidentified, Catherine Louise Hoff, Mary Olive Pidgeon, and Mildred Basye; (second row) Charles Matthews, Evelyn Deem, Eugene Painter, George Brooks, and Irvin Brooks; (third row) three unidentified, Edith Hoover (teacher), Ruth Applegate, unidentified, Eugene Rifner, and Lowell Painter.

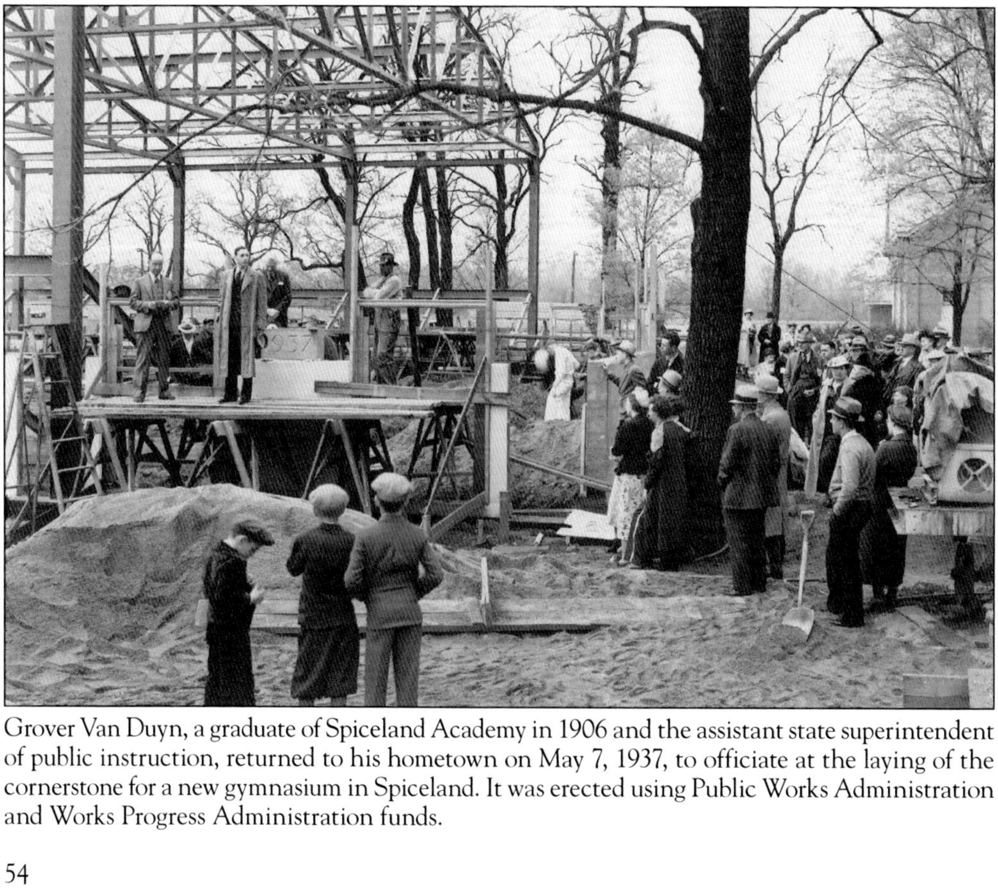

Grover Van Duyn, a graduate of Spiceland Academy in 1906 and the assistant state superintendent of public instruction, returned to his hometown on May 7, 1937, to officiate at the laying of the cornerstone for a new gymnasium in Spiceland. It was erected using Public Works Administration and Works Progress Administration funds.

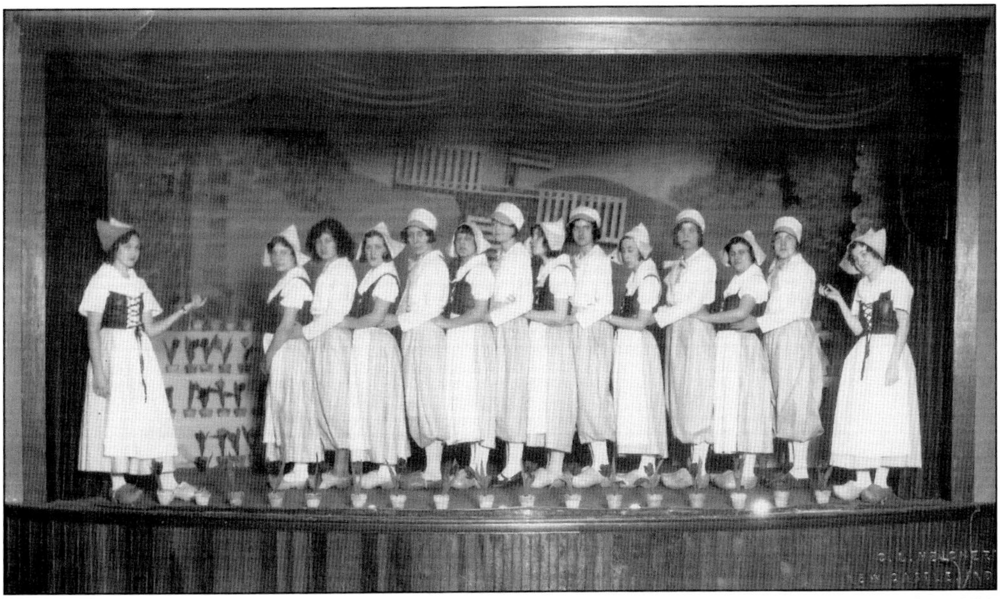

Even though it was staged in the town hall, located above Evans & Wilson grocery, the 1930 operetta *Tulip Time* was a high school production. The cast included students from the classes of 1930 through 1933.

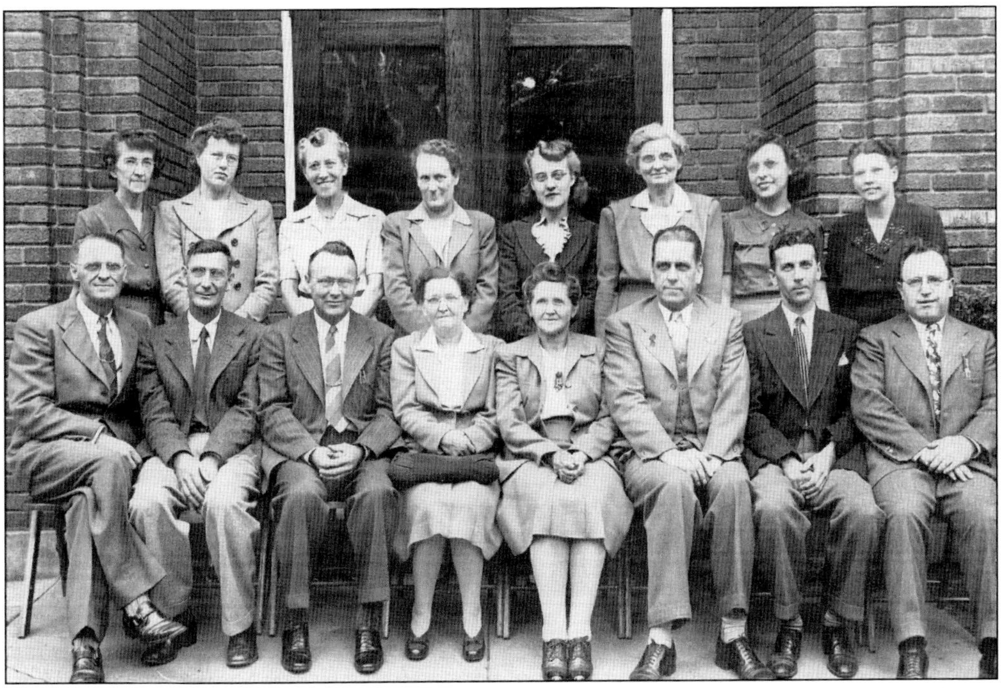

These elementary and high school teachers were photographed during the 1945–1946 school year. From left to right are (first row) Loring A. Eilar, Harvey Davidson, Will K. Kinkaid (principal), Olive Kelly, Lena Holtsclaw, Roydon Gordon (Spiceland Township trustee), Robert Wade, and Estel Miller; (second row) Florence Bundy, Betty Williams Gordon, Berniece Eilar, Grace Gastino Hall, Ruth Donahue, Helen Rockhill, Pauline Merryman Poer, and Dorothy Davidson.

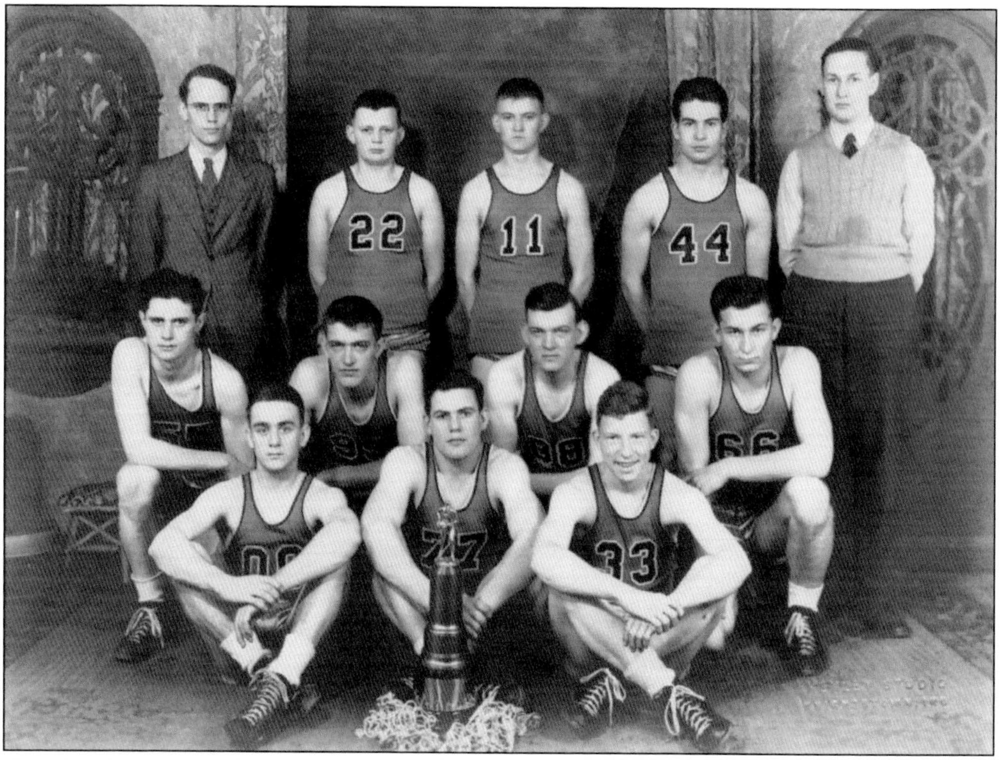

The 1944 Spiceland Yellow Jackets strived for success on the basketball court. The team included, from left to right, (first row) John "Johnny" Johnson, Kash Kissick, and Max McCorkle; (second row) Paul "Bus" Copeland, Charles "Chuck" Wells, Glen Wright, and Arthur "Art" Lykins; (third row) Carl Puhlmann (coach), James Copeland, James Poer, Russell Bridges, and Theodore "Ted" Applegate (manager).

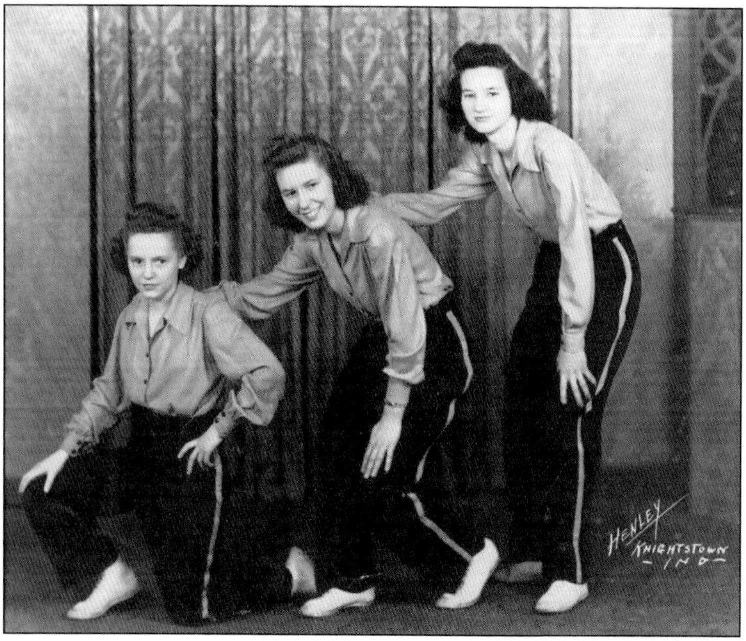

Although they are now called cheerleaders, they were once referred to as yell leaders. These gals led yells for Spiceland in 1945. From left to right are Joan Murphy, Betty Hayes, and Myra Hayes.

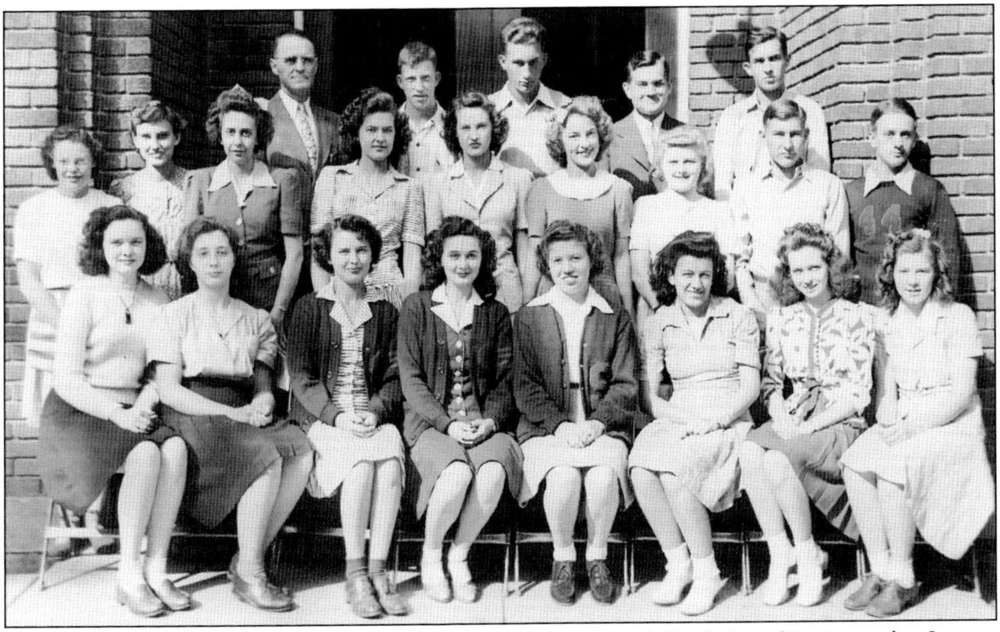

Members of the class of 1944 at Spiceland High School pose with English and Latin teacher Loring A. Eilar and school principal Jesse Frazier. From left to right are (first row) Yvonne Campbell, Eloise Nugen, Mildred Moffitt, Lois Anderson, Eva Lou Lockridge, Phyllis Heffernan, Harriett Hopkins, and Dorothy Schweikhardt; (second row) Ruby Sammons, Alice Warren, Anita Painter, Shirley McGregor, Ruth Smith, Mildred Lewman, Geraldine McDonald, George Conrad, and John Johnson; (third row) Eilar, Max McCorkle, Arthur Lykins, Frazier, and Max Moffitt.

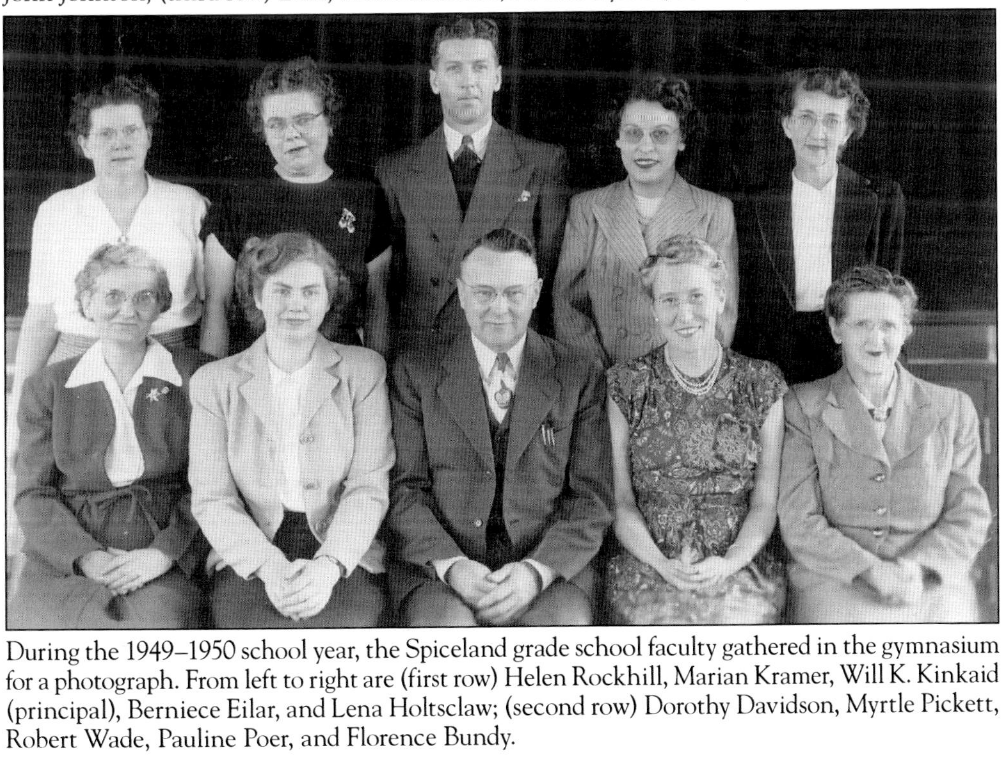

During the 1949–1950 school year, the Spiceland grade school faculty gathered in the gymnasium for a photograph. From left to right are (first row) Helen Rockhill, Marian Kramer, Will K. Kinkaid (principal), Berniece Eilar, and Lena Holtsclaw; (second row) Dorothy Davidson, Myrtle Pickett, Robert Wade, Pauline Poer, and Florence Bundy.

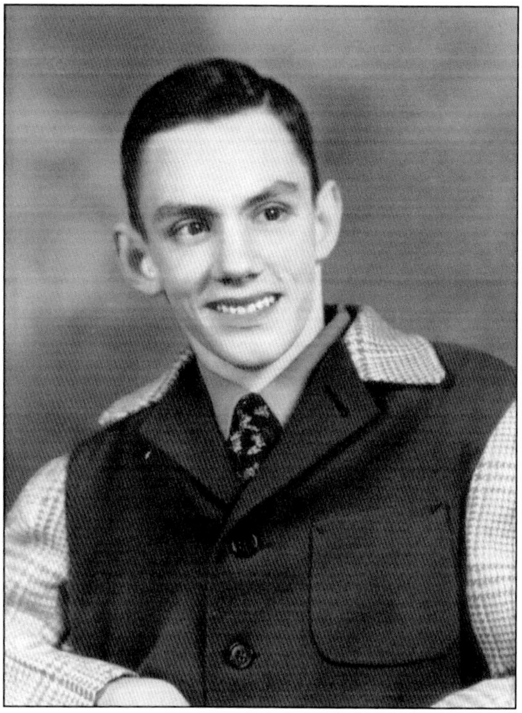

John Lynn Scovell, afflicted with infantile paralysis, was the only child of Macy and Murl Scovell. Through hard work and with the cooperation of his teachers, John Lynn was able to graduate from Spiceland High School in 1946. He died on August 2, 1948.

Erected in 1914 to replace the old brick building, this structure served as Spiceland Academy until the academy closed in 1921. Then, from 1922 until 1969, when the school district was consolidated into a larger district, it served as Spiceland High School. It was razed in October 1973.

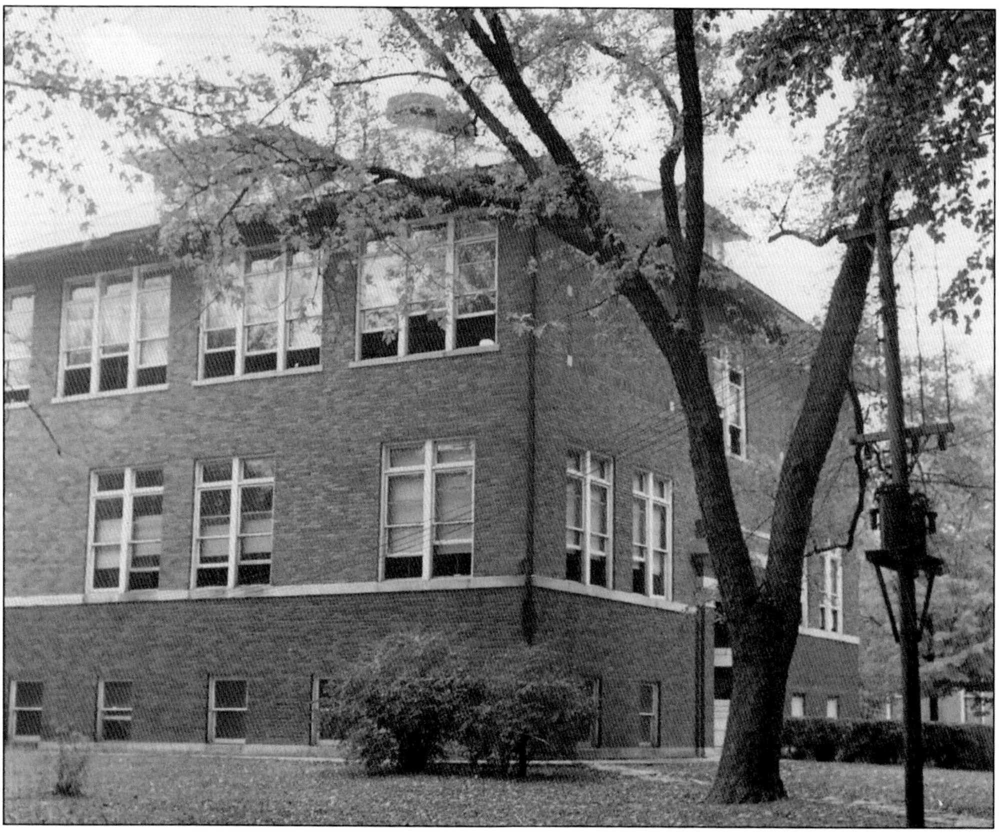

Known for years as simply Spiceland Elementary, in the 1950s, this school was named in honor of S.E. Pickering, who taught in the grade school in Spiceland for over 50 years. The building was erected in 1917, vacated in 1969, and razed in October 1973.

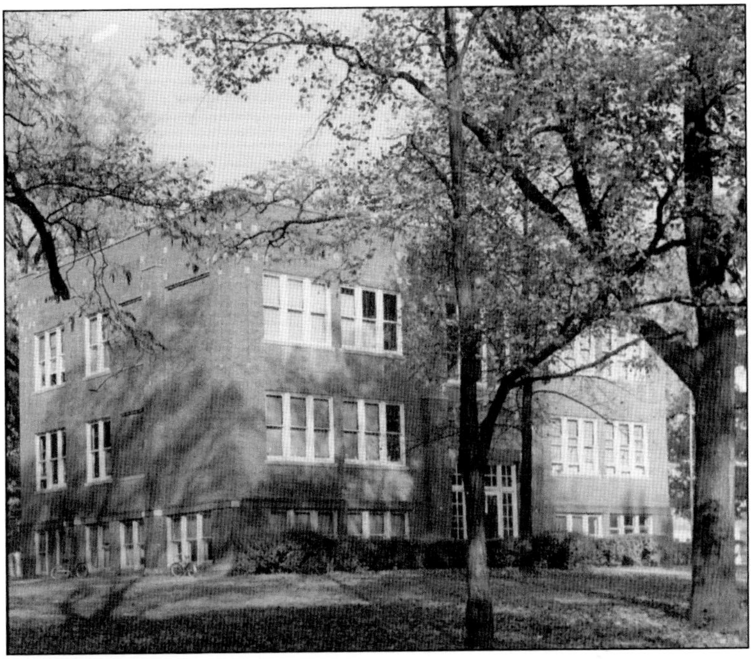

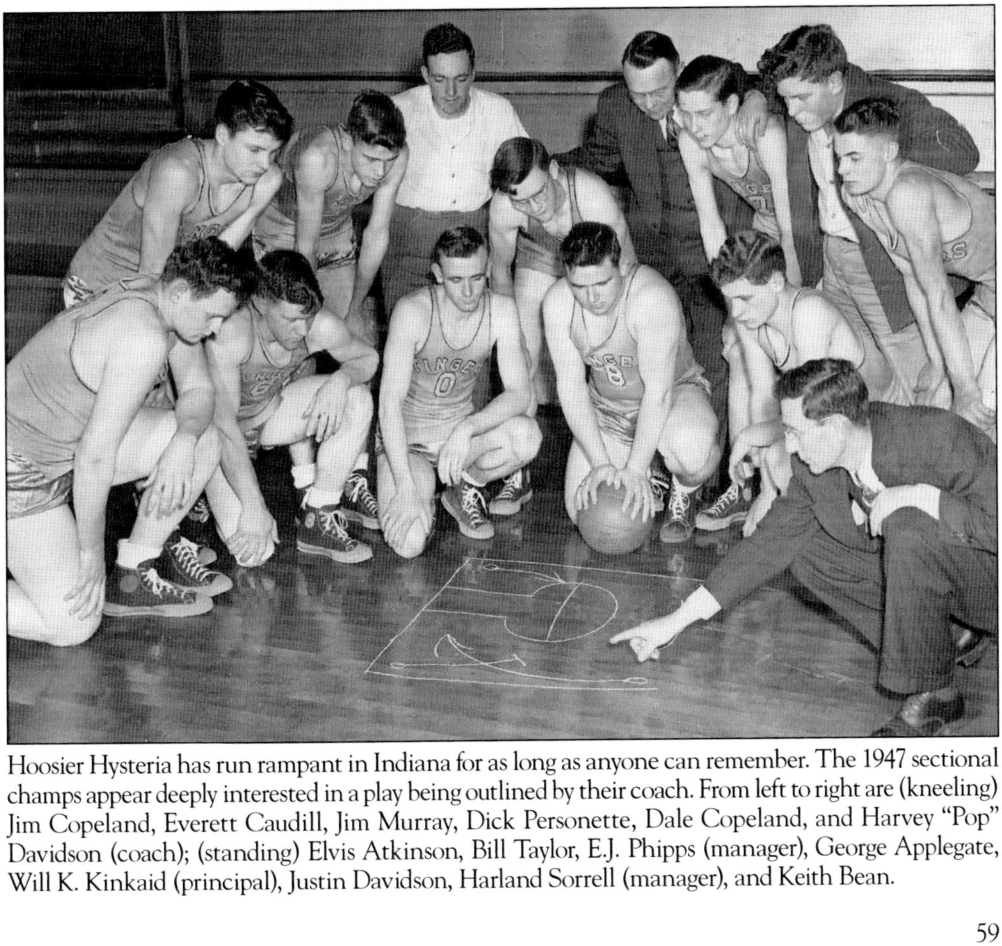

Hoosier Hysteria has run rampant in Indiana for as long as anyone can remember. The 1947 sectional champs appear deeply interested in a play being outlined by their coach. From left to right are (kneeling) Jim Copeland, Everett Caudill, Jim Murray, Dick Personette, Dale Copeland, and Harvey "Pop" Davidson (coach); (standing) Elvis Atkinson, Bill Taylor, E.J. Phipps (manager), George Applegate, Will K. Kinkaid (principal), Justin Davidson, Harland Sorrell (manager), and Keith Bean.

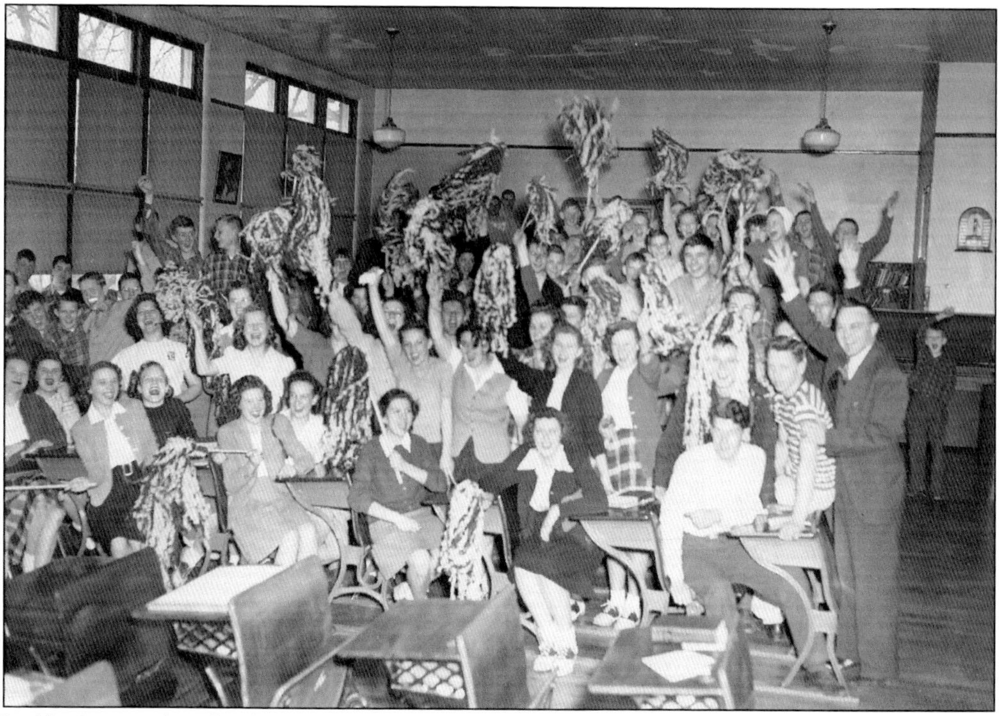

Led by Principal Kinkaid (far right), Spiceland High School students appear all fired up and ready to cheer on their 1947 basketball team.

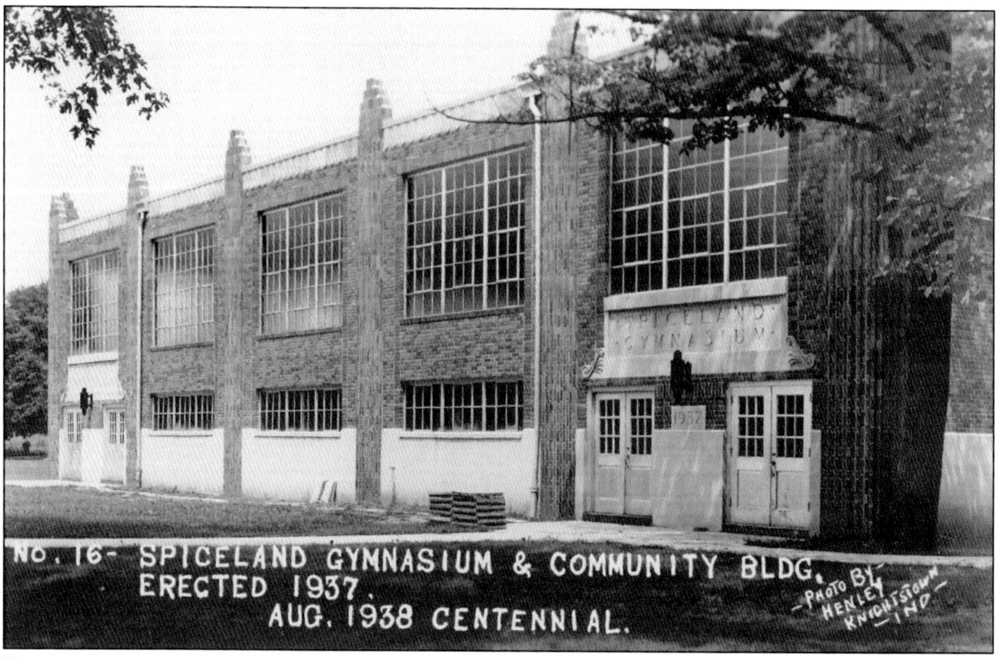

This photograph, taken during the 1938 Spiceland centennial, shows the gymnasium. In his book *Hoosier Temples: A Pictorial History of Indiana's High School Basketball Gyms*, Donald E. Hamilton featured the building and mentioned that unemployed brick masons and stonecutters did some very detailed work during the Depression on the exterior of this shrine to Spiceland basketball.

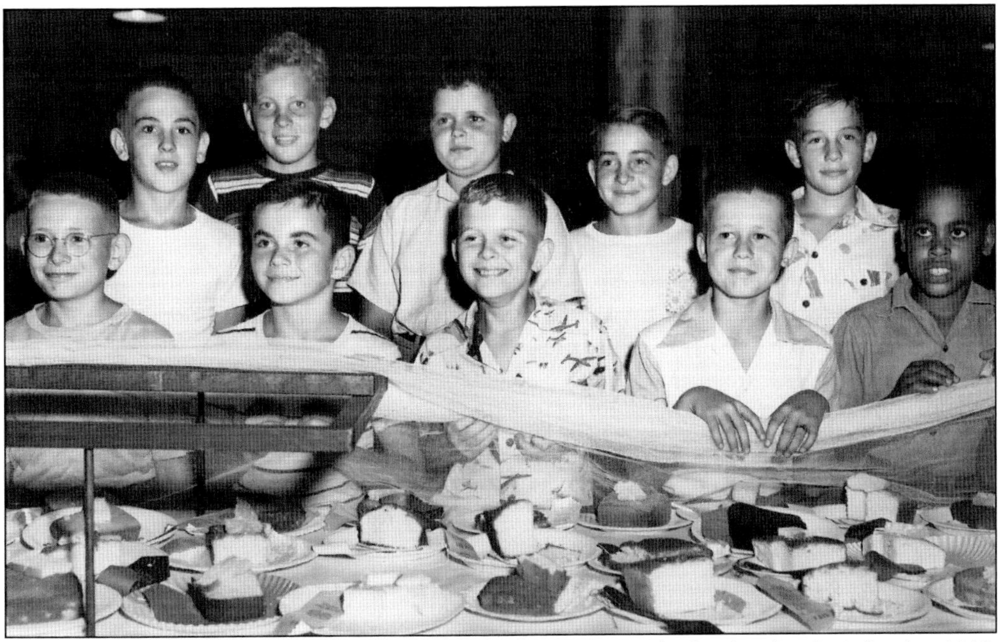

These young lads took a cooking class when they were in junior high school at Spiceland in 1948. Proudly showing their pies and cakes at the county 4-H fair are, from left to right, (first row) Earl Applegate, Paul Adams, Norman Cooley, David Van Hoy, and Herbie Meredith; (second row) Lynn Barlow, Ed Bryson, Dick Copeland, Ray Cable, and Don Scroggins.

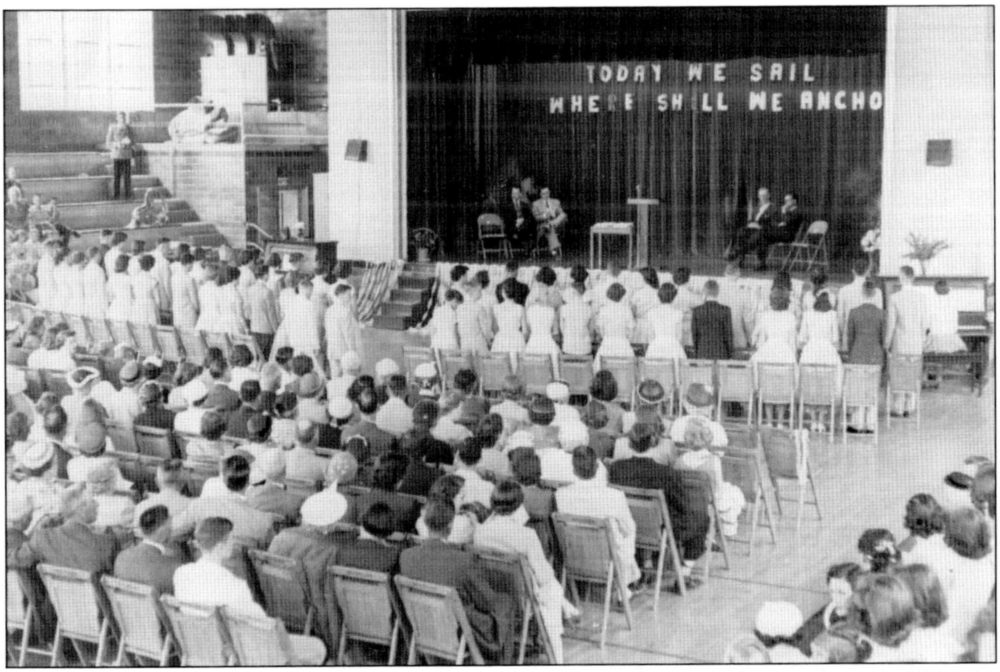

One of the highlights of field day was eighth grade graduation, which was always held in the morning as a way to begin the day's activities. This photograph, taken inside the gymnasium, shows the 1956 class ready to receive their diplomas.

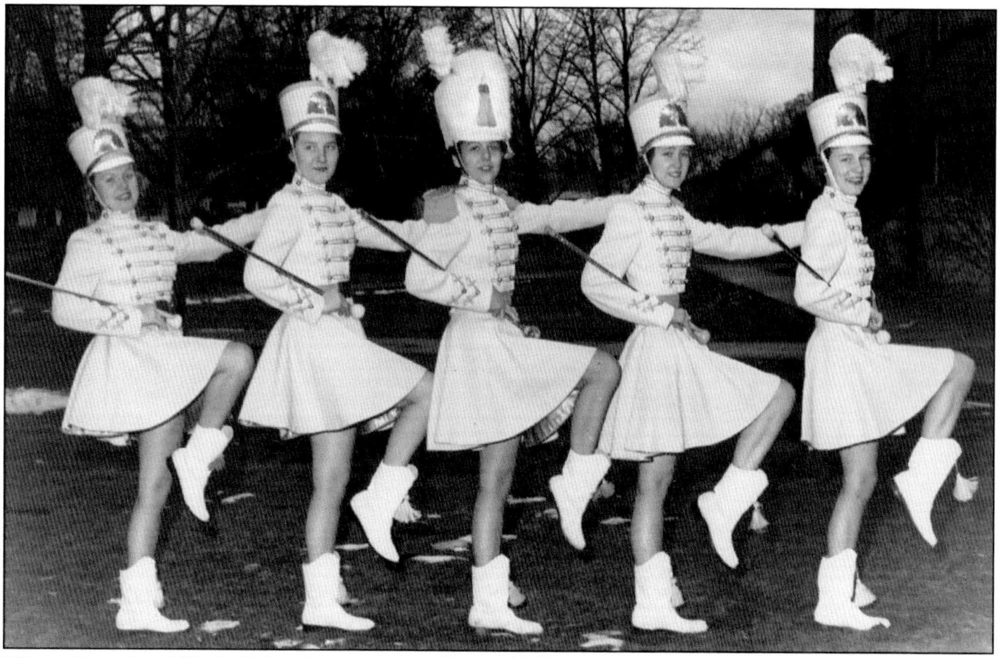

These Spiceland High School majorettes show off their new uniforms and appear ready to lead the high school band. These young ladies were members of the classes of 1954 and 1955. From left to right are Joan Brock, Carolyn Bryson, Shirley Archibald, Nancy Miller, and Joyce Garner.

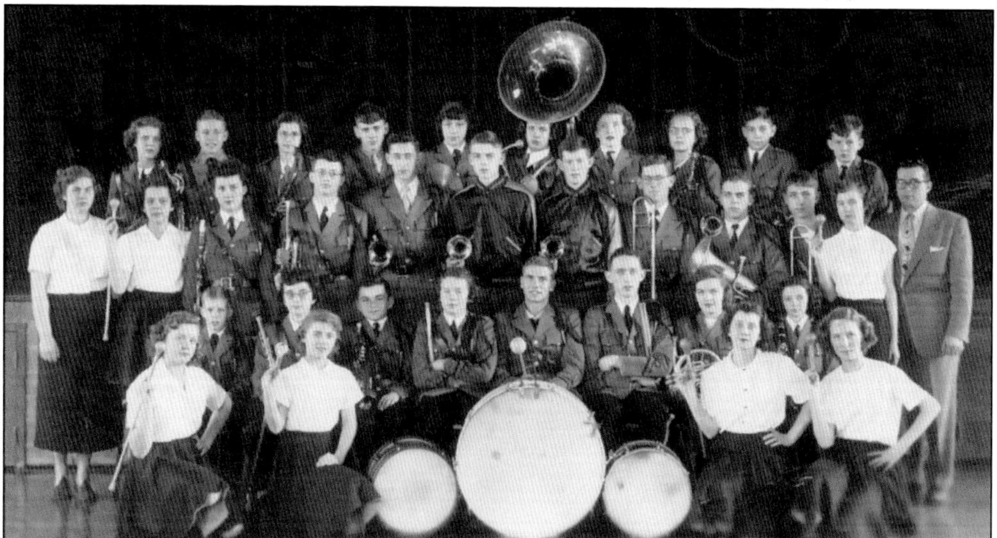

Carl Smolik was the director of the Spiceland High School band, shown here around 1950. The band members and twirlers are, from left to right, (first row) Joan Brock, Marilyn Wade, unidentified, and Carolyn Bryson; (second row) Jon Bogue, Deanna Crosier, Paul Adams, Nancy Adams, Walter Cramer, Don McCoy, Joyce Barlow, and Barbara Clapp; (third row) Marian Cramer (teacher), Shirley Archibald, Donna Nicoson, Byron Coffin, Walter Clay, Roger Ward, Norman Talbott, Keen Talbott, Tom Weber, unidentified, Nancy Miller, and Smolik; (fourth row) Ellen Kay Ward, David Van Hoy, Rosalyn Coffin, Jerry McClinic, unidentified, Patsy Bean, Mary Jane Catt, Doris Jo Applegate, Don Scroggins, and Tom Applegate.

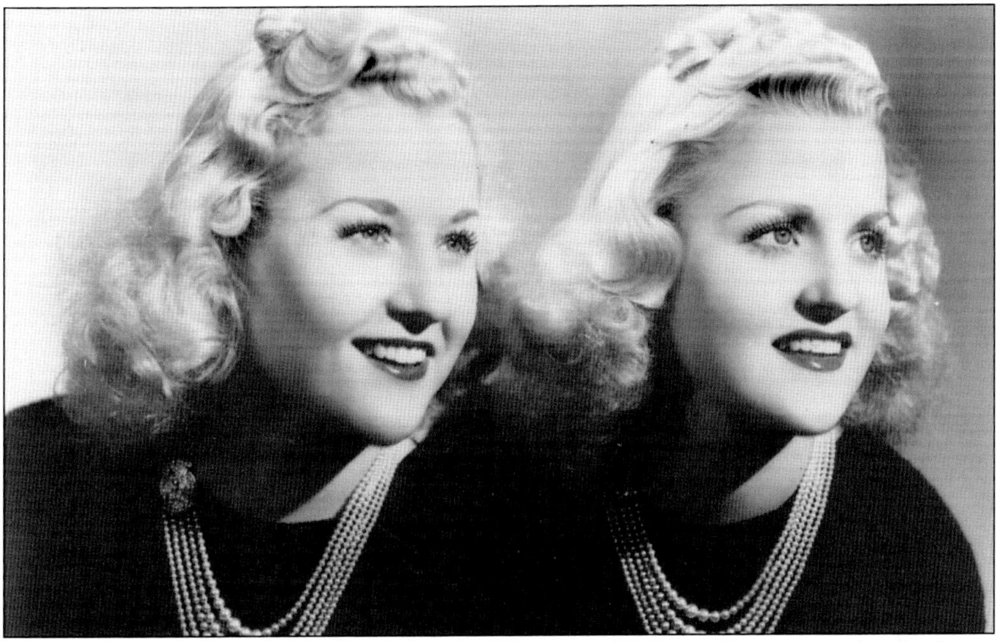

The Hoff sisters, Jean (left) and Catherine Louise (known as "Sis"), got their start as cheerleaders at Spiceland High School in the late 1930s. Leaving school, they toured the country as an acrobatic dancing team known as the Blondell Sisters. While performing in Chicago clubs for gangsters, an agent saw the act, and they were soon on their way, singing and dancing right through World War II on various USO tours. Eventually, Jean returned home to marry her high school sweetheart, but Sis continued in show business, performing on Broadway and in nightclubs. She appeared in the 1970s in many television commercials, touting such products as Post Raisin Bran cereal, Maxell House coffee, Pall Mall cigarettes, Oxydol, and Fruit of the Loom underwear.

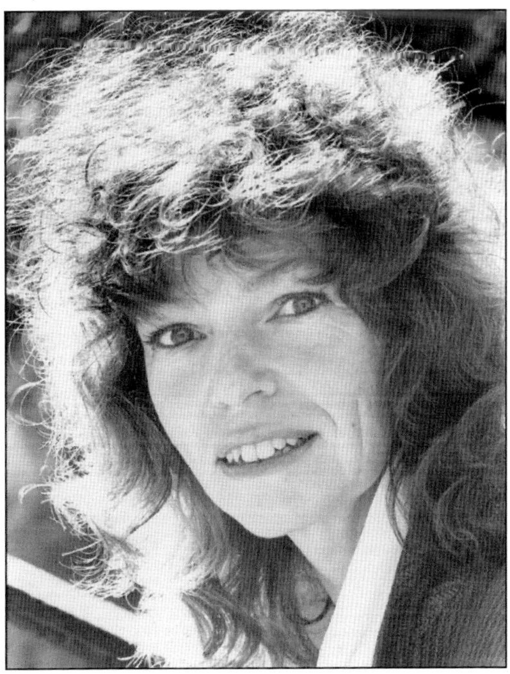

Gretchen (Kiger) Cryer, a 4-H girl from Dunreith, has had a successful career on Broadway. A graduate of and former teacher at Spiceland High School, she has written the lyrics for several productions. Her career in New York City, where she has appeared in several plays and on television, dates to the 1960s.

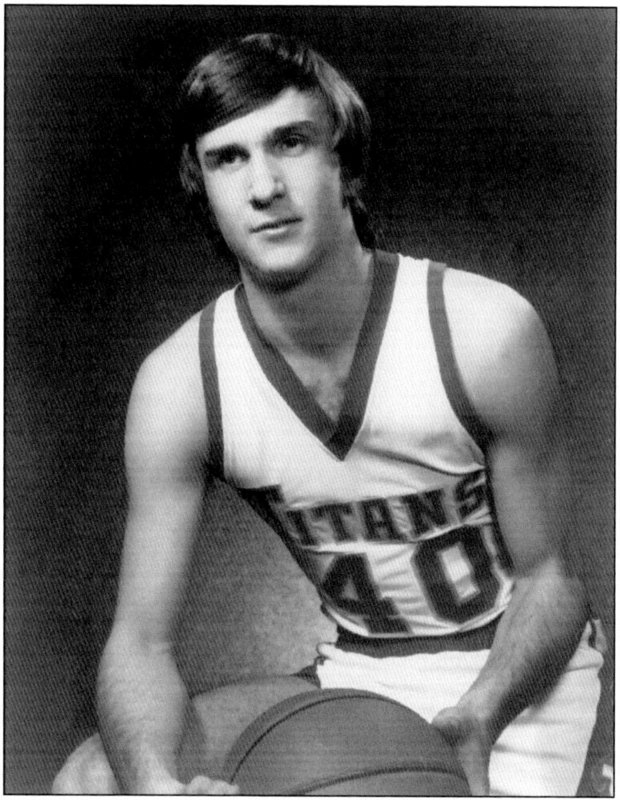

Randy Reece attended Spiceland Elementary School and graduated from Tri Junior-Senior High School in 1977. Tri is the consolidated school that Spiceland Township students currently attend. An outstanding basketball player, he holds the school record for most points scored and is one of the top scorers in Henry County basketball history.

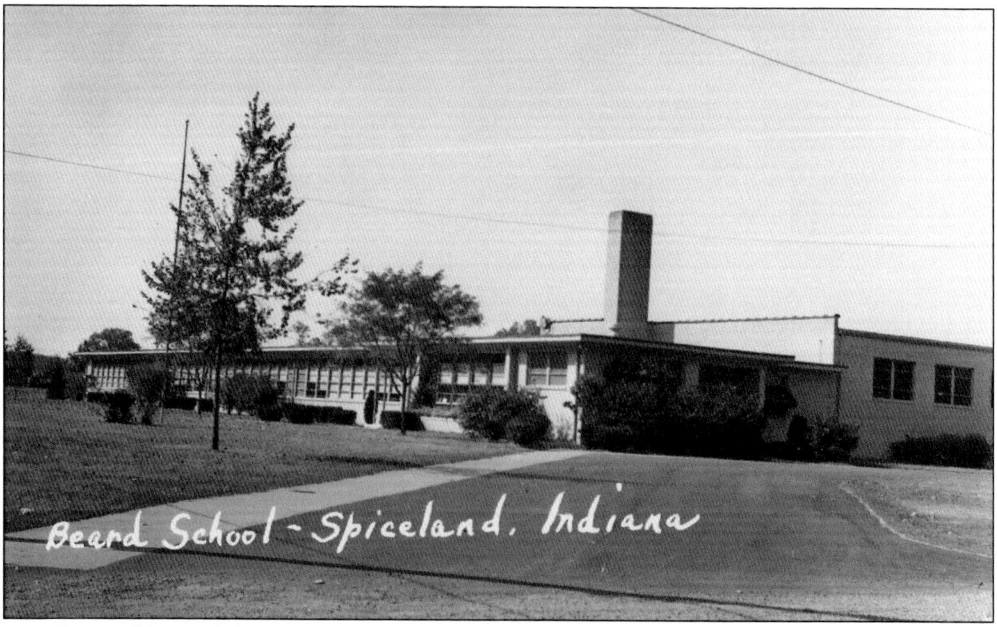

In 1953, an additional elementary building was added to the school campus at Spiceland. Originally named the Beard School after famed historian Charles A. Beard, who once attended the academy, the name was later changed to simply Spiceland Elementary. This photograph was taken in 1963. The school closed in 2008.

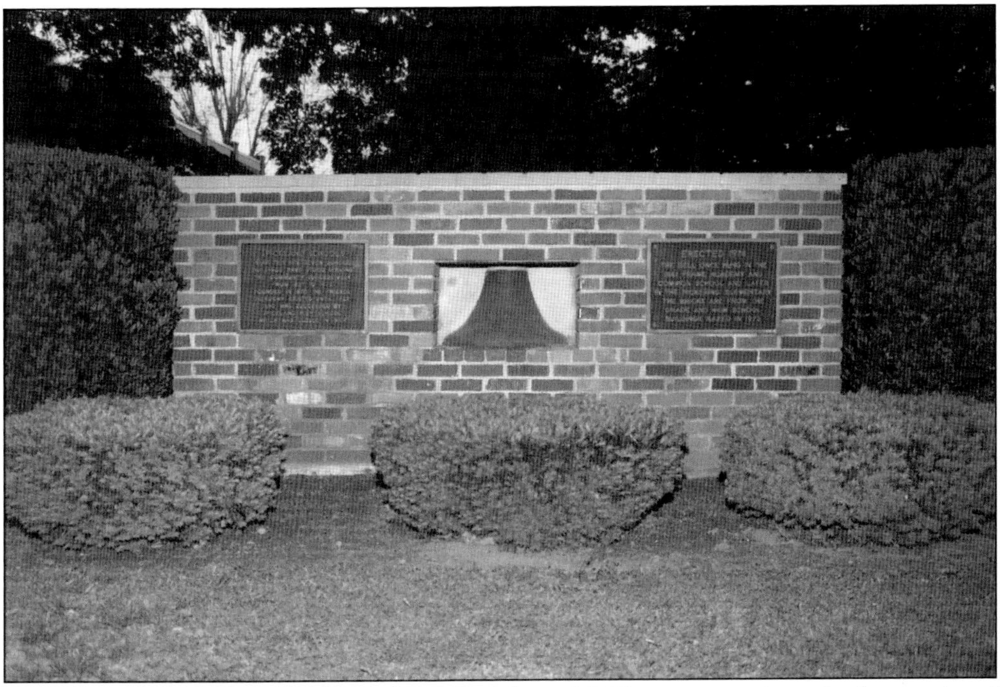

In 1974, a memorial designed by Walter Clay, class of 1950, was erected on the former site of several Spiceland school buildings. Made from bricks taken from the high school and Pickering Elementary, the memorial serves as a tribute and reminder that education was paramount in the minds of Spiceland and Spiceland Township residents for nearly 150 years.

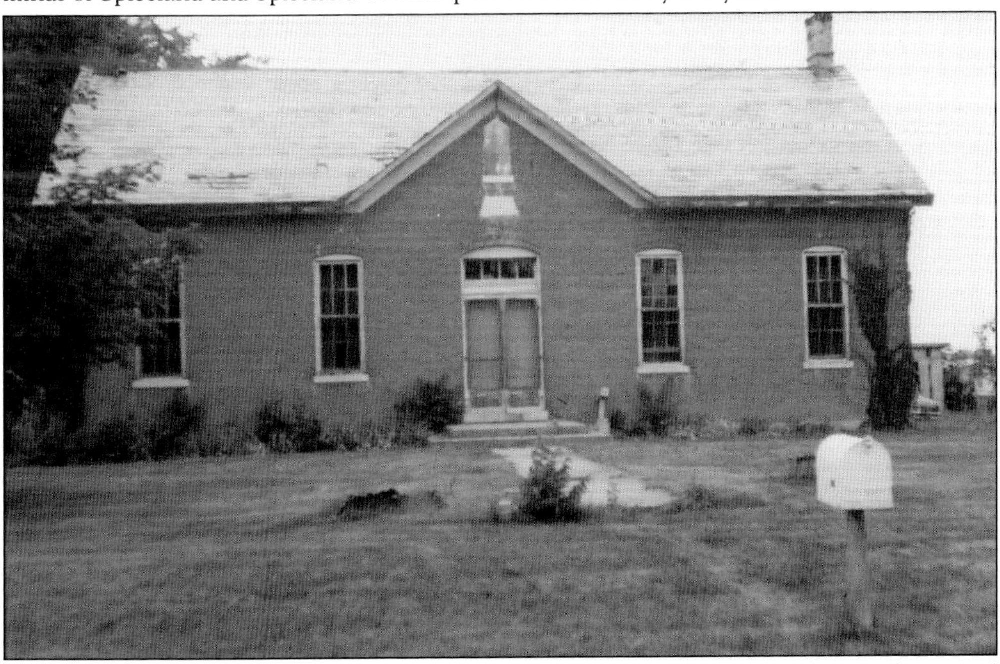

This 1970s photograph shows the former Ogden School. Erected in 1878, it has not been used for school purposes for years. At one point, a tavern known as the Bucket of Blood was housed in the building. Today, it is a private residence.

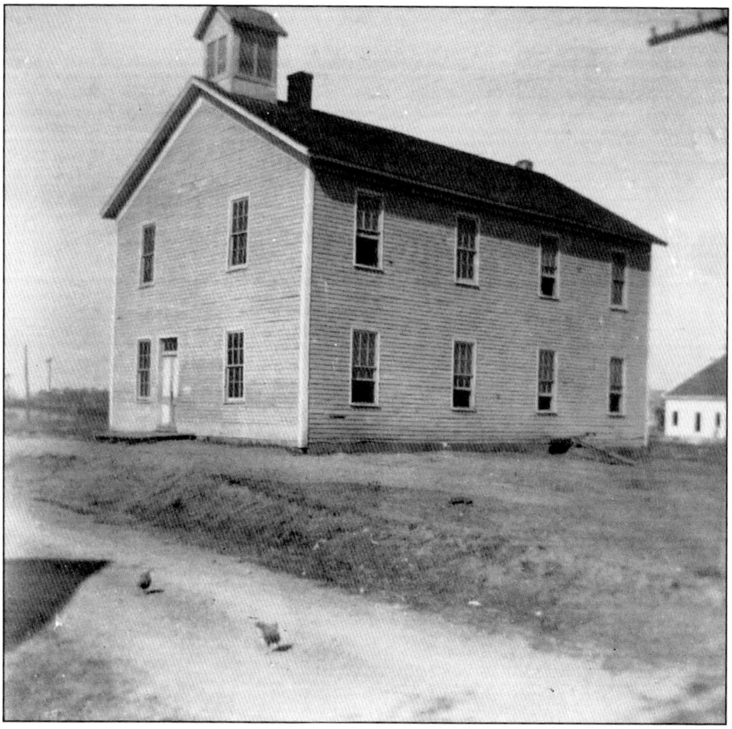

The Dunreith School was erected in 1864 and replaced with a brick building in 1908. The words to the first stanza of the Dunreith community song are sung to the tune of "The Old Oaken Bucket": "How dear to my heart are the scenes of my childhood, / When fond recollections present them to view; / The school of my youth, and the playground near by it / Was all dear to me as to you."

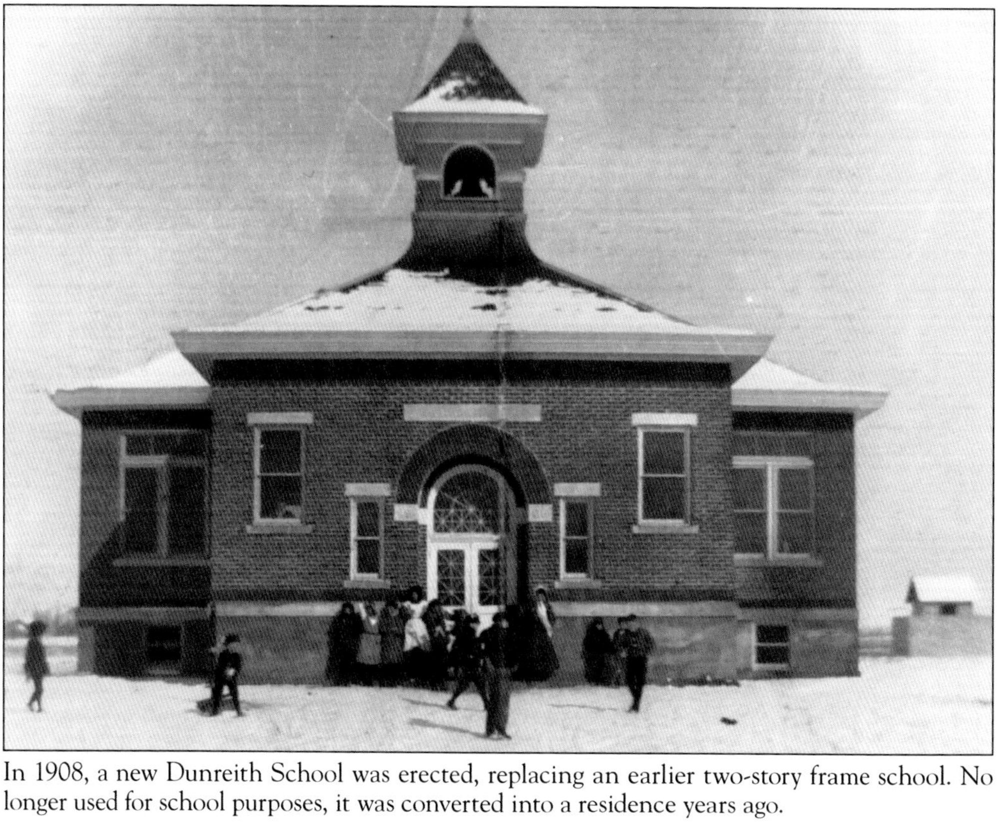

In 1908, a new Dunreith School was erected, replacing an earlier two-story frame school. No longer used for school purposes, it was converted into a residence years ago.

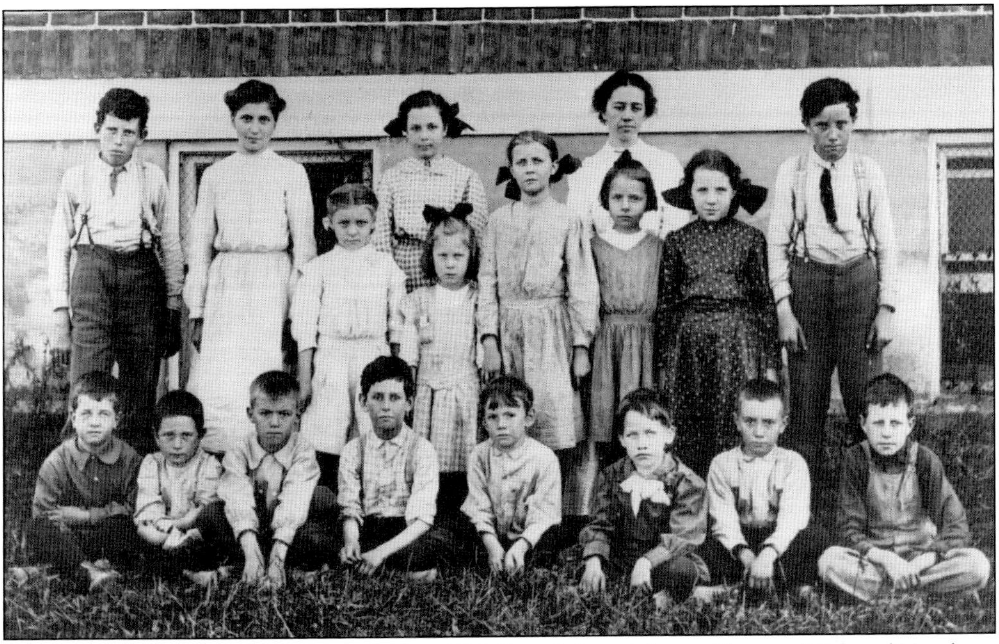

Students at Dunreith were photographed in 1910. From left to right are (first row) Howard Henshaw, Charley Hudelson, Carl Kassen, Julian Crum, "Little Buck" Harrold, Loring Gotchall, unidentified, and Russell Owens; (second row) two unidentified, Gladys Saul, Dorothy Deem, Marie Harter, and Sheridan Sorrell; (third row) Shirley Sorrell, Ruby Ledbetter, unidentified, and Lillian E. Hayes (teacher).

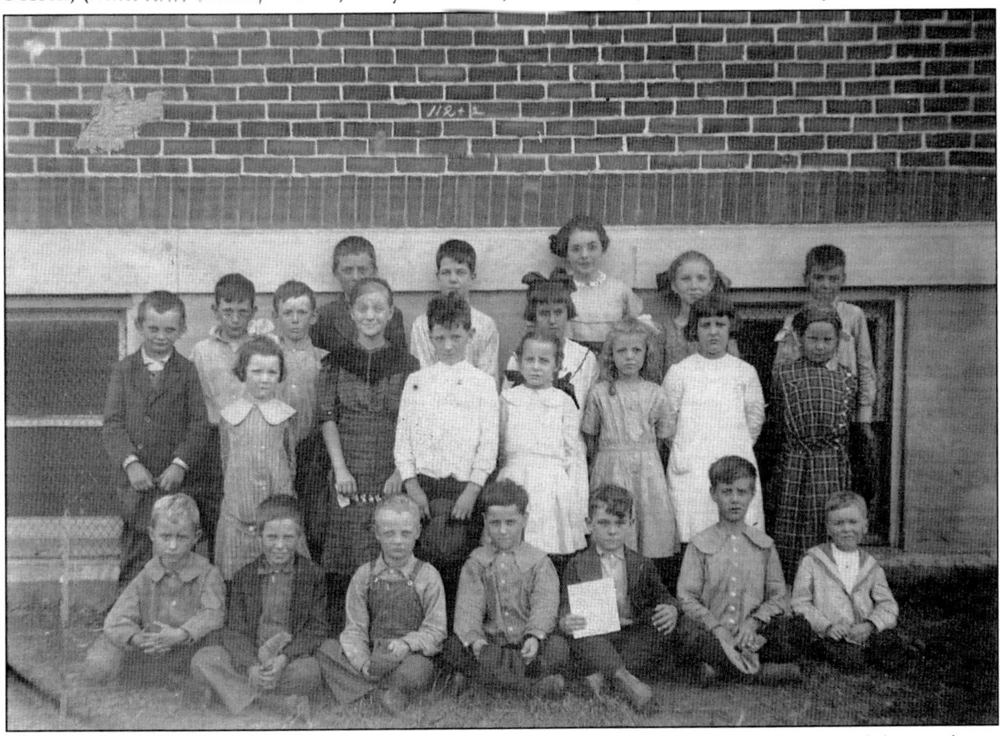

This photograph of students at Dunreith was taken around 1912. Sadly, only one of the students is identified: Agnes (Holtsclaw) Essington, fifth from left in the second row.

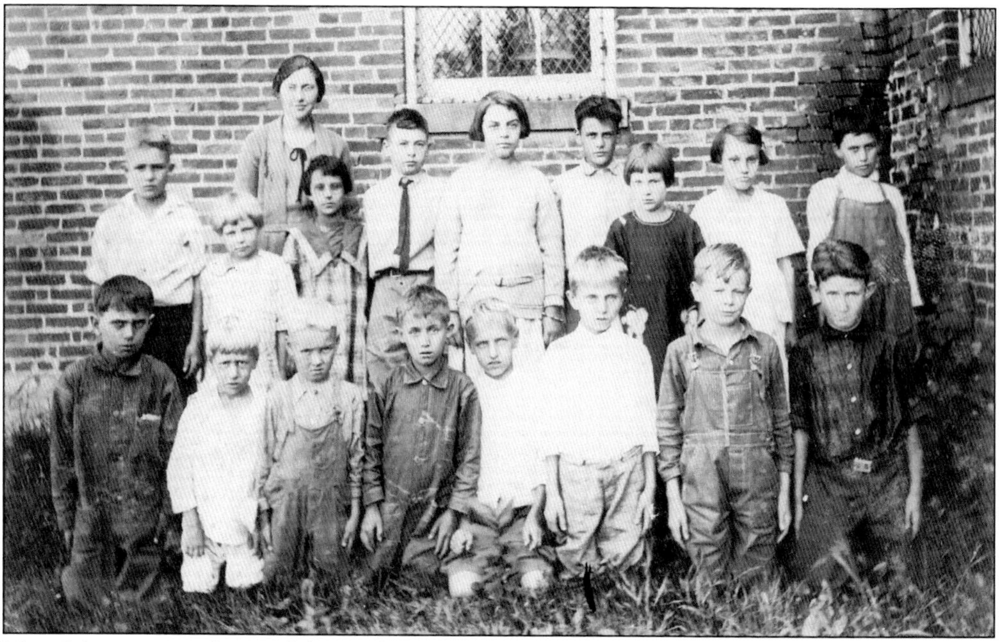

Marie Johnson is seen here with her students at Ogden in 1922. From left to right are (first row) ? Hedrick, Charles Longwell, Charles Brown, ? Hedrick, Oliver Longwell, John Longwell, Hugh Roberts, and Harry Richards; (second row) Marion Brown, Lois Rogers, Barbara Pheneger, James Moffitt, Nevada Williams, Roscoe Pheneger, Rosemary Moffitt, Martha McIntyre, and Clarence Leonard.

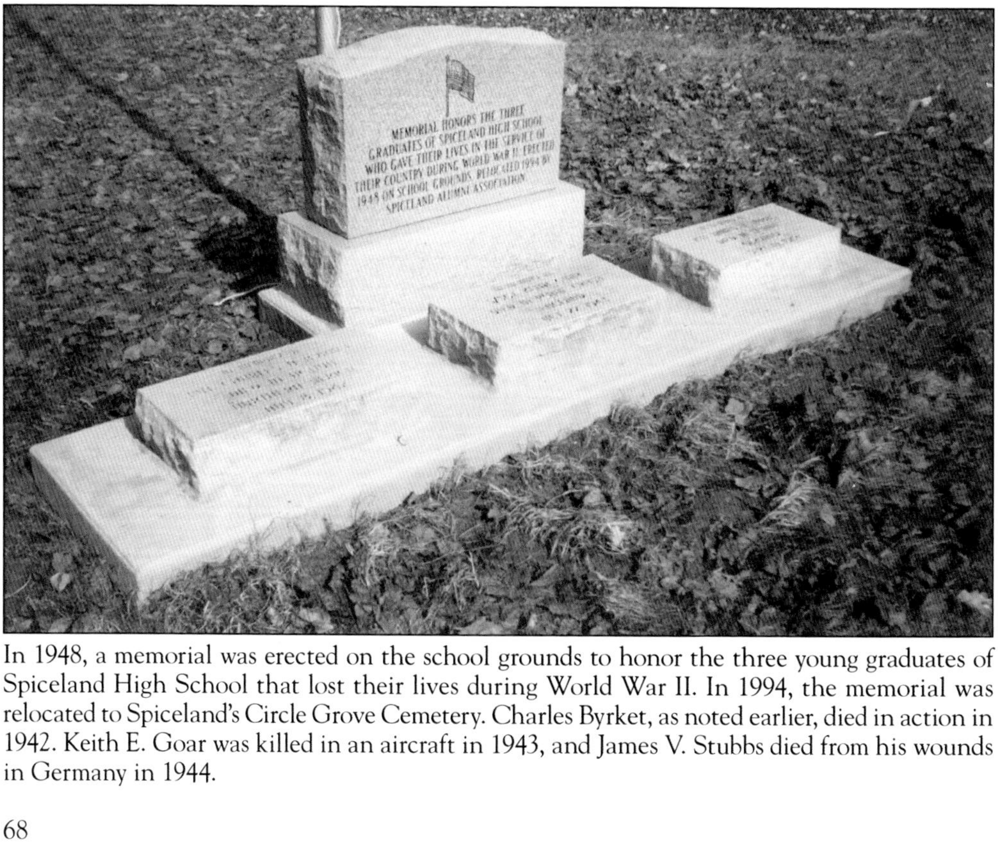

In 1948, a memorial was erected on the school grounds to honor the three young graduates of Spiceland High School that lost their lives during World War II. In 1994, the memorial was relocated to Spiceland's Circle Grove Cemetery. Charles Byrket, as noted earlier, died in action in 1942. Keith E. Goar was killed in an aircraft in 1943, and James V. Stubbs died from his wounds in Germany in 1944.

Robert V. Mathes came to Spiceland to teach in 1950. In 1955, he was made principal of Spiceland High School, and he continued in that position until the high school closed in 1969. From 1969 until his retirement in 1987, he was principal of both Spiceland Elementary and Tri Elementary.

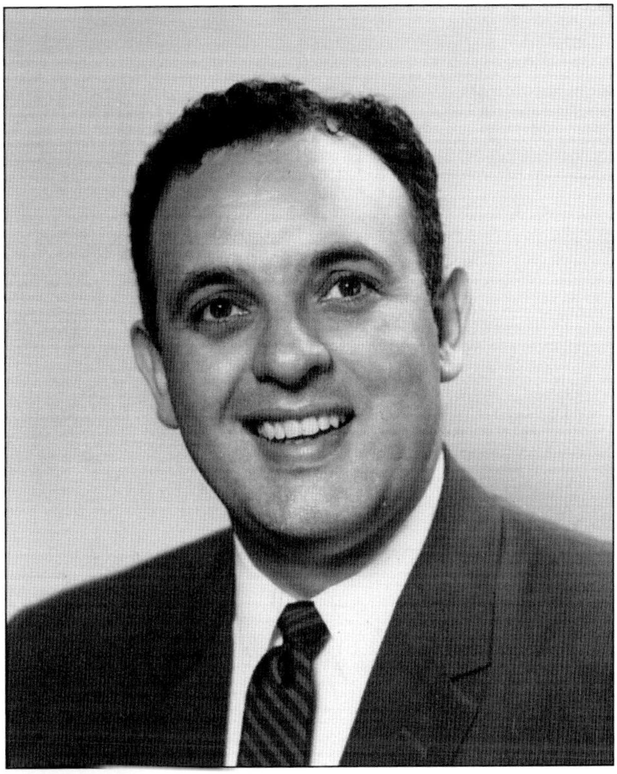

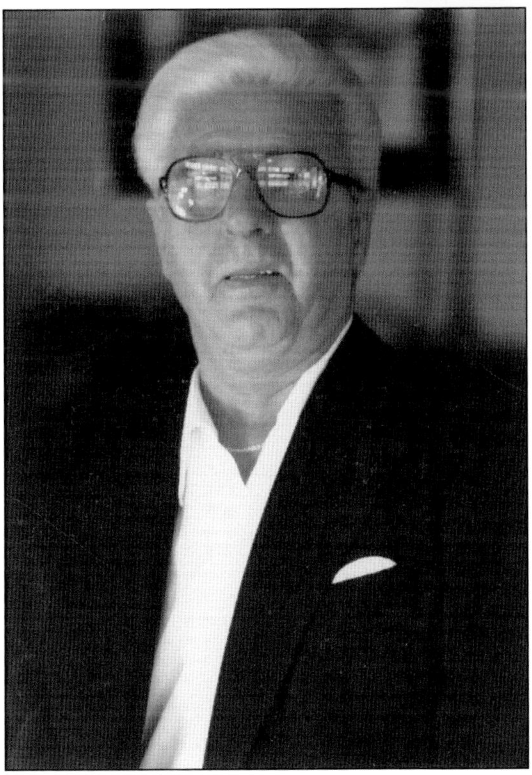

Robert Beck Wade (1910–1996) was a much-loved junior high school teacher at Spiceland, where he taught for 36 years. This photograph was taken at his 75th-birthday open house in 1985.

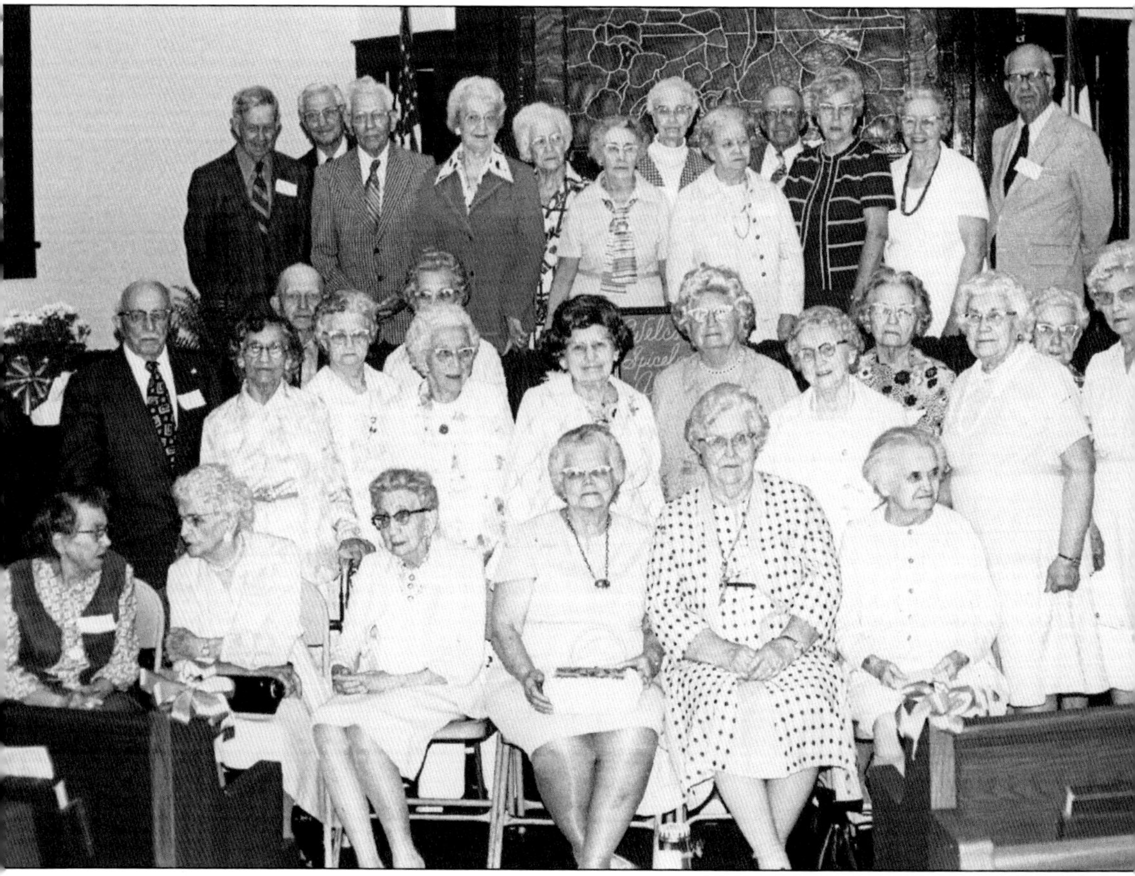

At the May 15, 1976, Spiceland alumni meeting, 31 graduates of Spiceland Academy assembled for this group photograph. This was the last time this many graduates were able to attend the annual meeting of the association. Those pictured graduated between 1900 and 1921. From left to right are (first row) Emma Smiley, Alnetta Ward, Gertrude Catey, Mildred Hardin, Irene Titus, and Edith C. Moffitt; (second row) Perry Wilson, Ada Hinshaw, Venton Brenneman, Emogene Harrold, Mary Wilson (partially hidden), Mary Chenoweth, Flossie Crum, Minnie Boyd, Pauline Haisley, Edith S. Moffitt, Exie Collins, Mary Smith, and Violet Bird; (third row) Ed Poer, Horace Shepherd, Dwight Shepherd, Opal Stobaugh, Nellie Stafford, Hazel Taylor, Ruby Brenneman, Mossie DePew, Dorsey Poer, Mary Hollensbe, Faye Vanderbeck, and Franklin Henshaw.

Five

Entrepreneurs, Spiceland Township Style

Certain residents of Spiceland Township have long been known for their initiative and their capacity to be productive and economically successful. Some businesses are still known for their longevity, while others that dated back for decades have only recently closed.

Draper, Inc., is now in its 12th decade. The Oliver C. Steele Manufacturing Company existed for 94 years. Wilson Market is currently over 100 years old, and Spiceland had a drugstore for 98 years. For approximately 115 years, Dunreith had a blacksmith shop, and barbers have been cutting hair in Spiceland for as long as the town has existed. Until 2013, there had been a bank in Spiceland for 120 years.

So, the long and the short of it is that some businesses have been, or were, around for quite a long time. Some, of course, had but a short existence. Over the years, a large number of groceries and restaurants in the township were not successful. Competition, a lack of good management, the economy, and a small clientele caused many would-be entrepreneurs to fail.

In this section of the book, the successful, the unsuccessful, and the businesses that only lasted for a short time will all be highlighted.

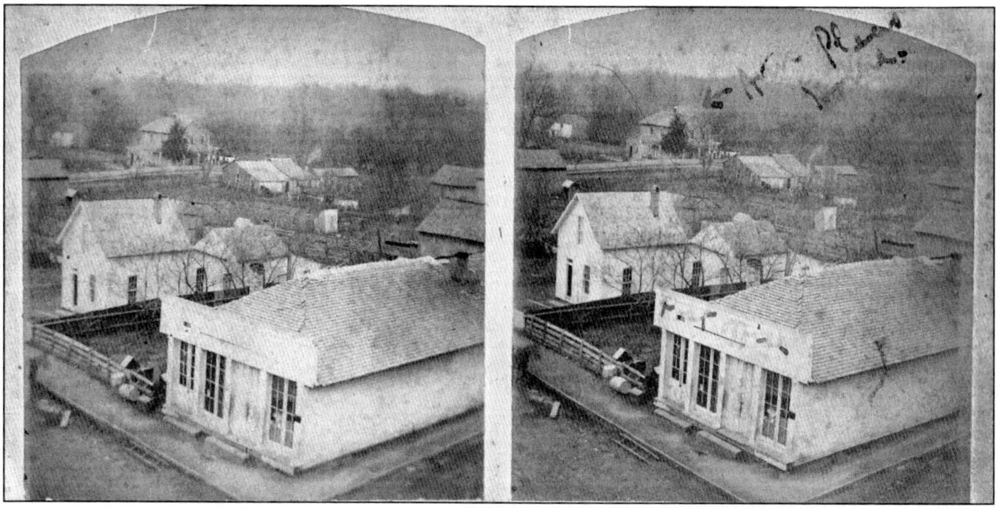

Tradition has it that Solomon Sweet (1800–1839) was Spiceland's first merchant. What he sold in his store remains a mystery, but it was probably dry goods and an assortment of general merchandise. After the store was removed, Oliver Nixon's drugstore was erected on the site in 1878.

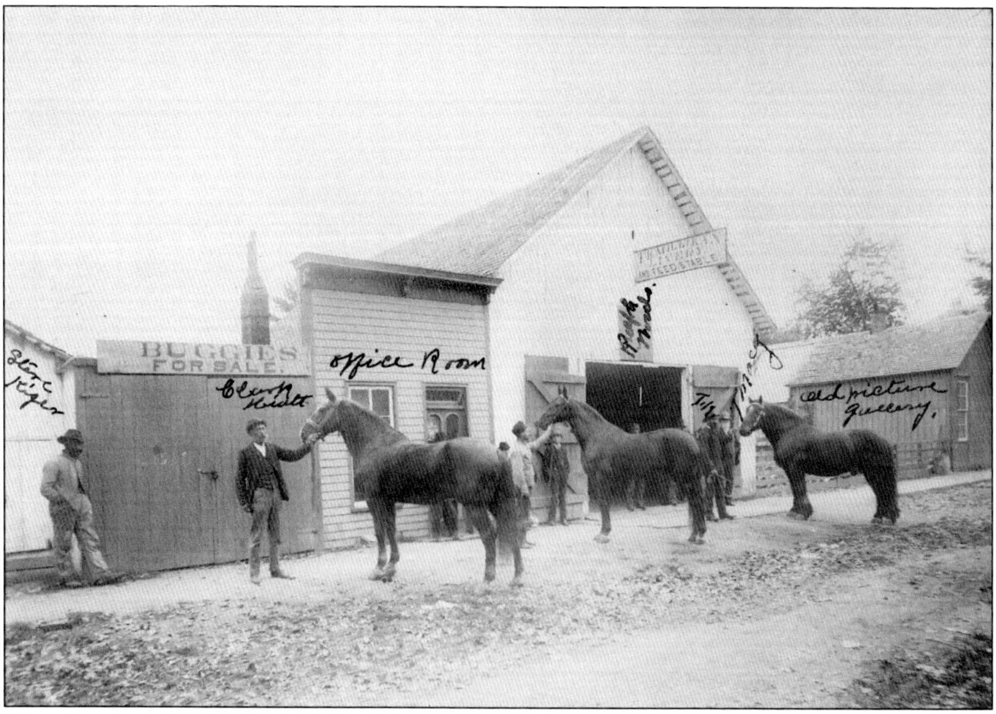

This photograph, probably taken in the 1880s, shows a number of buildings along the east side of North Pearl Street in Spiceland. The taller building housed T.K. Millikan's livery and feed stable. Robert Gordon's photography studio is seen on the far right. Standing on the far left is Steve Kiser, a former slave.

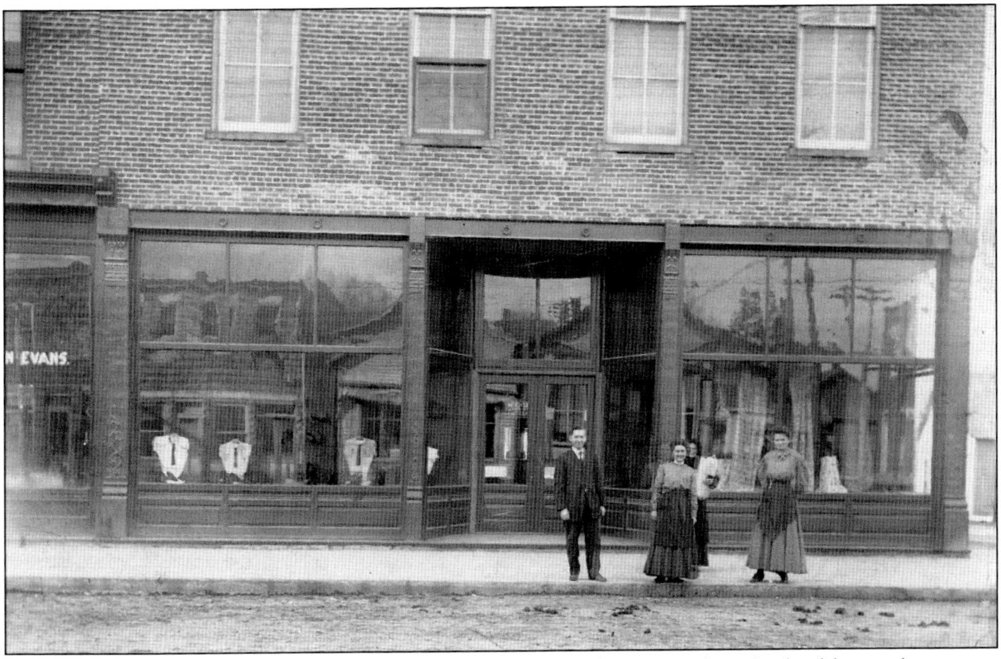

Alton Evans is seen in front of his dry goods store around 1910. Today, the building is known as Hoover Hall.

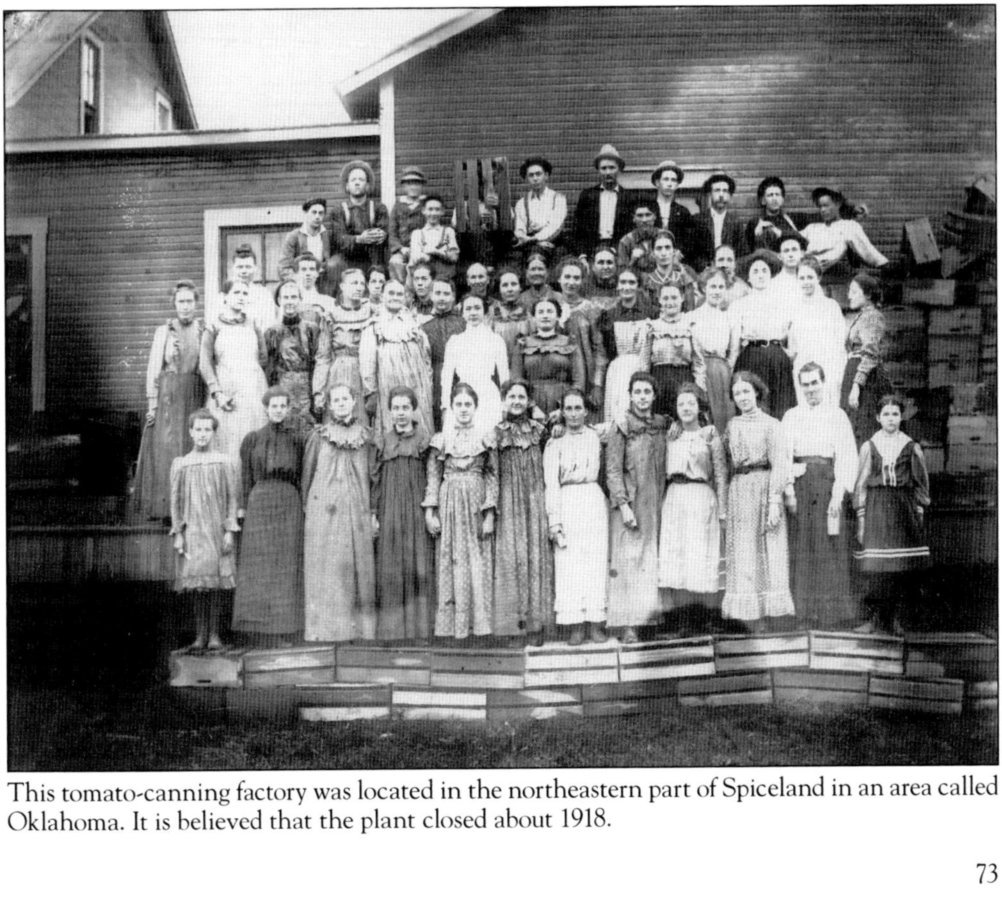

This tomato-canning factory was located in the northeastern part of Spiceland in an area called Oklahoma. It is believed that the plant closed about 1918.

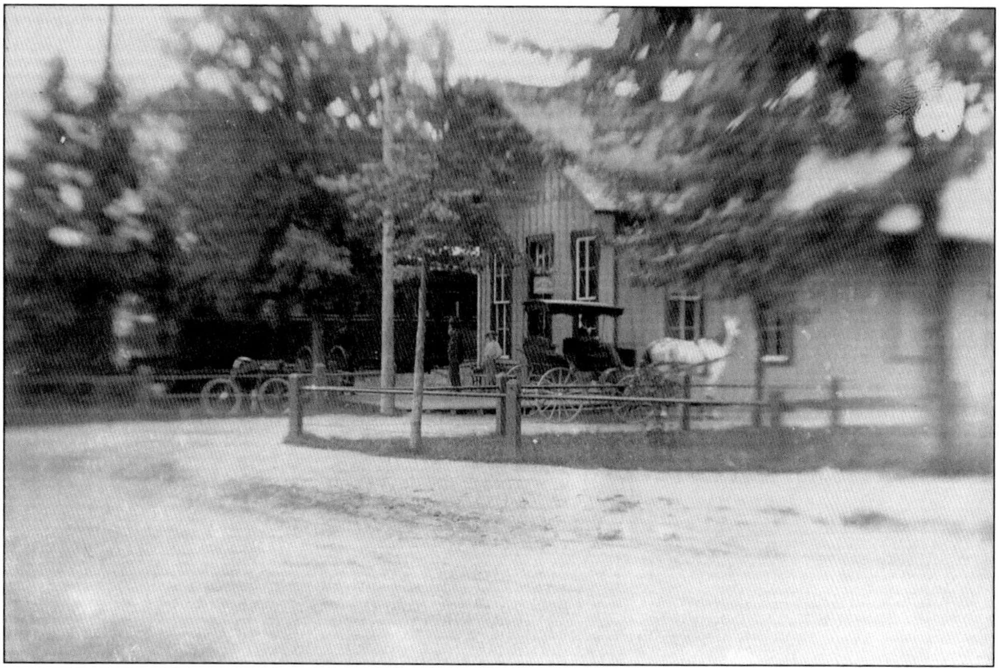

The coming of the railroad to Spiceland in 1881 gave impetus to the growth of the town. The Lake Erie & Western Railroad, and, later, the Nickel Plate Railroad, gave Spiceland an economic boost. The depot was erected between 1882 and 1883. Residents would go to the depot to see the evening train arrive and depart for Rushville. The passenger train was known locally as "Old Spooney." Many aspiring young swains courted their ladies while riding the train, "spooning" being another name for courting at the time. The depot closed in 1961, and the building was eventually razed.

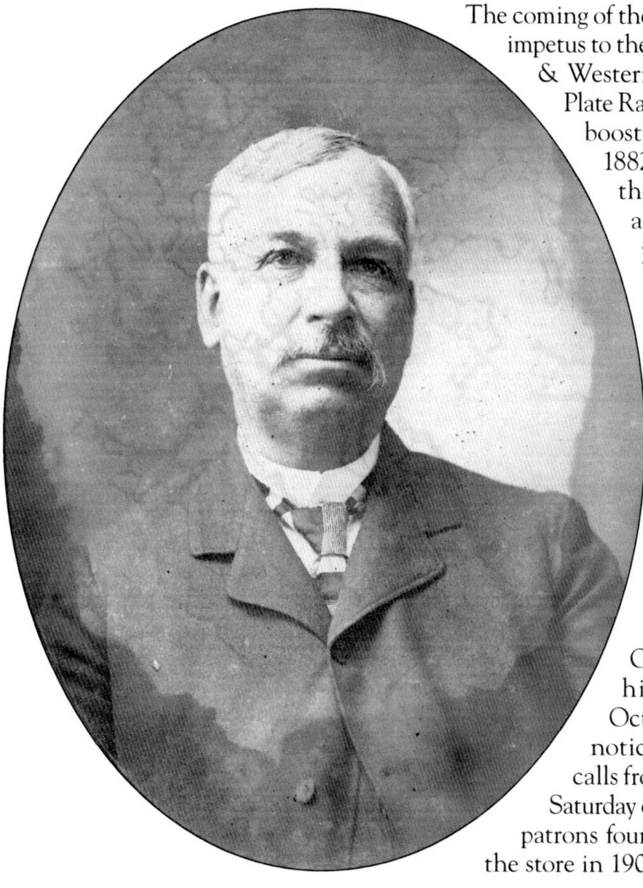

Oliver Hobbs Nixon opened his drugstore in Spiceland on October 18, 1878, with the following notice: "I shall be pleased to receive calls from my friends in my business room Saturday evening from 7 to 9." Unfortunately, patrons found him dead behind a counter in the store in 1906.

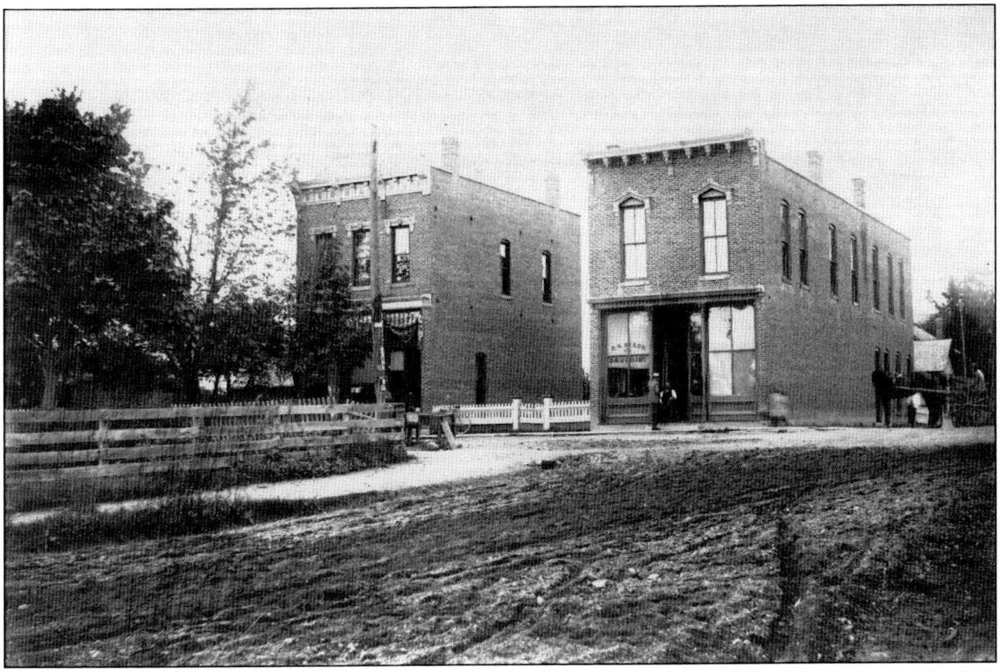

This 1896 photograph shows the Bank of Spiceland (left) and Oliver Nixon's drugstore (right). Note the rutted, unpaved street.

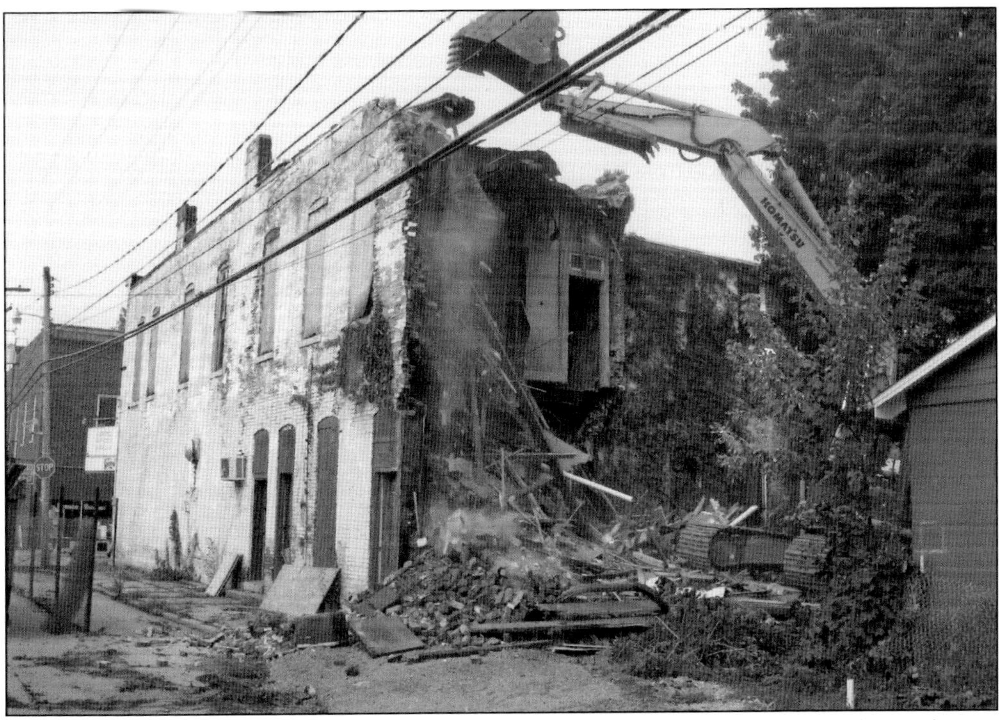

After serving three successive druggists, Oliver Nixon, Clyde Smith, and F.M. "Andy" Anderson, this building fell to the wrecking ball on July 22, 2010. The building had been crumbling since March 2006.

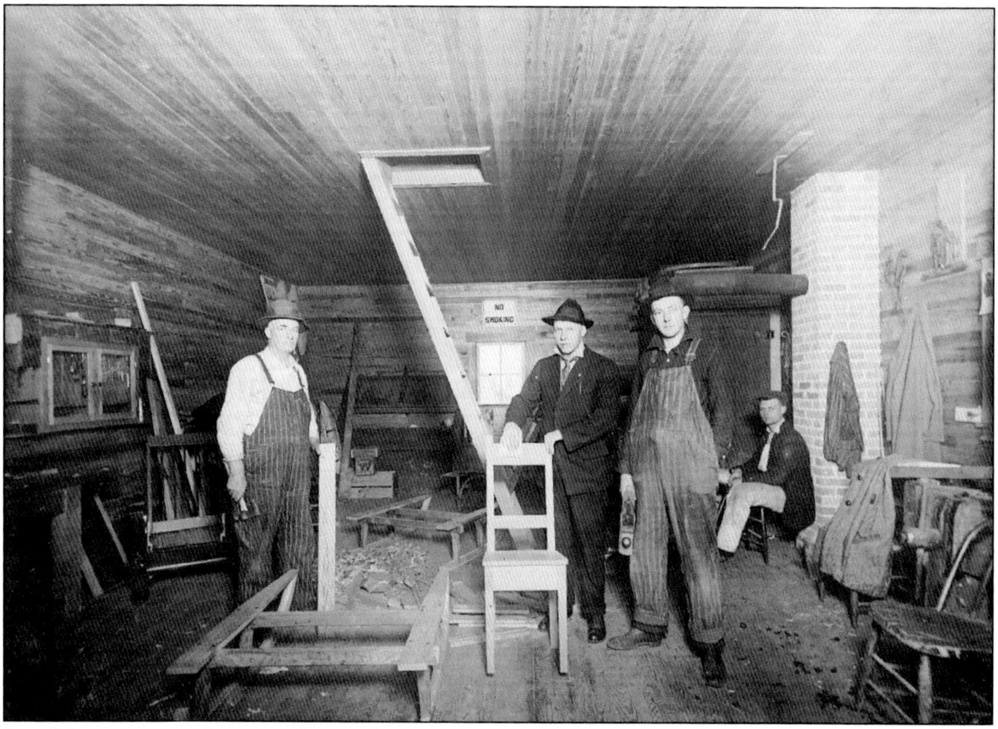

Bundy's carpenter shop was located on South Pearl Street in Spiceland. From left to right are Frank Bundy, Lem Rifner, Floyd Bundy, and Carroll Copeland.

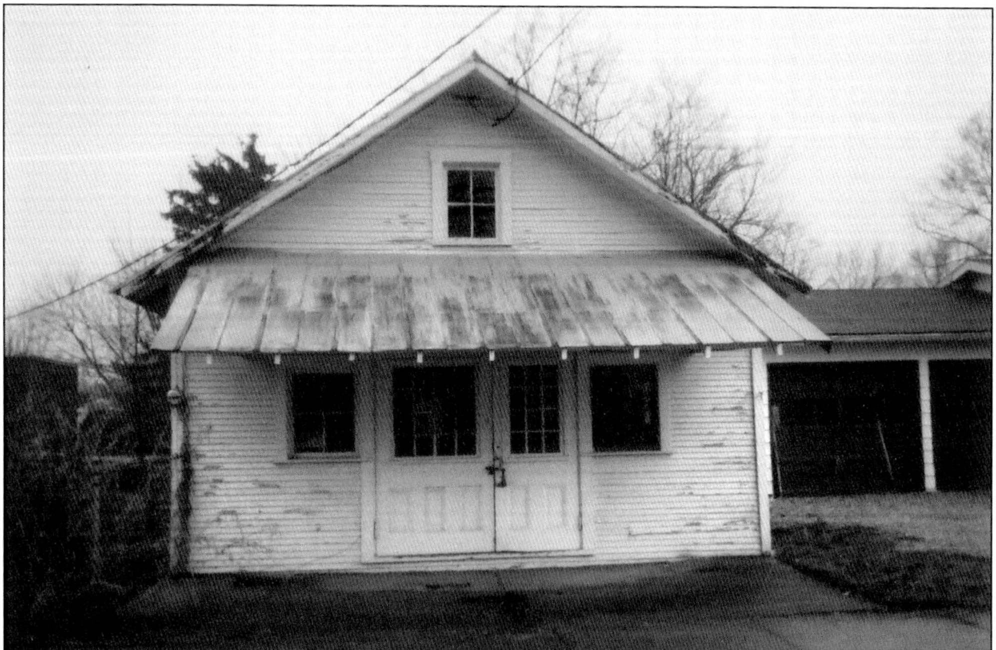

The former Bundy's carpentry shop has seen little activity in nearly 50 years and remains unoccupied today.

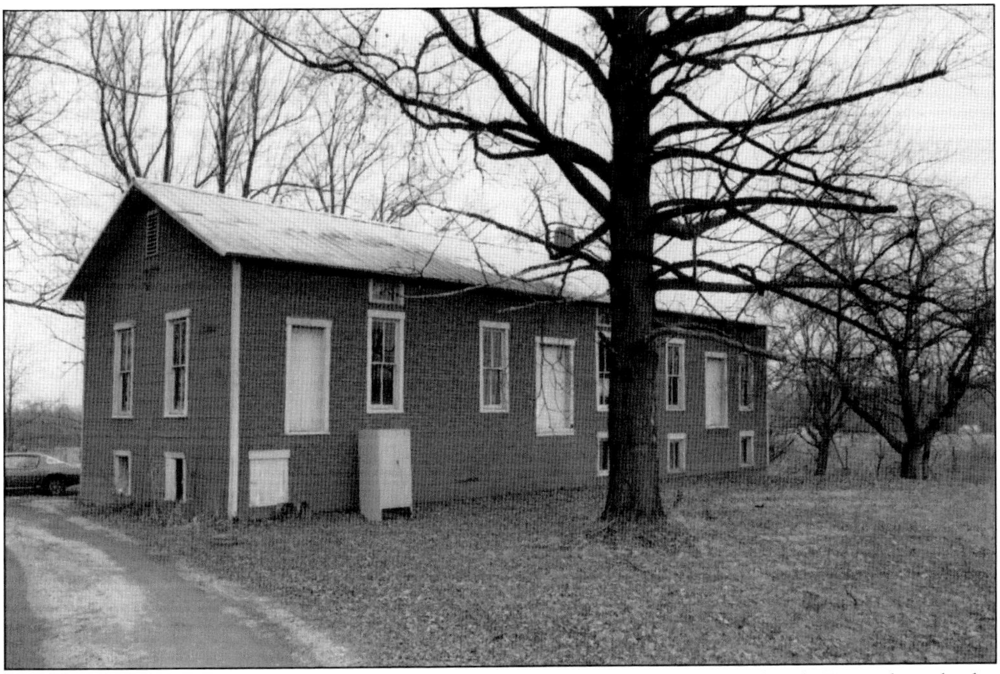

For many years, Albert Symons operated an orchard northeast of Spiceland. Even though the orchard has been gone for over 60 years, the apple storage house remains.

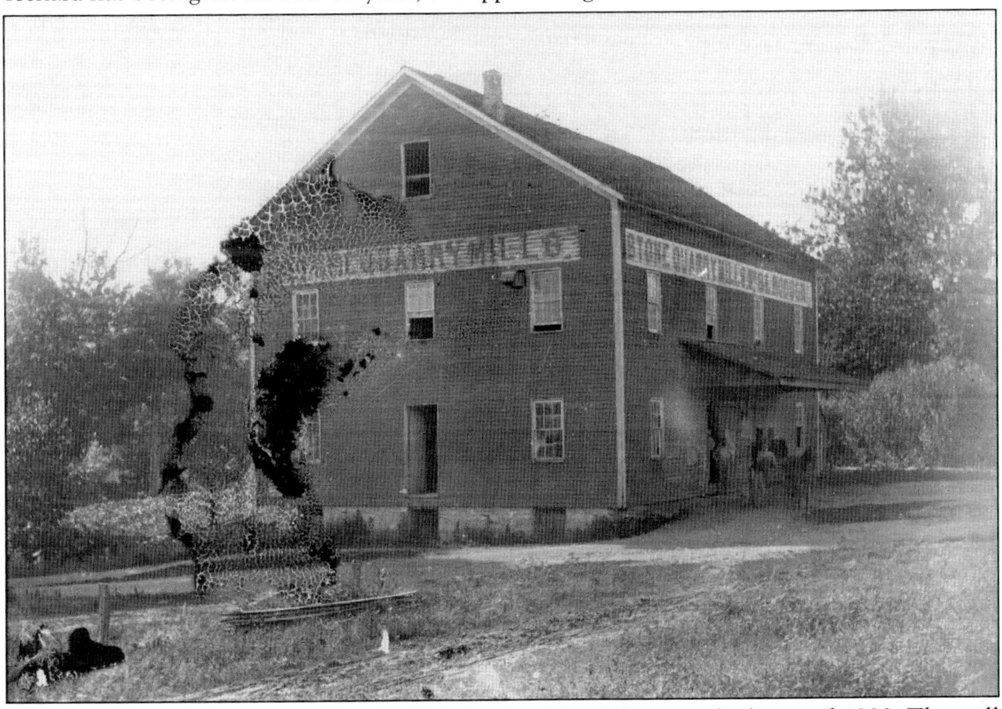

The Stone Quarry Mills, located west of Spiceland, was photographed around 1900. The mill burned down in 1911, when Rankin Bert Reece was operating it. William Hodson, Reece's father-in-law, had been one of the earlier millers. Timbers from the old upper mill on the Big Blue River were moved and reassembled to complete the current mill, which is no longer used.

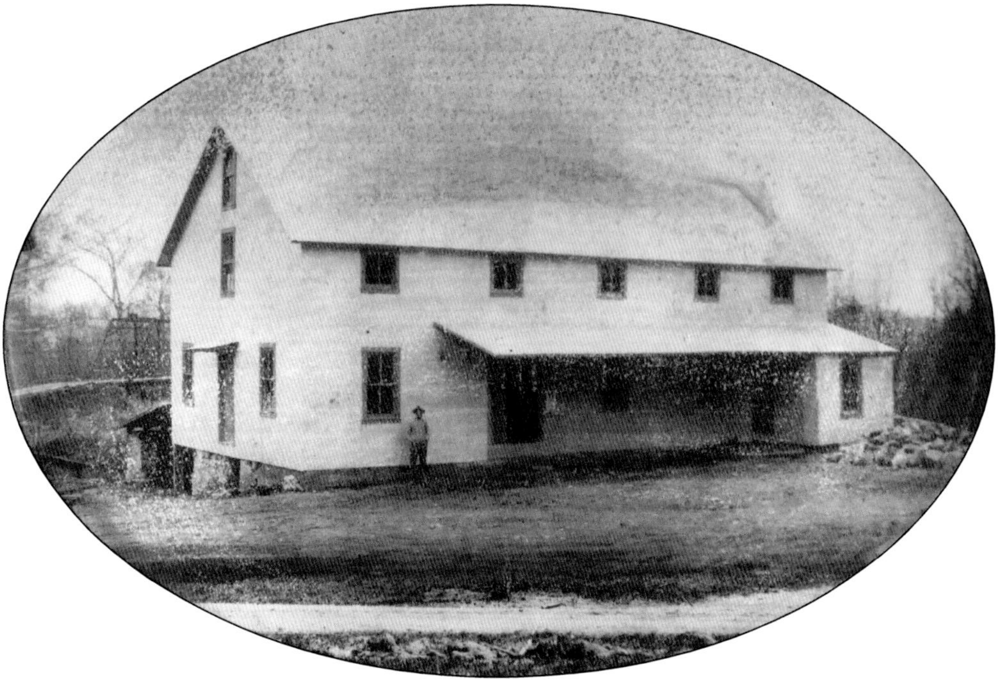

After the original structure burned down, a new Stone Quarry Mills was erected the next year. Still standing today, it has been converted into a residence in recent years. (Courtesy of Martha Resler.)

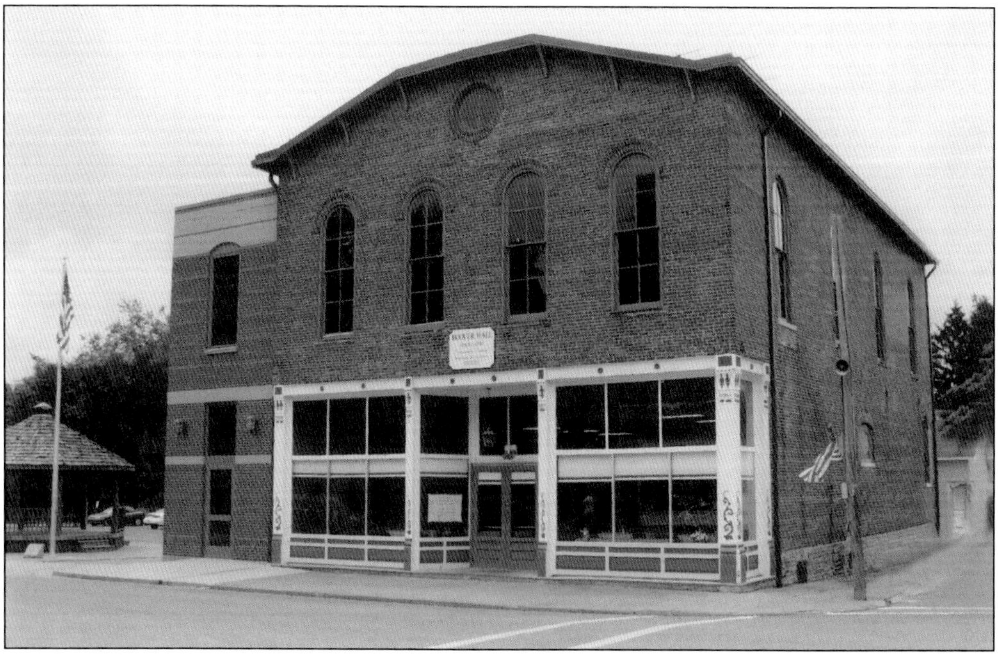

Hoover Hall was erected in the center of Spiceland in 1875. Although the building has been used by several businesses over the years, it was mostly used as a dry goods store. Currently, it is the home of the Spiceland Preservation and Tourism Society and serves as Spiceland's community center, museum, and art gallery.

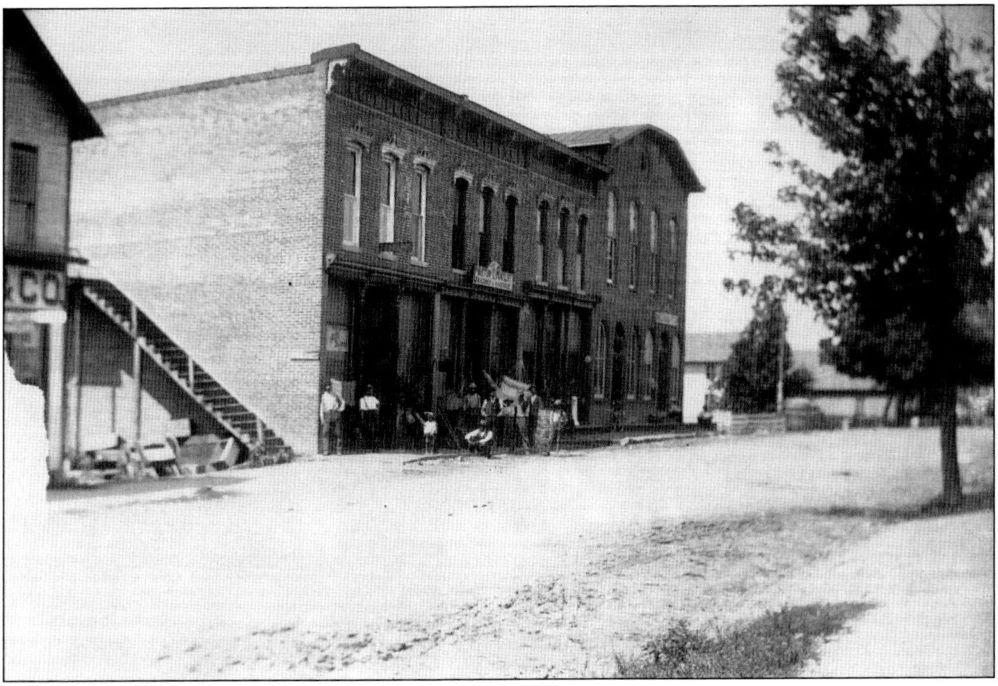

This business block on East Main Street in Spiceland was photographed around 1898. Hoover Hall is the taller of the brick buildings. All of the adjoining brick buildings were razed in 1982.

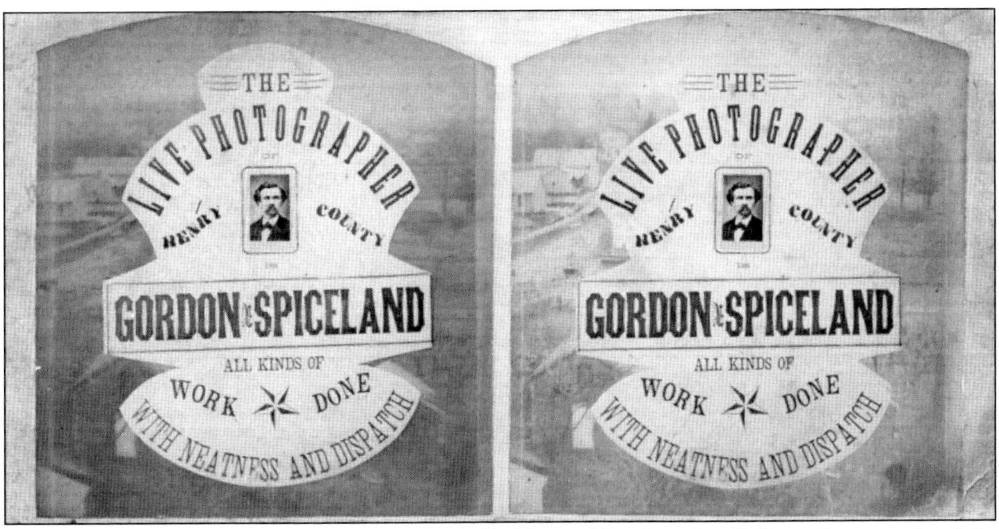

It is interesting to note that Robert Gordon billed himself as Spiceland's "live photographer." At some point, he left Spiceland and continued his business in Indianapolis.

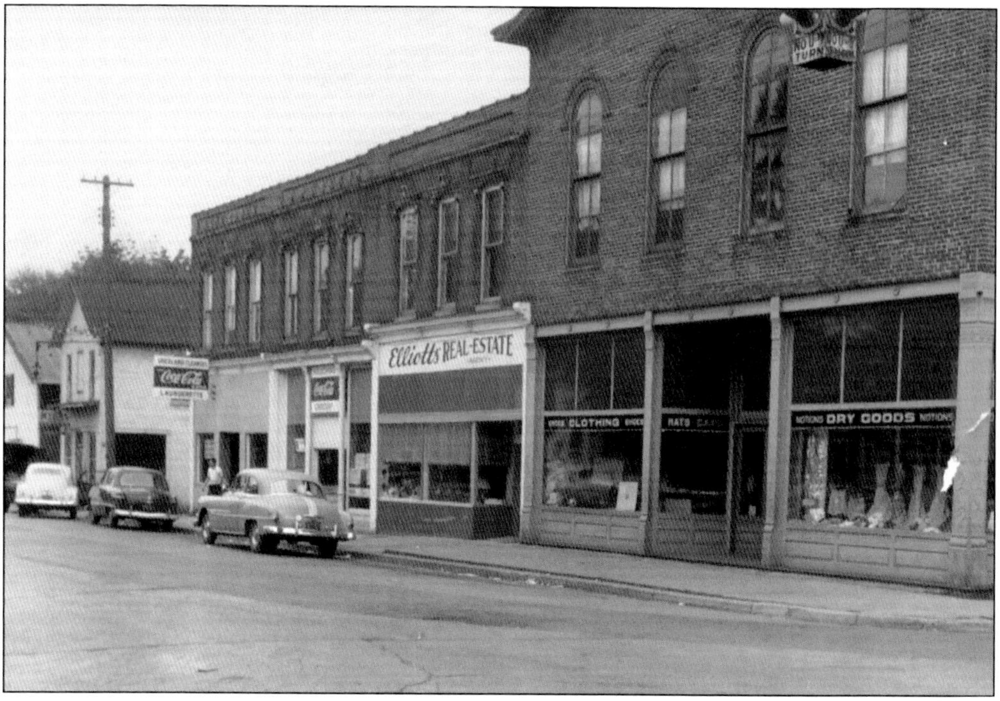

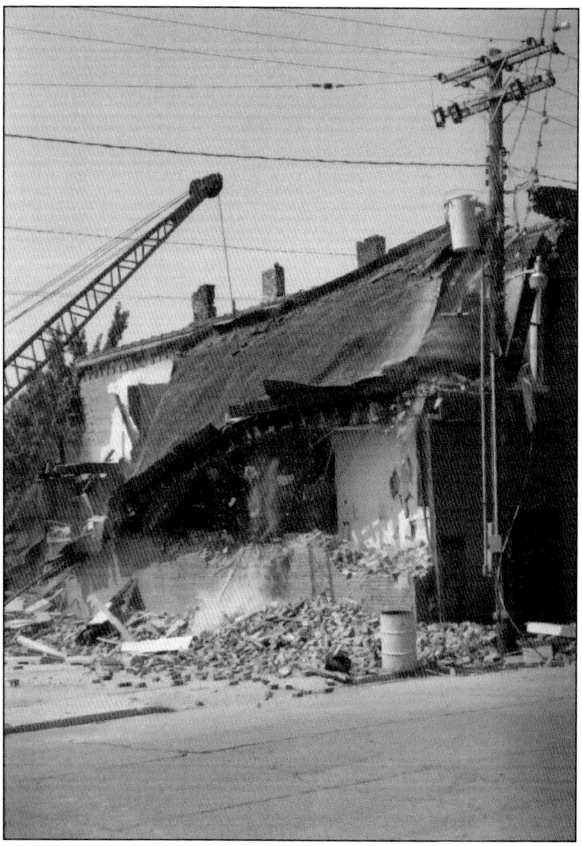

This 1956 photograph shows some of the businesses on East Main Street in Spiceland. Hoover Hall is the building on the right advertising dry goods.

On August 16, 1982, several business buildings adjacent to Hoover Hall on Spiceland's Main Street were razed due to safety concerns and health hazards. These buildings had housed mainly groceries and restaurants over the years.

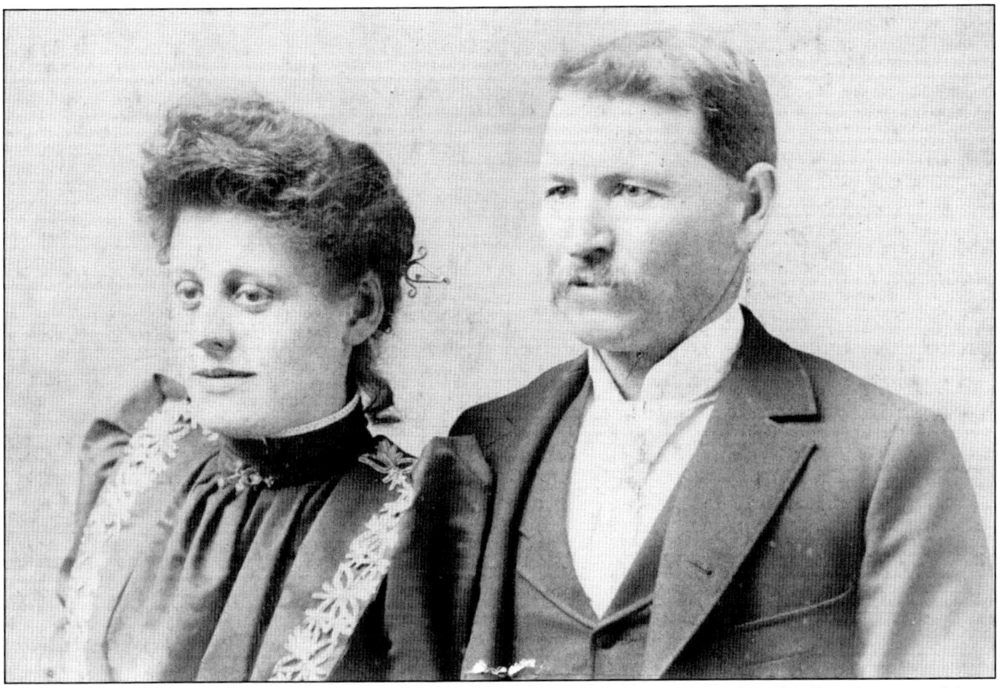

On October 1, 1891, John Stigleman took young Lora Simmons as his bride; their wedding photograph is shown here. Stigleman was a Civil War veteran. Several years after the war, he started a furniture factory in Spiceland, the J. Stigleman Manufacturing Company.

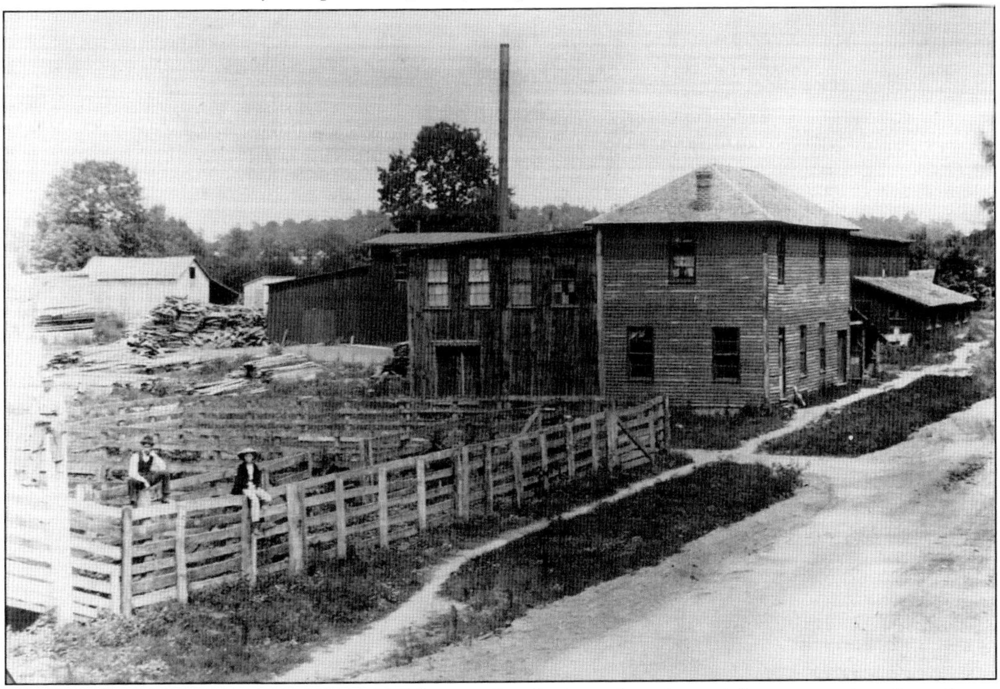

The Stigleman factory manufactured house finish (woodwork and fancy carvings), caskets, cupboards, folding chairs, doors, and washing machines. The factory, pictured here, was destroyed by fire in 1918.

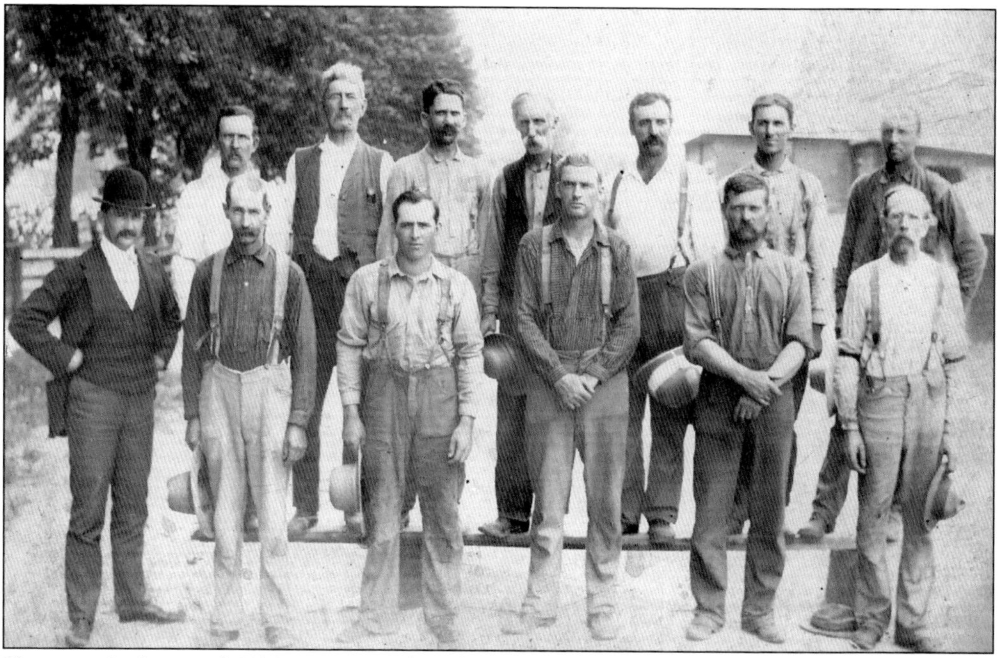

Photographed around 1896 are some of Stigleman's employees. From left to right are (first row) Clarence Hall, Harry Millis, Harry Rife, Frank Bundy, Tom Hodson, and Joe Barber; (second row) Thomas Clarkson Gordon, J. Addison Unthank, Marcellus Taylor, Clark Antrim, Charles Ballenger, Lon Manifold, and Charles Ward.

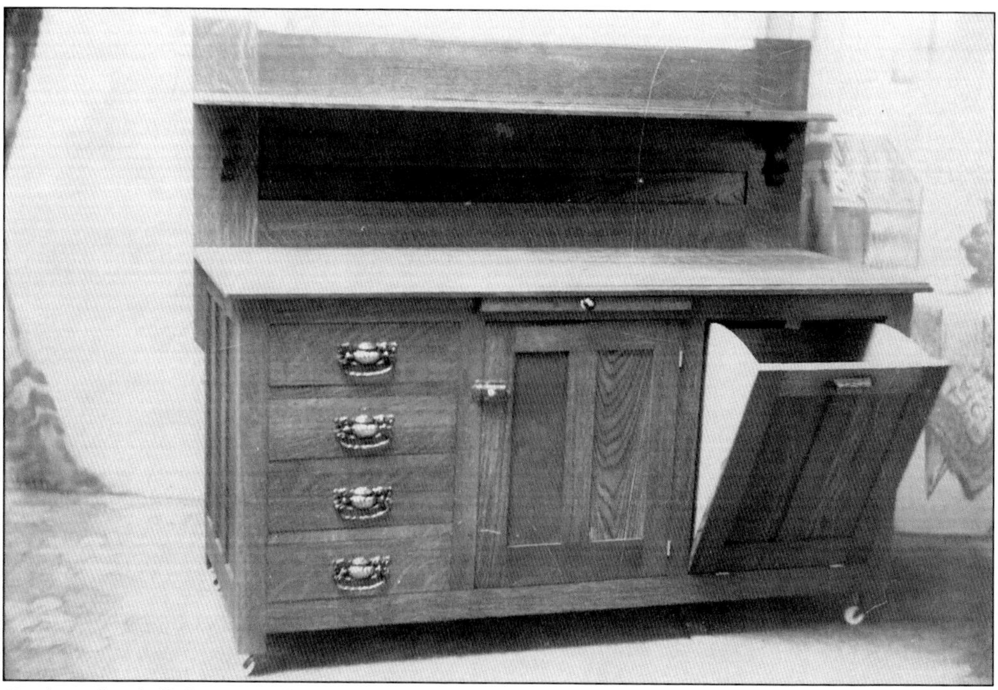

Cupboards of all shapes and sizes were manufactured at the Stigleman factory. A cupboard very similar to the one shown here can be seen at the Henry County Historical Society Museum in New Castle.

Pictured here is an oak door made at the Stigleman factory. The Spiceland Friends Meeting has two cupboards that were made at the factory, both of which are very different in design.

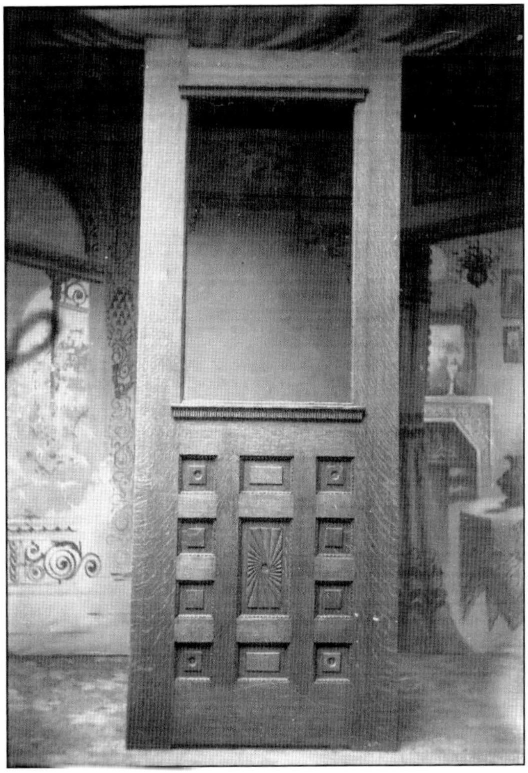

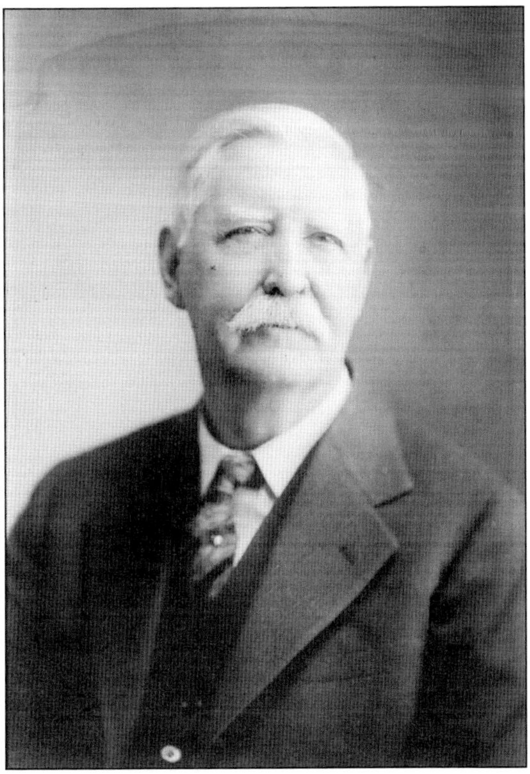

In 1900, Oliver C. Steele (1862–1945) founded the Oliver C. Steele Manufacturing Company in Spiceland. The firm mainly manufactured window shades and, later, gymnasium equipment. The business closed in 1994.

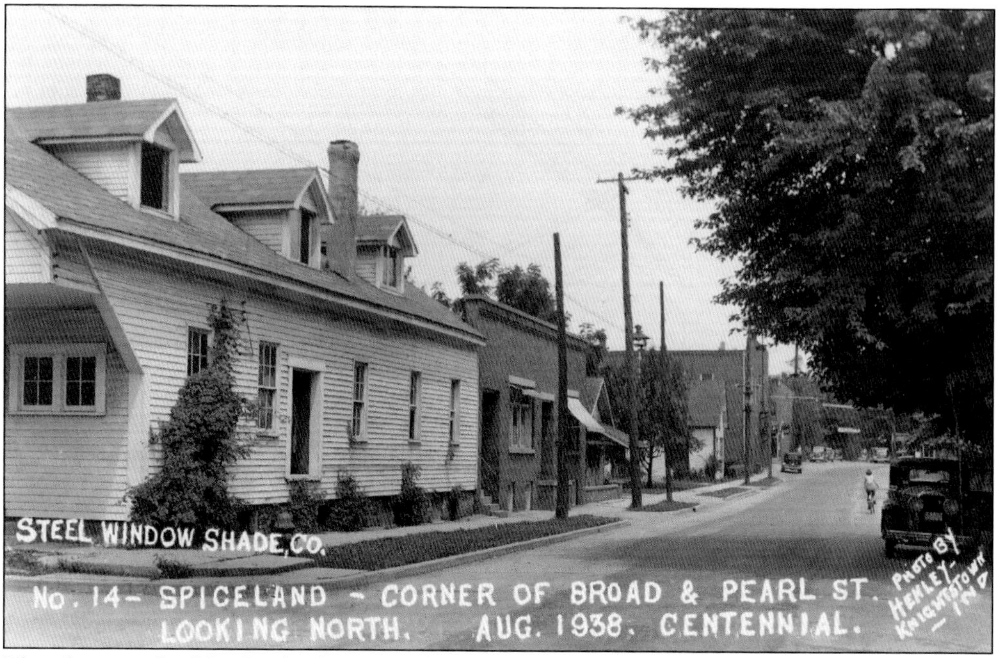

This photograph of the Steele plant was taken in 1938 during the Spiceland centennial. The frame building was originally used for grain storage, and washing machines were later manufactured there. Alexander Steele, Oliver C. Steele's father, once had a blacksmith shop in the basement.

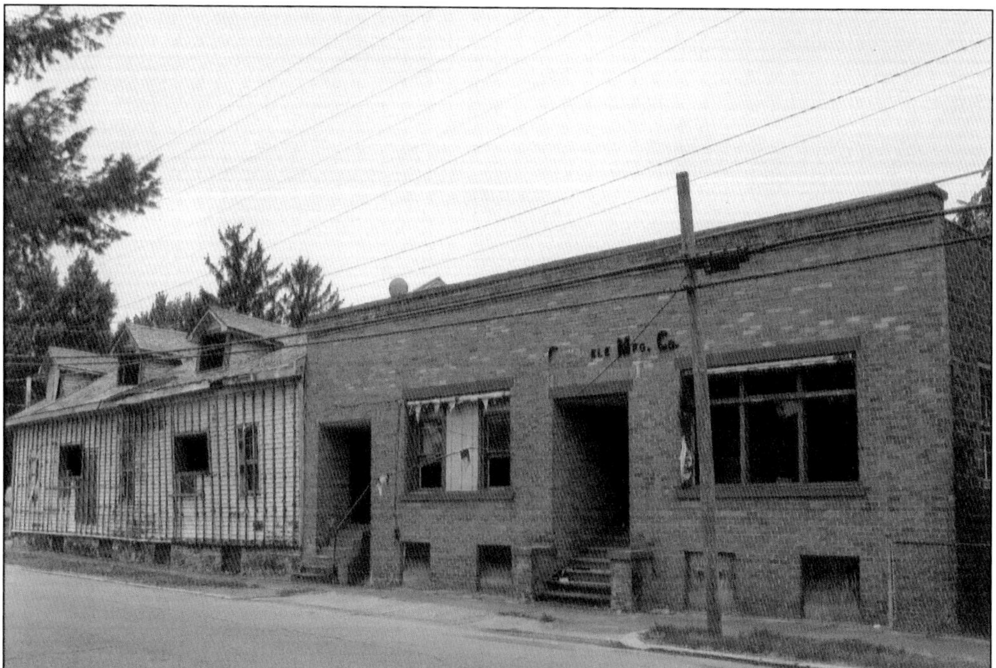

On September 17–18, 2013, the former Steele complex was razed. Basically unoccupied since the factory closed in 1994, the buildings had deteriorated to the point that removal was inevitable. This photograph was taken just before demolition began.

This advertisement for the Steele factory dates from the 1950s. During this period in the firm's history, Meriweather Steele Hamilton, a nephew of Oliver Steele, was the owner of the company.

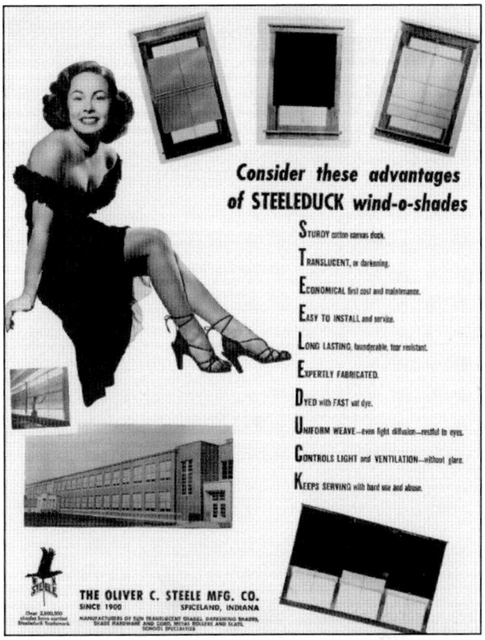

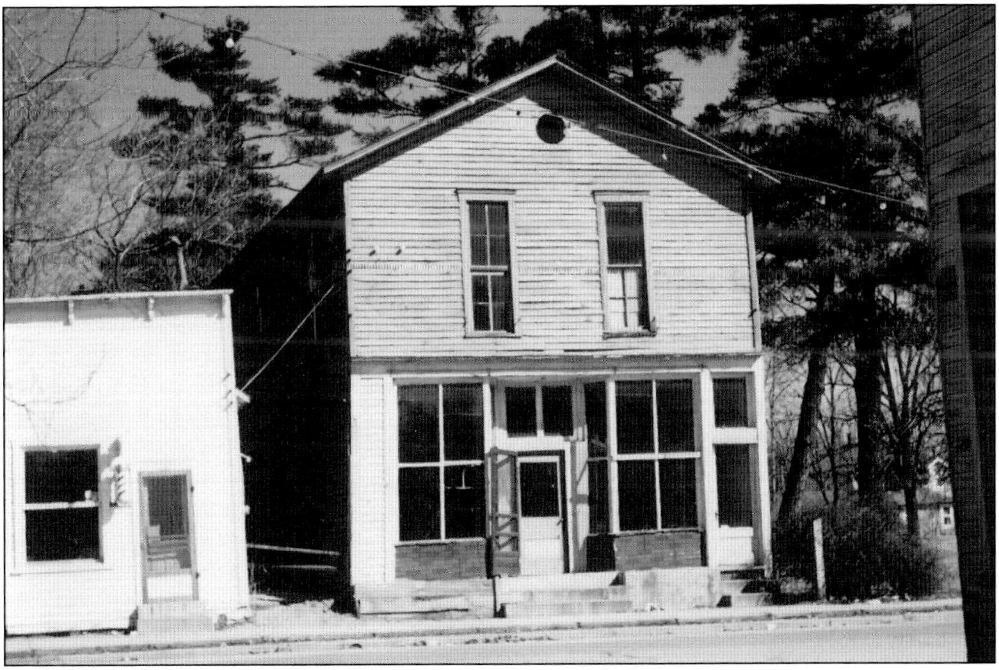

These two frame buildings in Spiceland had many uses over the years. The building on the left once housed a shoe shop, followed by a lunchroom, a barbershop, and, finally, a coin laundry. The back half of the larger building was built by Samuel Lane for a painting and carpentry shop. Lane painted buggies and wagons on the upper story. He constructed an incline on the east side of the building so he could take the items to the second story. A rope and winch built at the top of the stairs pulled the buggies and wagons up to the second floor. The front half of the building was constructed about 1891. Over the years, the building was used as a harness shop, a meat market, a grocery, and, finally, a secondhand store. The building was dismantled in 1959.

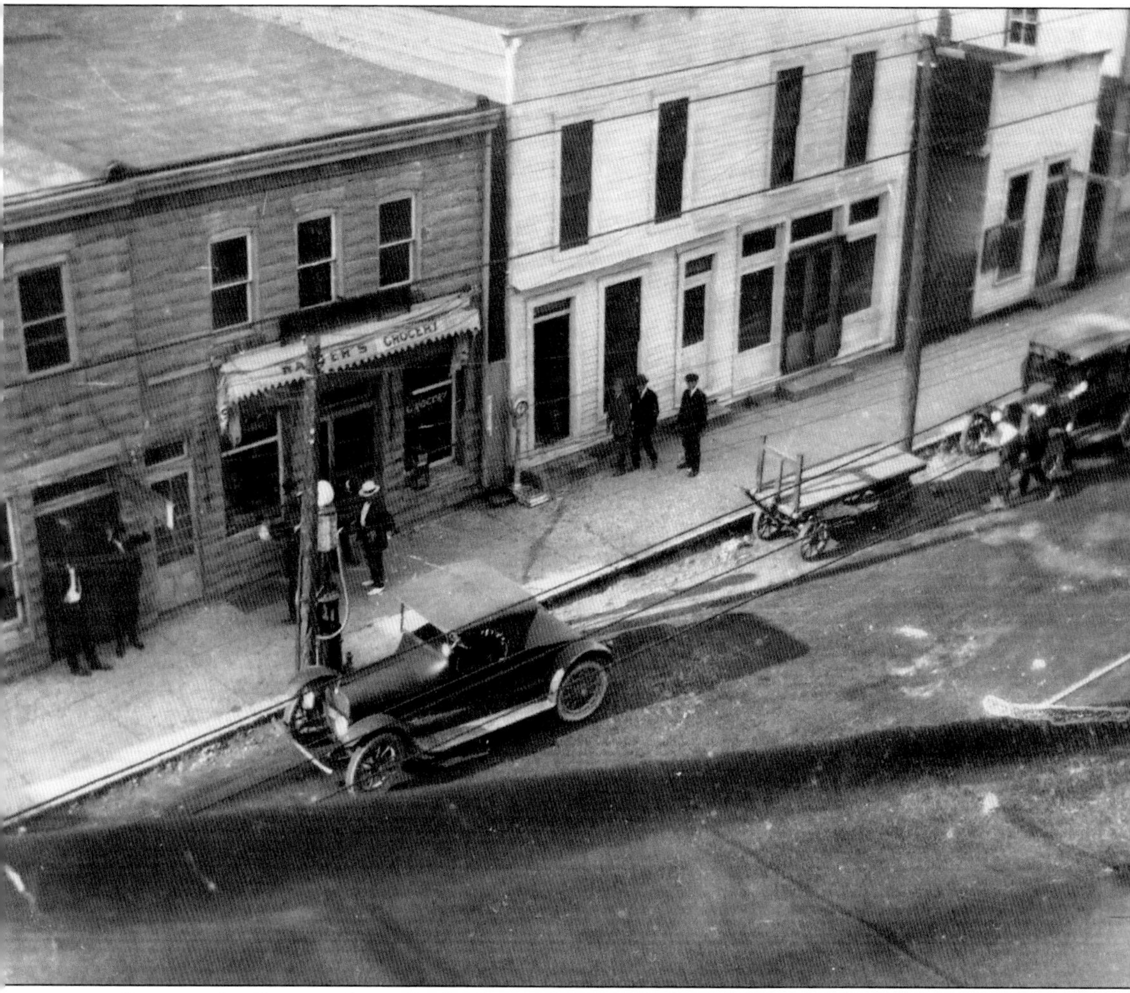

Photographed here in the early 1920s is a portion of Spiceland's business district. The businesses are, from left to right, a cream station, a grocery, the interurban station and lunchroom, a meat market, a barbershop, a shoe-repair shop, and another meat market.

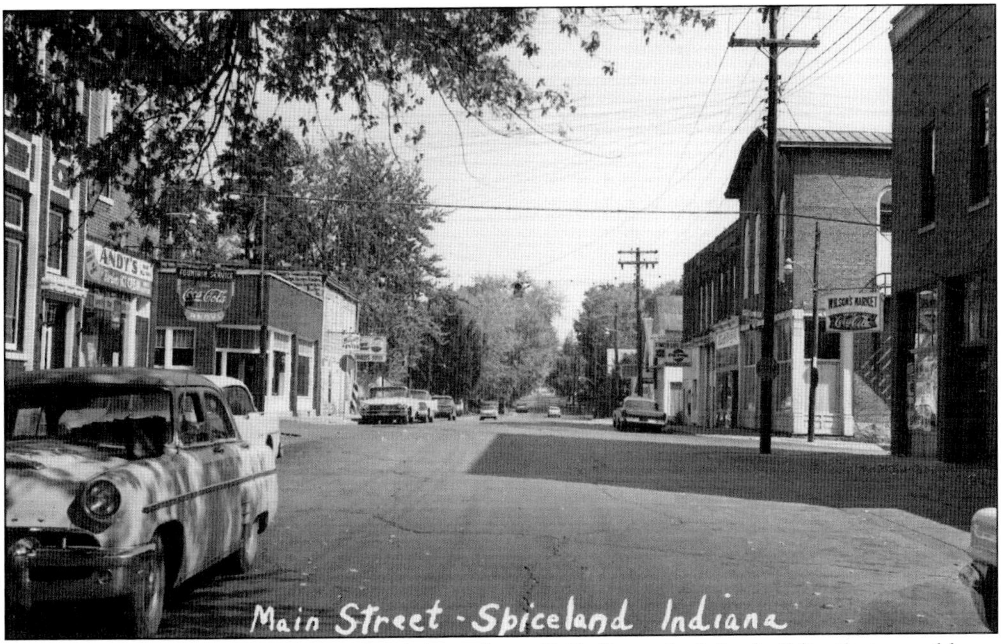

This view of Main Street in Spiceland dates from 1963. Several of the buildings pictured have either burned or been razed since this postcard was produced.

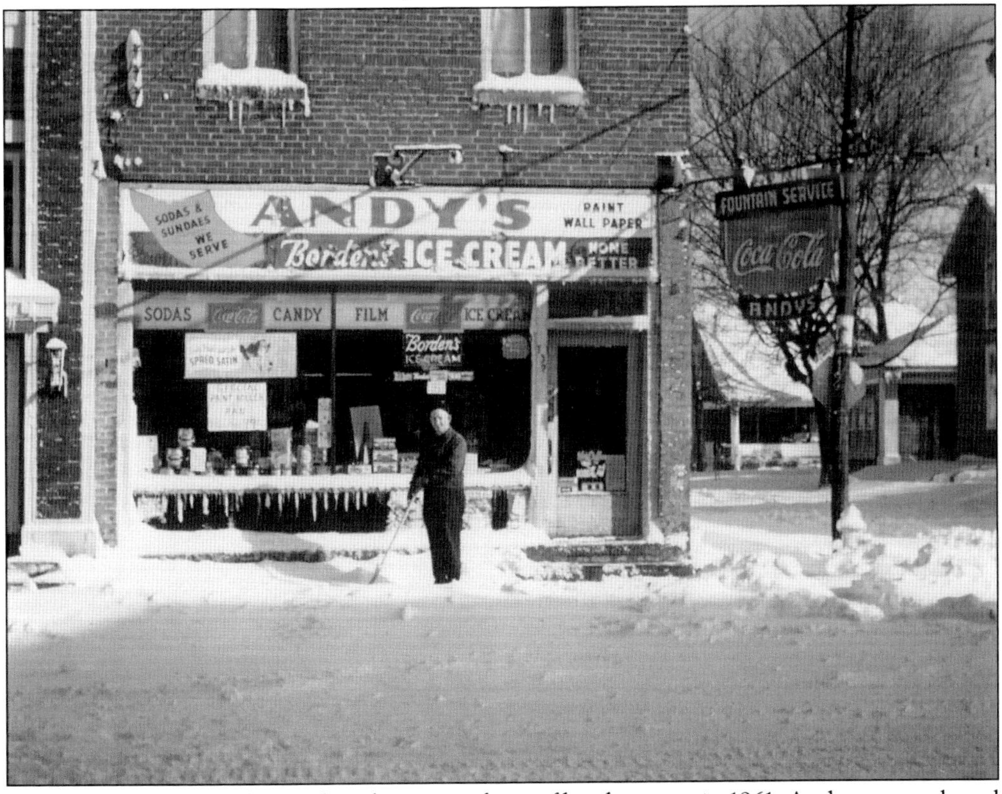

Francis M. "Andy" Anderson shovels snow in front of his drugstore in 1961. Anderson purchased the business from Clyde Smith in 1946 and continued in business until his retirement in 1976.

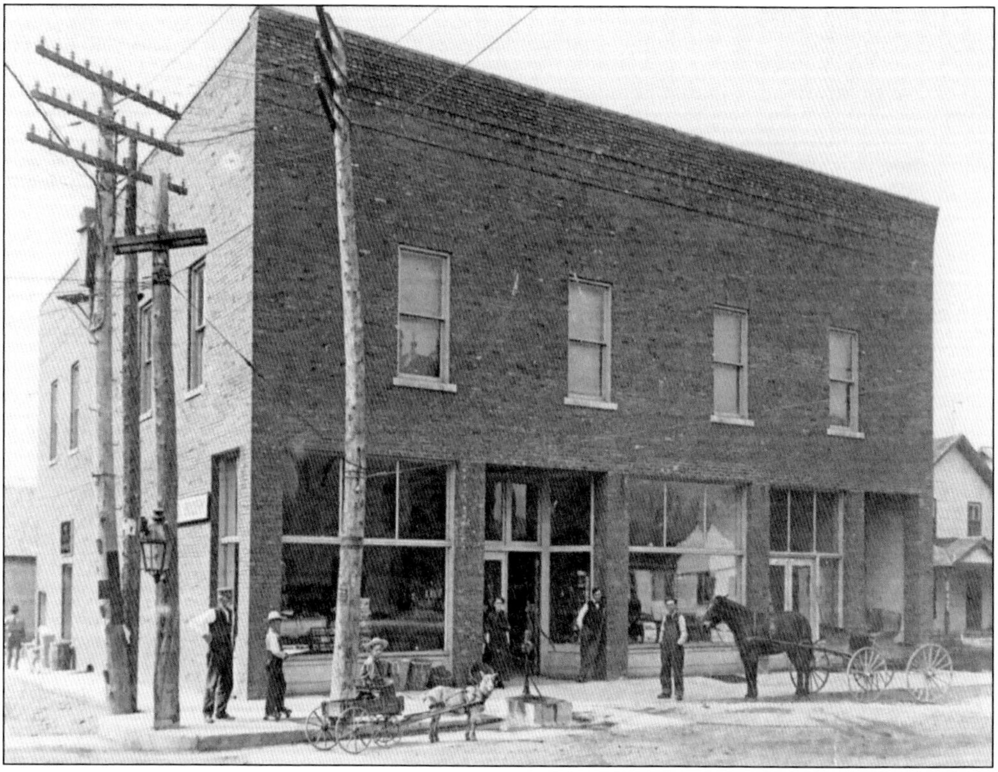

Erected in 1911, Evans grocery was later known as Evans & Wilson grocery and is now simply called Wilson Market. The town hall, complete with a stage, theater seats, and dressing rooms, was located on the second floor. Co-owners George Evans, leaning against the building, and Kerney E. Wilson, standing in front of the horse, are pictured shortly after the building was erected.

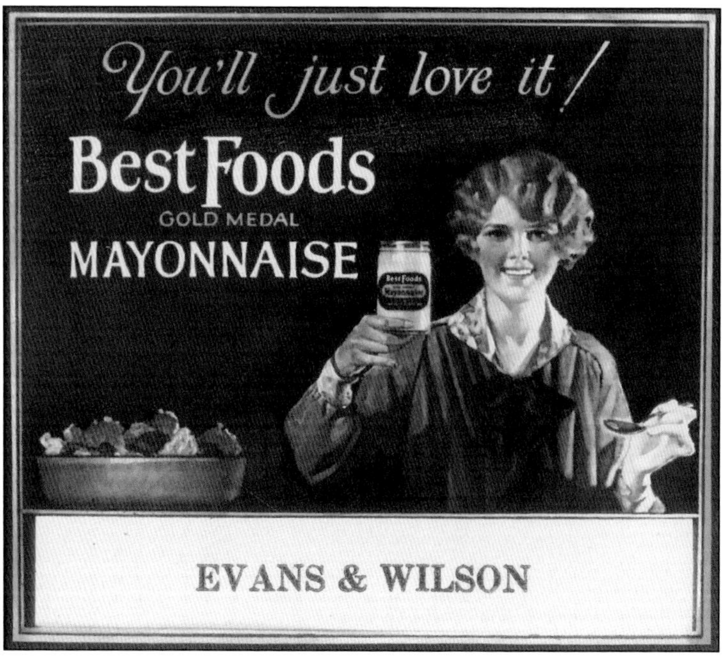

Taken from a glass slide, this advertisement for Evans & Wilson grocery probably dates from the 1930s.

Luther O. Draper (1867–1938) was the founder of Draper Shade Company, now known as Draper, Inc. He started the enterprise in 1902, traveling by interurban and bicycle to call on school officials in Indiana and Ohio. Now, 112 years later, the company is the largest industry, the largest employer (with over 500 employees), and the largest exporter in Henry County. (Courtesy of John D. Pidgeon.)

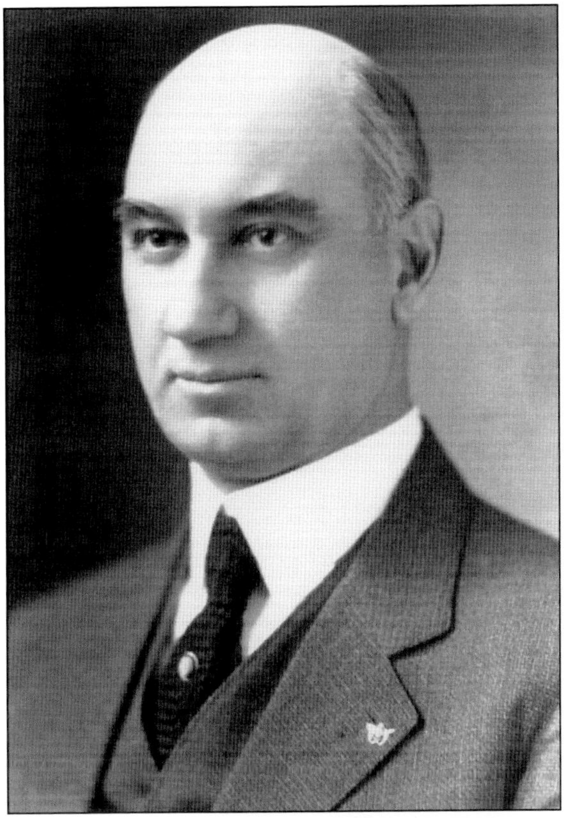

The original Draper shade factory was located on North Pearl Street in Spiceland. Luther Draper is pictured standing on the far right. (Courtesy of John D. Pidgeon.)

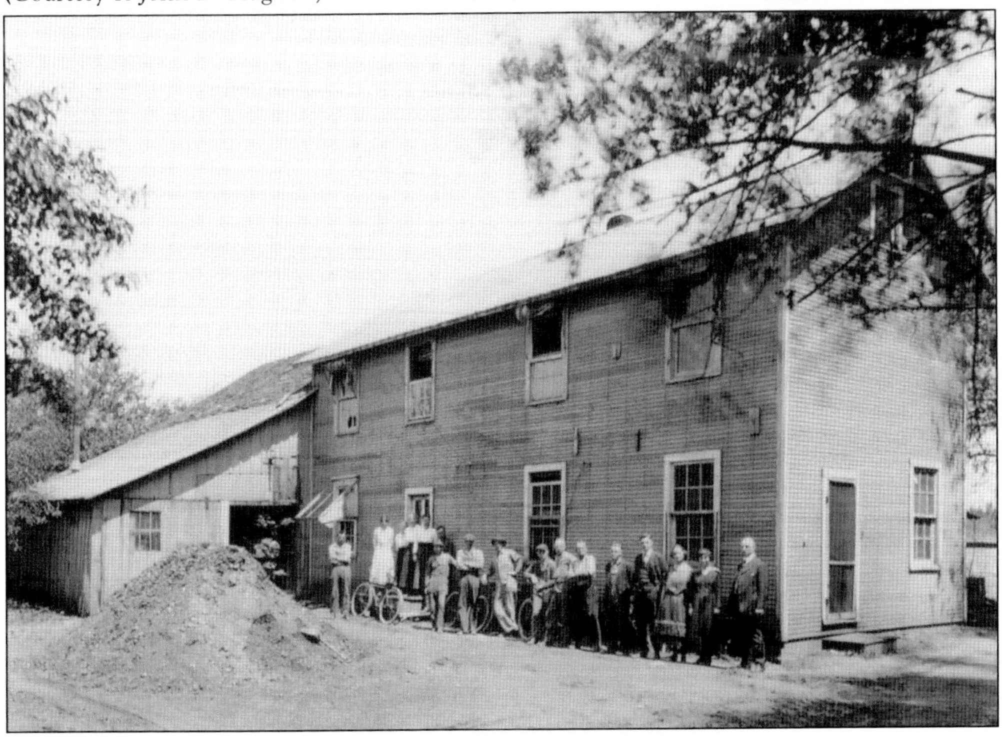

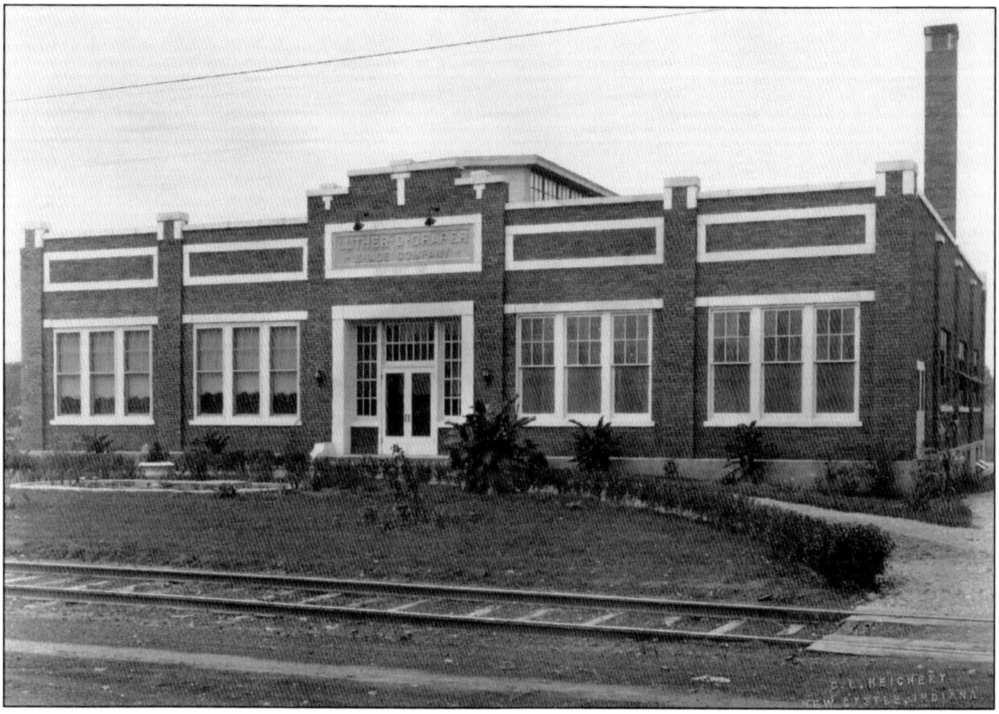

The second building to house the Draper factory was erected on South Pearl Street in 1921. The tracks of the interurban that ran between Spiceland and Dunreith are clearly visible.

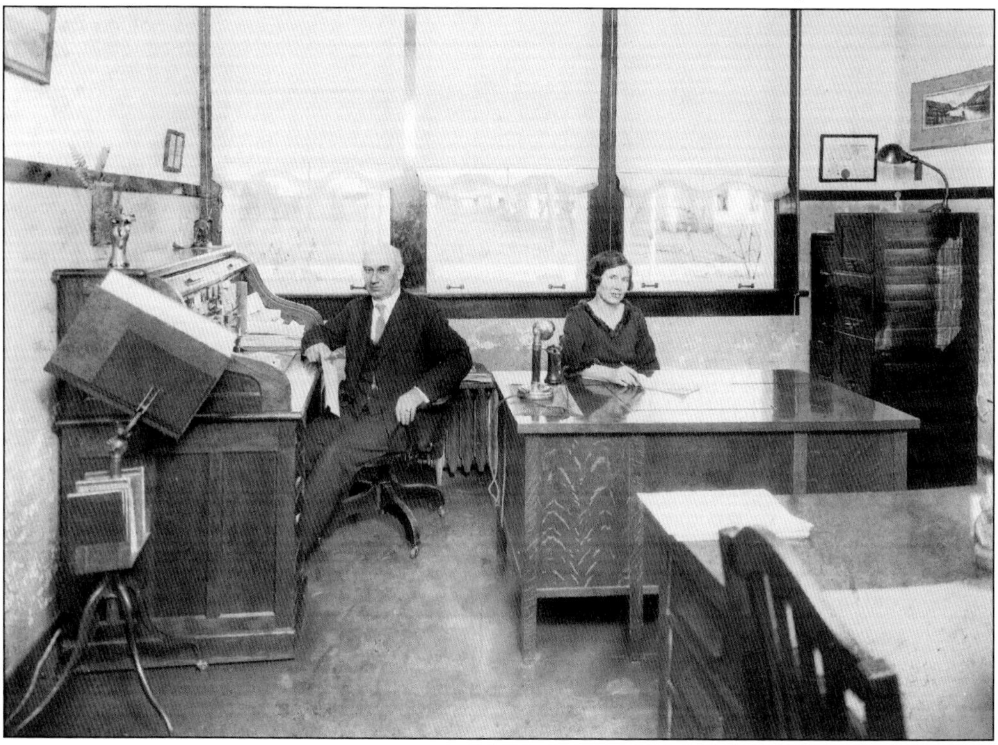

Luther O. Draper works at his desk alongside his secretary Loma (Delon) Humphrey Niles in 1924.

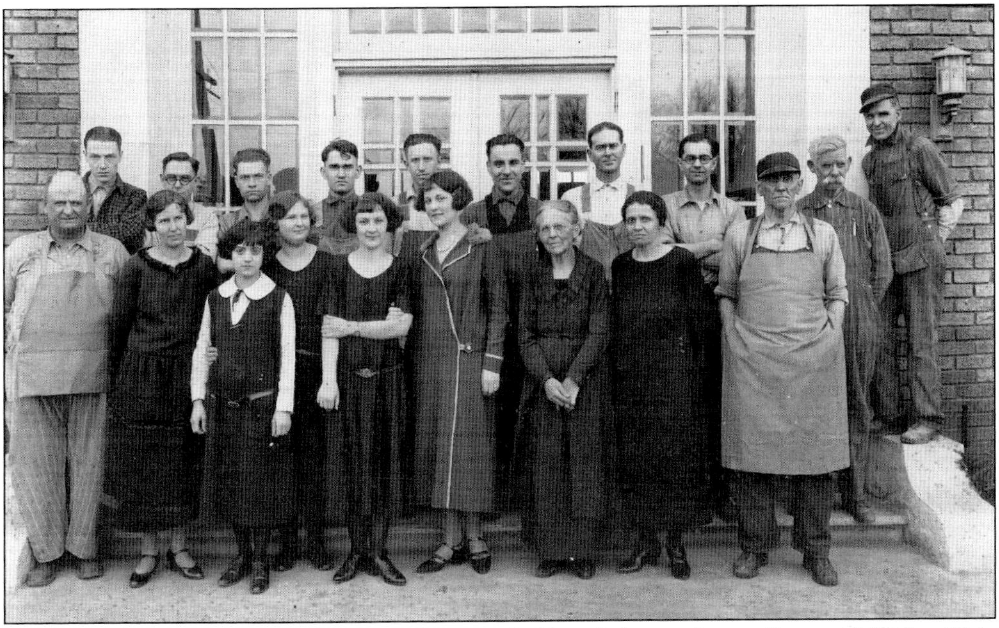

Draper's employees posed for this 1924 photograph. From left to right are (first row) Walter Kirk, Loma Humphrey Niles, Ruby Meek, Esther Webster, Mildred Holloway, Ermie Risk, Harriett Antrim, Lenneth Smethers, and Walter Henley; (second row) Herman Magee, Howard Basye, Hobart Starbuck, Robert Applegate, Carlton Henry, Philip Applegate, William Johnson, Robert Myer, Daniel Brewer, and Walter Culbertson.

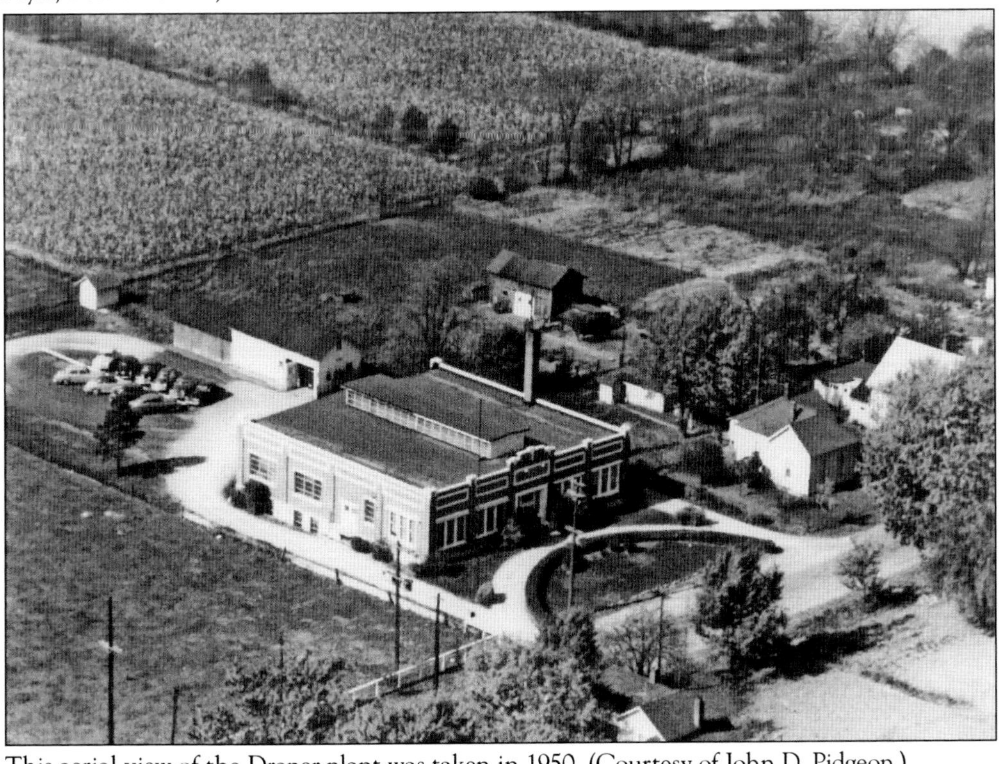

This aerial view of the Draper plant was taken in 1950. (Courtesy of John D. Pidgeon.)

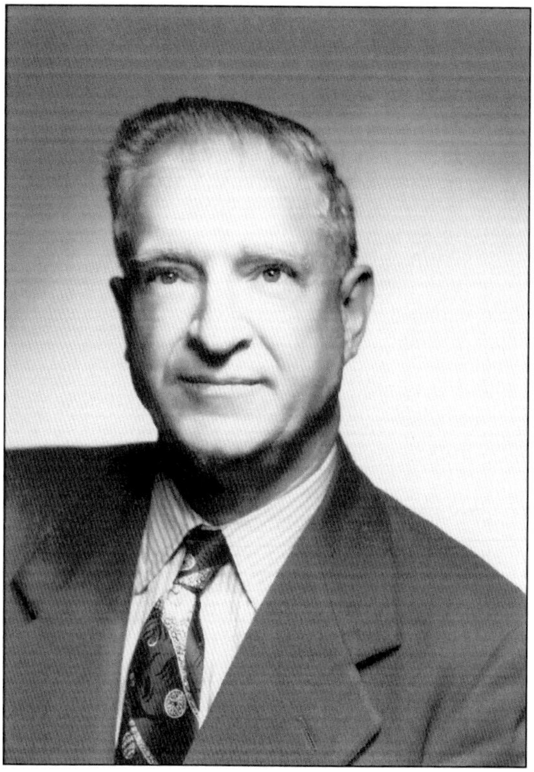

Elmer F. Pidgeon (1893–1971), the son-in-law of Luther O. Draper, became the president of the company after Draper's death in 1938 and served in this capacity until 1968. What started with Draper selling spring-roller window shades for schools has expanded to include a complete line of projection screens and related audiovisual products, such as project and flat screen lifts, commercial window shades, and gymnasium equipment. (Courtesy of John D. Pidgeon.)

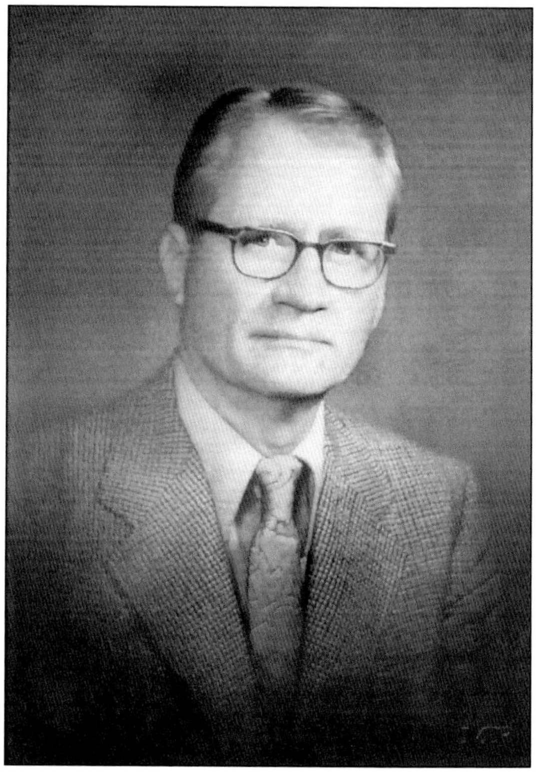

Luther A. Pidgeon (1918–2004), the grandson of Luther O. Draper, became president of the company in 1968. During his tenure, the company witnessed exceptional growth. The physical facilities and the number of different products manufactured expanded greatly. Additional Draper facilities can be found today in California, the United Kingdom, and Sweden, and Draper products are shipped to over 100 countries around the world. John D. Pidgeon, Luther Pidgeon's son and a great-grandson of Luther Draper, is the company's president. His cousin Michael Broome, another great-grandson of Luther Draper, is the company's vice president. (Courtesy of John D. Pidgeon.)

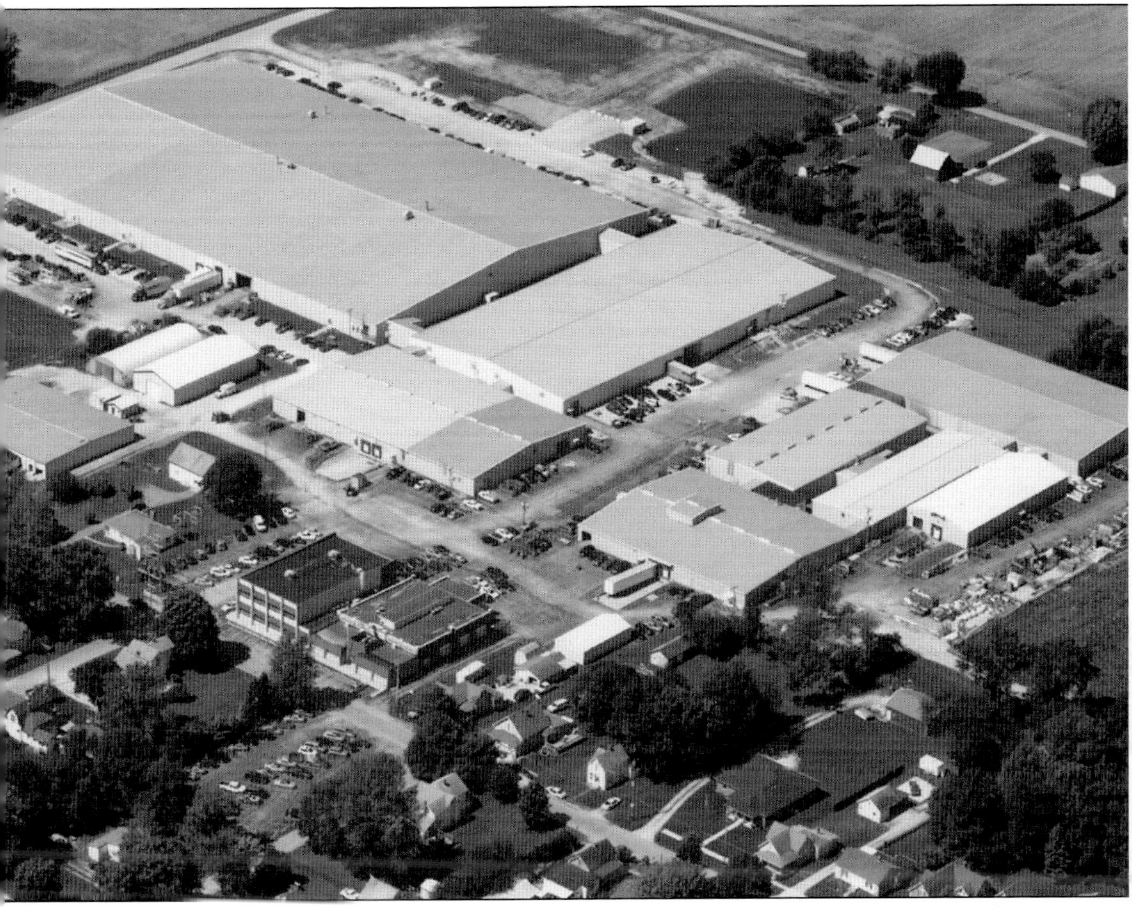

This aerial view of Draper's facilities was taken in 2010. Multiple buildings now comprise the company's complex. (Courtesy of John D. Pidgeon.)

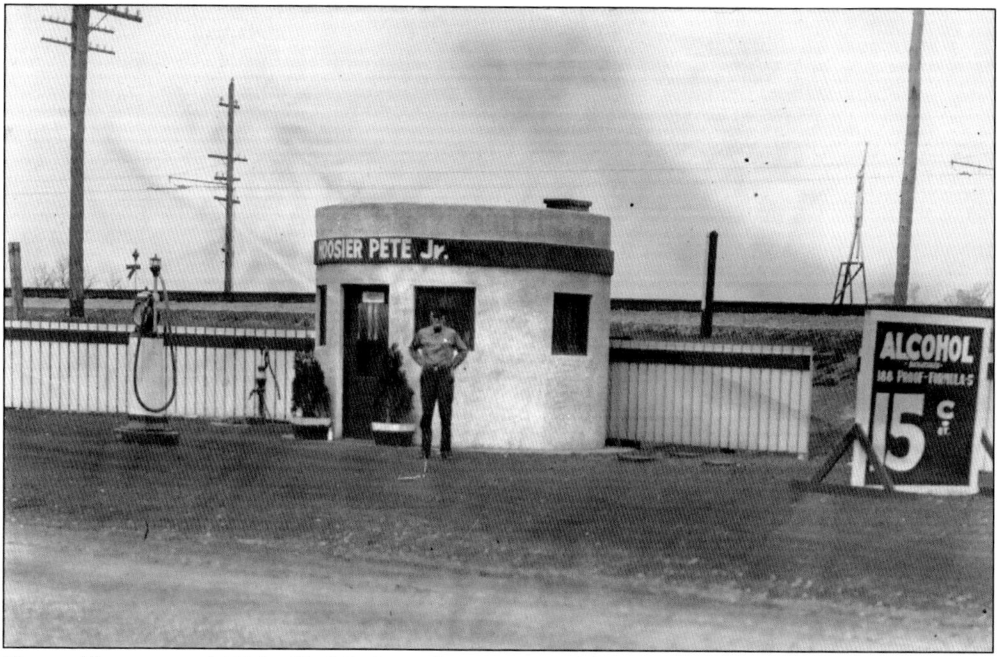

Pictured here around 1926 is Red Pickett, the operator of the Hoosier Pete Jr. filling station. It was located at the west edge of Dunreith, between the railroad and the National Road (US 40).

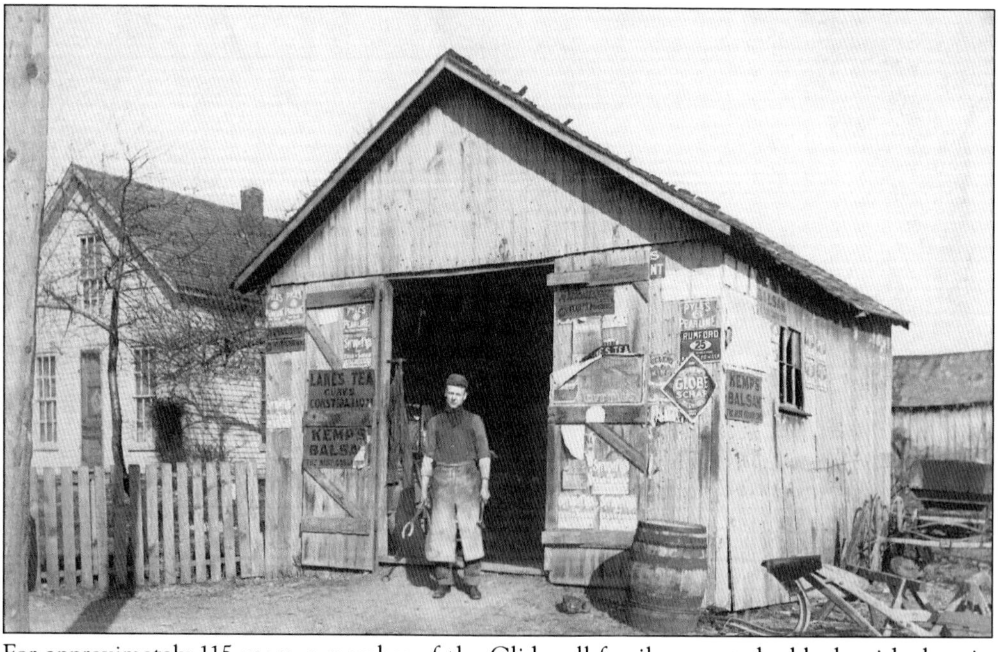

For approximately 115 years, a member of the Glidewell family operated a blacksmith shop in Dunreith. It all began in 1883 when Robert Glidewell (1851 or 1857–1908) opened for business. By the time he was 14 or 15, Robert's son Charles (1883–1965) had taken over the business. Charles is seen here in front of the original shop, which was located along the National Road (US 40) in Dunreith. (Courtesy of William Ed Pierce.)

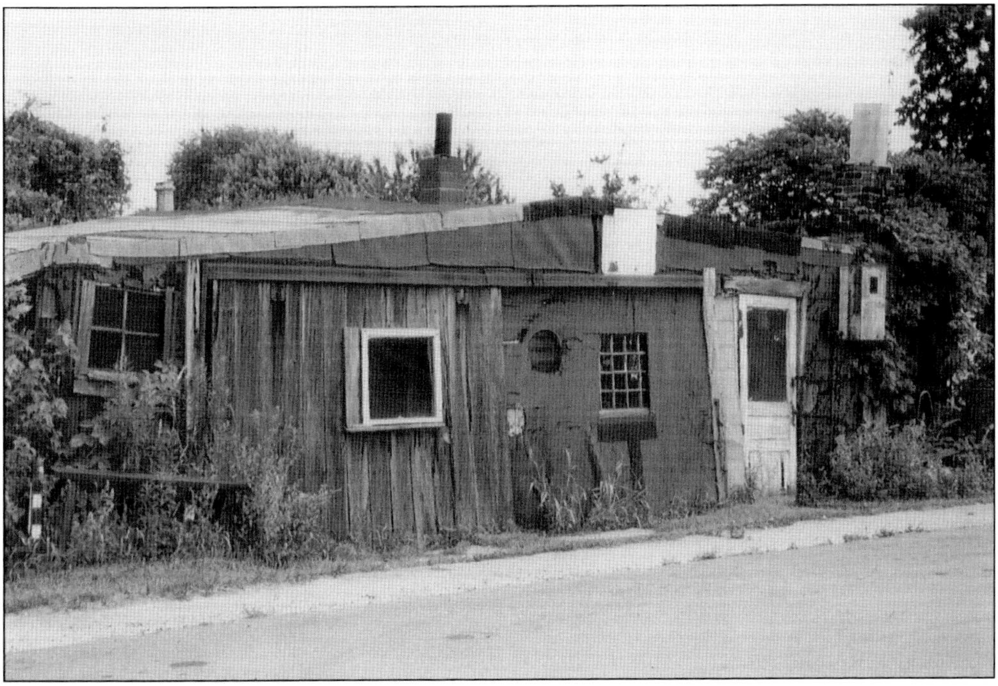

Eventually, Charles's son Howard (1908–2001) entered the picture, and he continued the family enterprise until age and ill health forced him to retire about 1999. This image of the second blacksmith shop was taken in 1994.

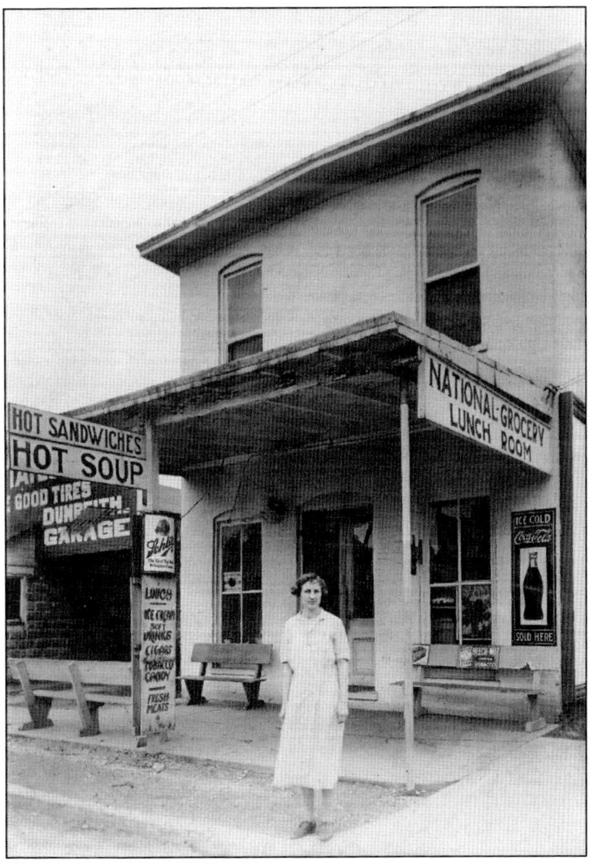

Sadie O'Melia is pictured in front of her grocery and lunchroom at Dunreith. The photograph was taken prior to 1928, as the National Road (US 40) was widened that year, which meant the front porch had to be removed.

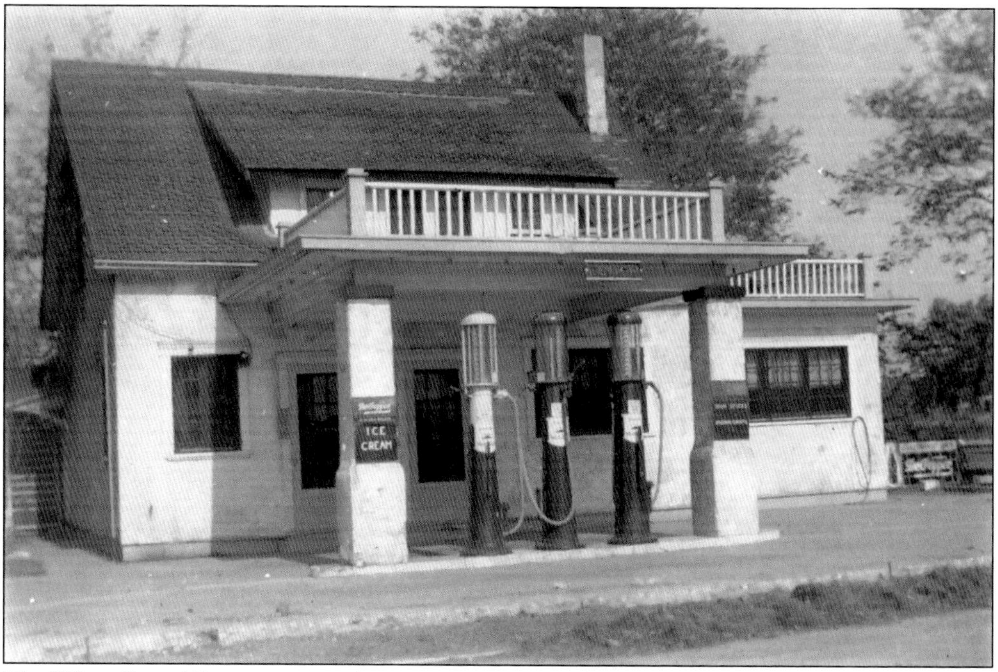

The White Rose filling station and restaurant in Dunreith, pictured here around 1930, was quite a notorious place in its day. It was operated by George and Sadie O'Melia and was later called the Chat and Chew Restaurant.

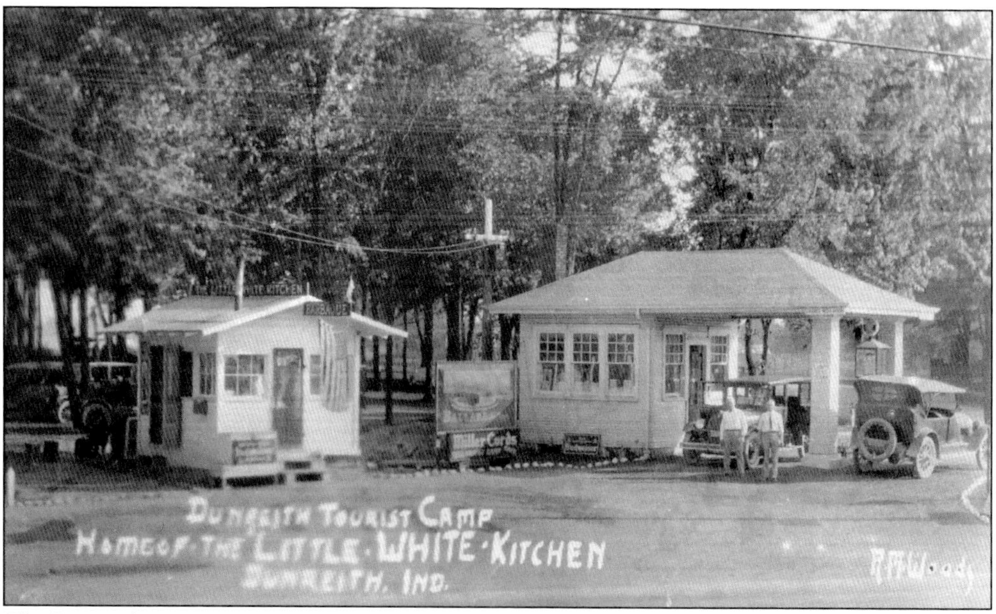

The Dunreith tourist camp and filling station is shown in this photograph, along with the original Little White Kitchen (left). A larger restaurant, a famous Henry County eatery, was built later but was destoyed by fire around 1958.

Worth Brown pumps gas at his D-X filling station in Dunreith in 1937. Later, he operated a Pure Oil station in the town. (Courtesy of Charlene Williams.)

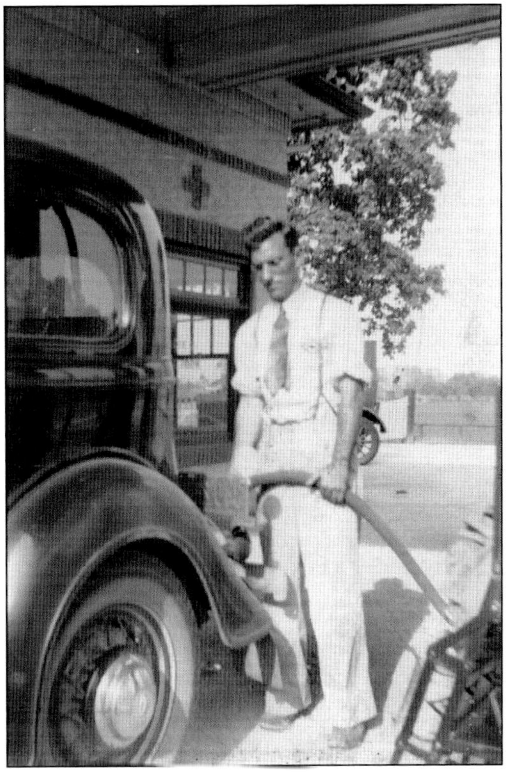

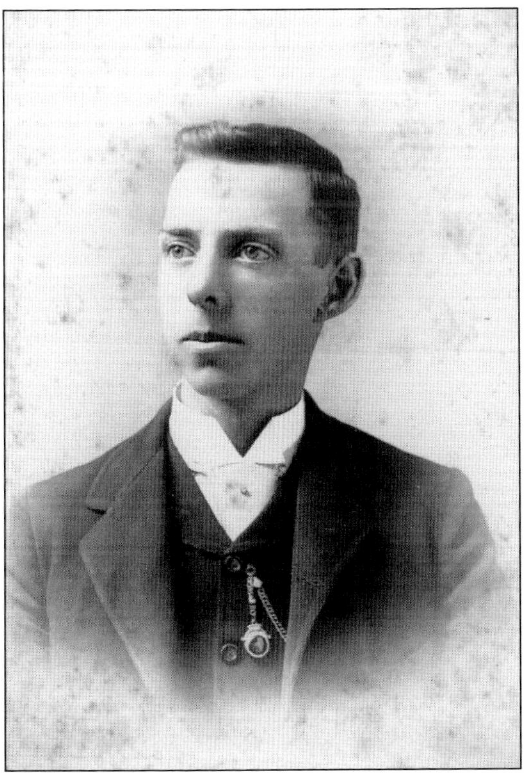

Ernest Deem (1867–1937) was the original owner and operator of the Dunreith Canning Factory. The factory processed tomatoes and was located along the Pennsylvania Railroad. It was destroyed on New Year's night in 1968 as the result of a huge train wreck and explosion. (Courtesy of Sylvia Salanitro.)

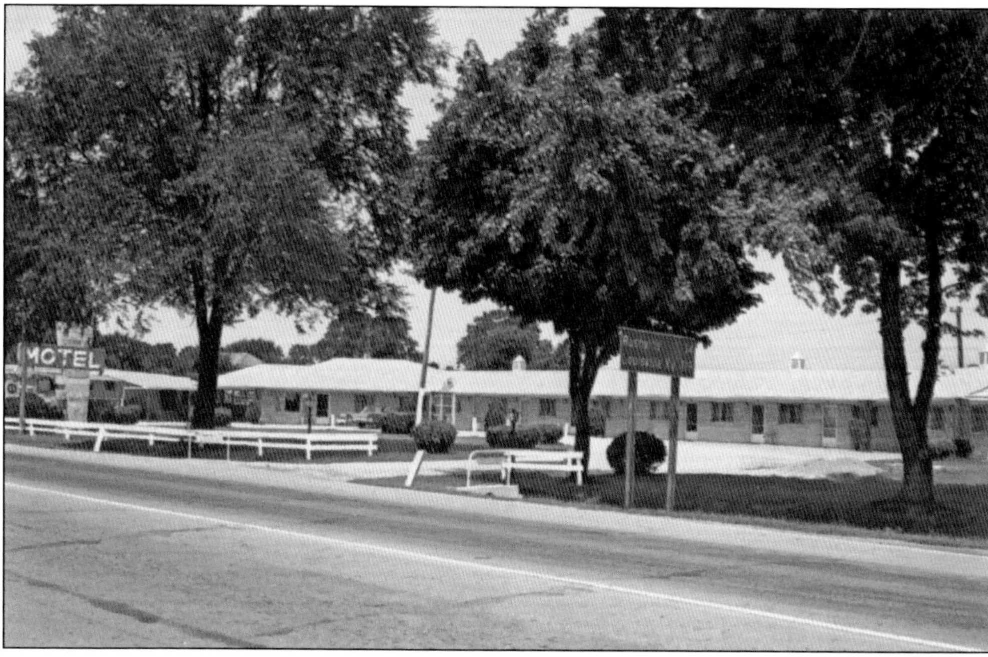

It is rare to find a flamingo in eastern Indiana, but that is the word used to identify the Flamingo Motel and Restaurant in Dunreith. The motel (above) opened in 1953 and is still welcoming overnight guests. The restaurant is a small-town café that respects the meat-and-potatoes sensibilities of its patrons. Several years ago, the *Indianapolis Star* nominated it as one of their favorite country restaurants. The restaurant was moved from US 40 west of town to its present location in 1946. That building burned in 1983, and a new building (below) opened on the same site in 1985. (Both courtesy of Lowell Jarvis.)

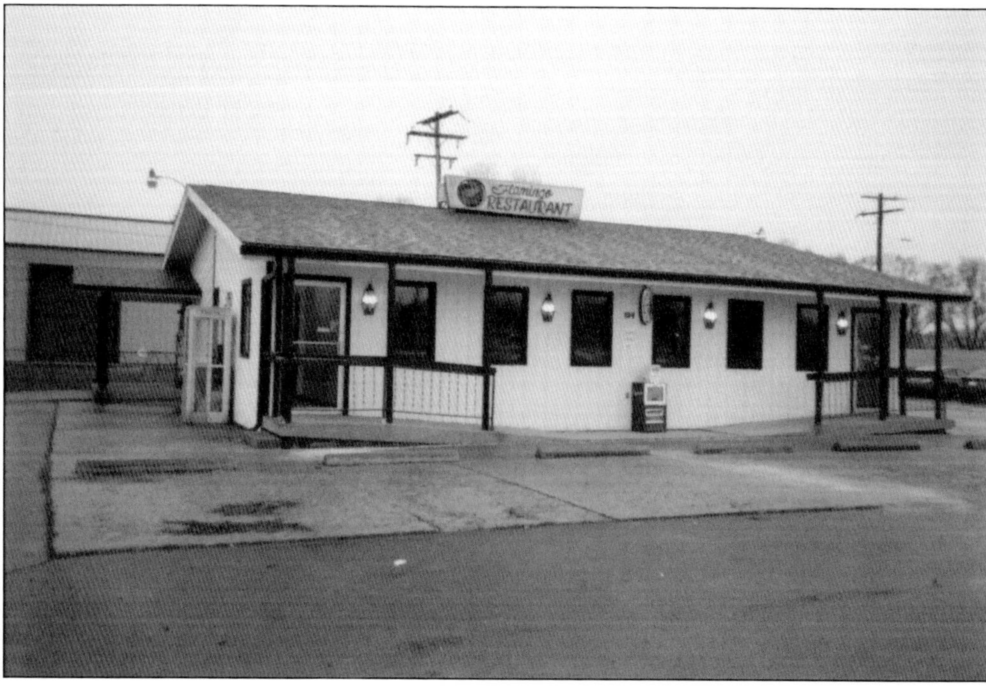

Six

Let Us Go for a Ride

The photographs in this chapter create a sense of being there that helps one enter into other time periods and localities. They provide a means to refresh one's memory. It is possible they might even provide gratification at first glance.

No single living person can remember the Spiceland Sanitarium and Mineral Springs or the Spiceland orphanage. One, perhaps, might remember their parents and grandparents making reference to them. For current residents, though, they are not even a memory. Images of these two institutions, along with the other photographs shown here, take the viewer back to a time and place one can only wish to remember. It is interesting how quickly some things fade from memory. Only a handful of township residents can remember root cellars, horses and buggies, outhouses, or the interurban. Soon, even these people will be gone.

The people pictured left an indelible mark on the history of Spiceland Township. They came from all walks of life and from a time period spanning nearly 200 years. The majority of them were not known beyond the safe confines of their home communities. They were selected for this pictorial history because they lived such varied lives—a barber, a doctor, a town handyman, a rabid abolitionist and town founder, a gentle lady adored by all who knew her, a star gazer, and a practicing atheist, to name only a few.

So, take a ride to Circle Grove Cemetery, down to Dunreith and Ogden, and out on the Spiceland Pike to Hoover's pond. Who knows, there might even be time to check out a book at the library or stop at the post office and pick up mail.

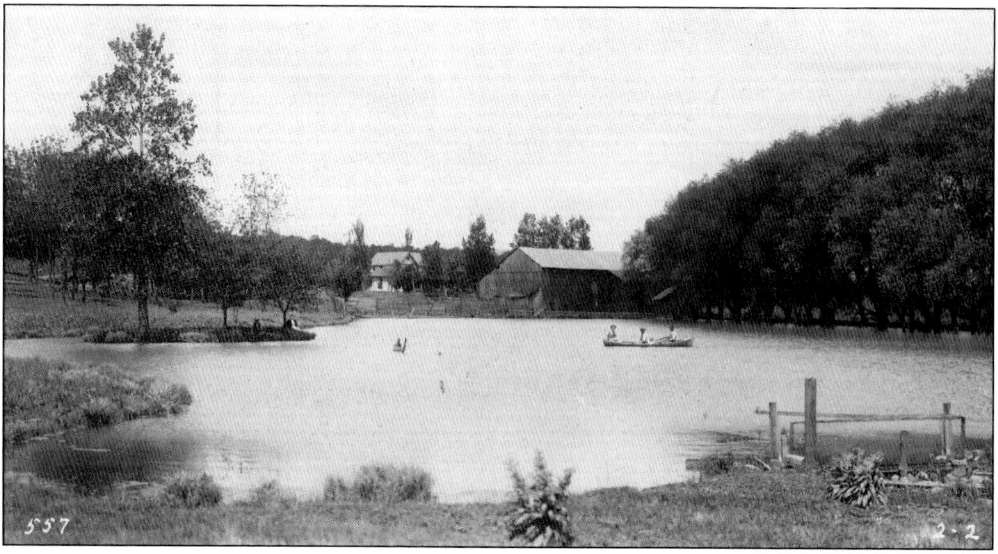

John and May Hoover's pond, located north of Spiceland on the pike, was a popular place to spend a few idle hours either in the summer or winter. Boaters are seen in this photograph, but ice-skating also attracted a lot of folks in the winter.

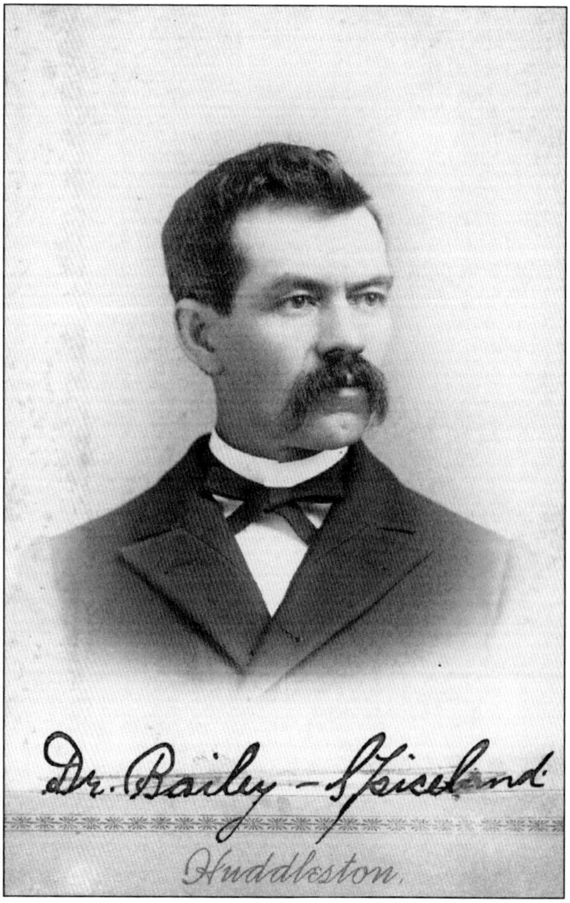

Dr. George D. Baily founded the Spiceland Sanitarium and Mineral Springs around 1893. He married Susan Fussell, who founded the orphanage at Spiceland.

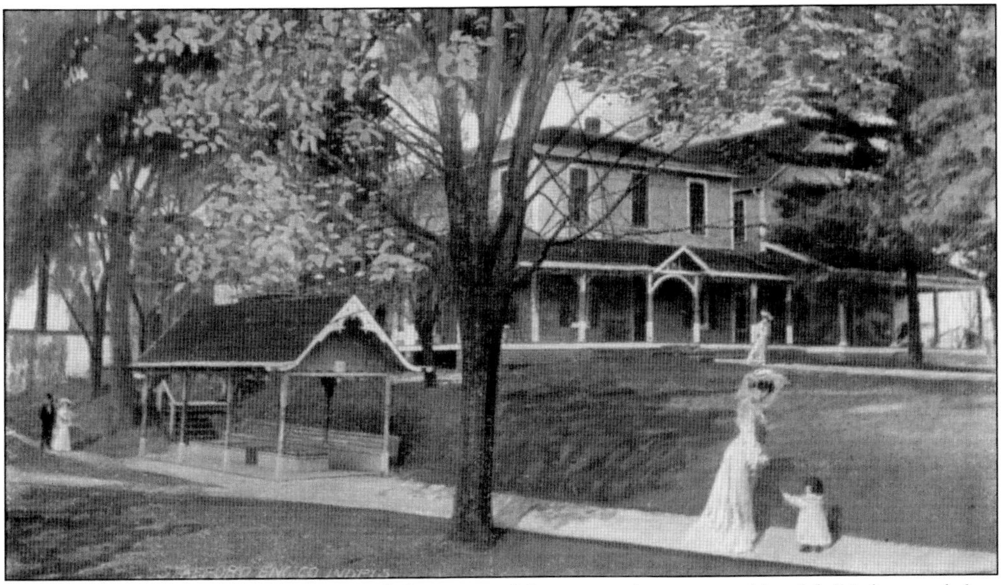

The Spiceland Sanitarium advertised that it was "the resort that restored health." It boasted that seven kinds of mineral water were available and that mineralized mud baths were supervised by capable attendants. In other advertisements, it boasted that it could successfully treat diseases of the liver, bladder, bowels, stomach, and kidneys.

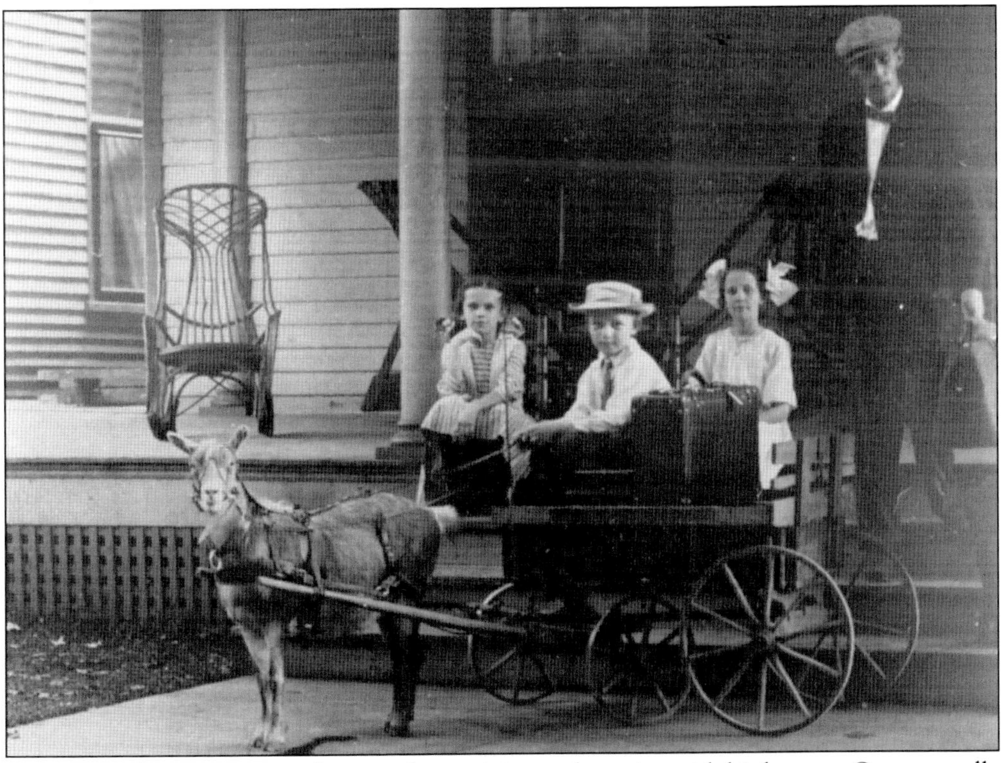

A visitor at the sanitarium is shown either arriving or departing with his luggage. Guests usually arrived in Spiceland on the interurban and were often transported to the sanitarium using Carr's goat wagon. It appears young Wilbur Carr and his goat are ready to perform their usual service.

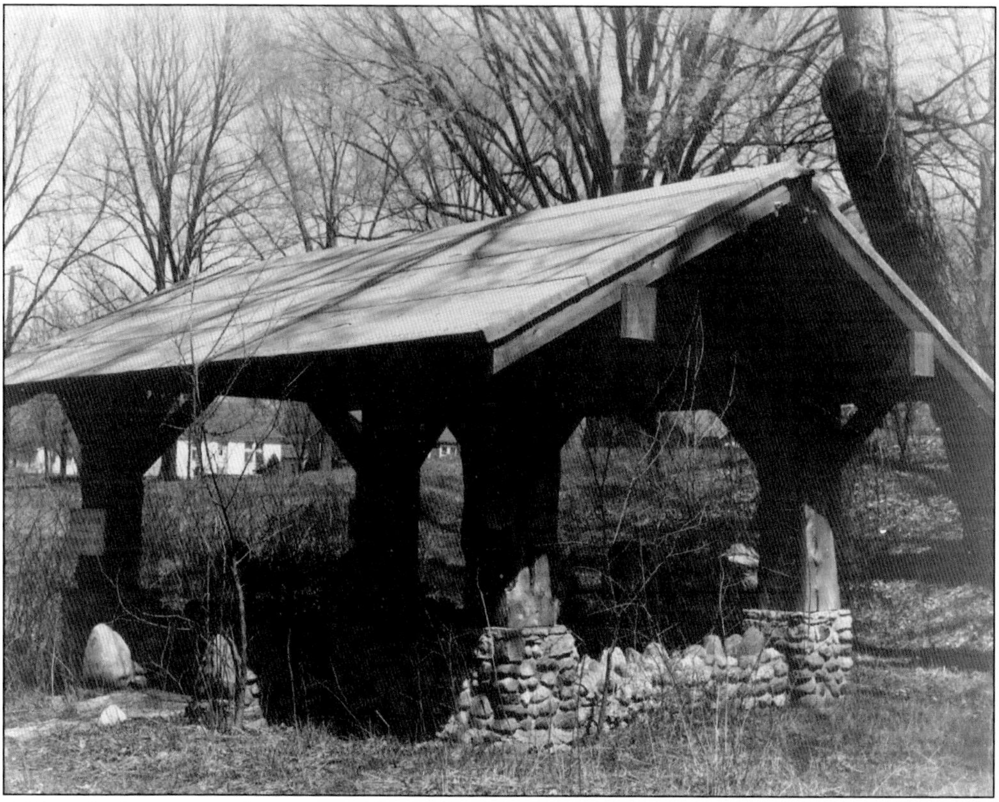

Although three springhouses were built after the sanitarium burned down in 1913, only one remains. Photographed in 1950, this springhouse has been renovated twice since this photograph was taken.

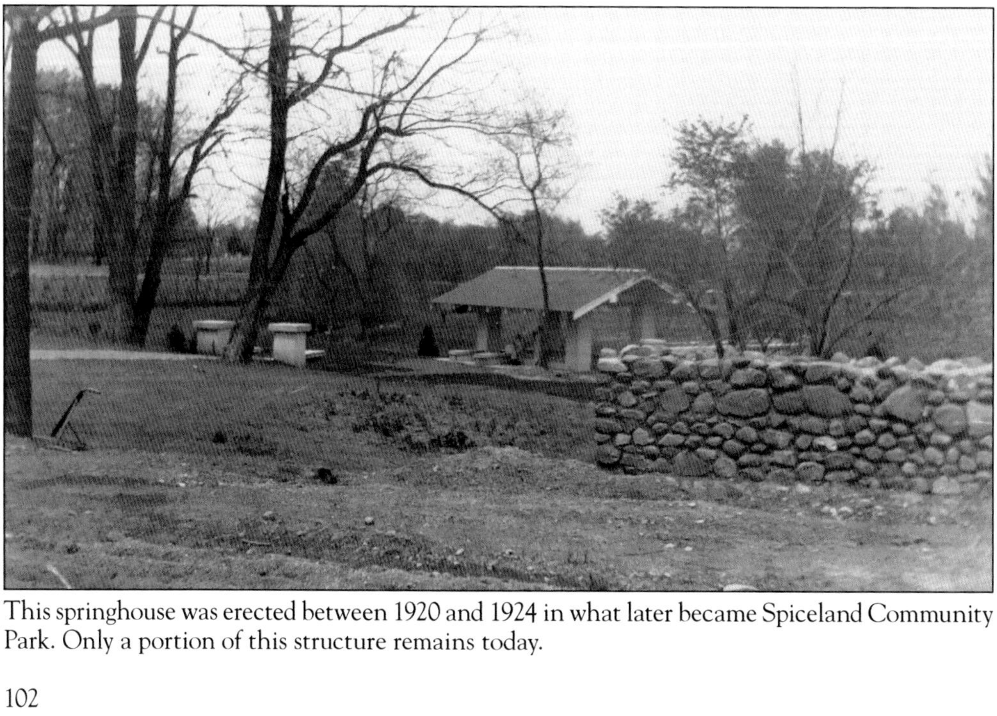

This springhouse was erected between 1920 and 1924 in what later became Spiceland Community Park. Only a portion of this structure remains today.

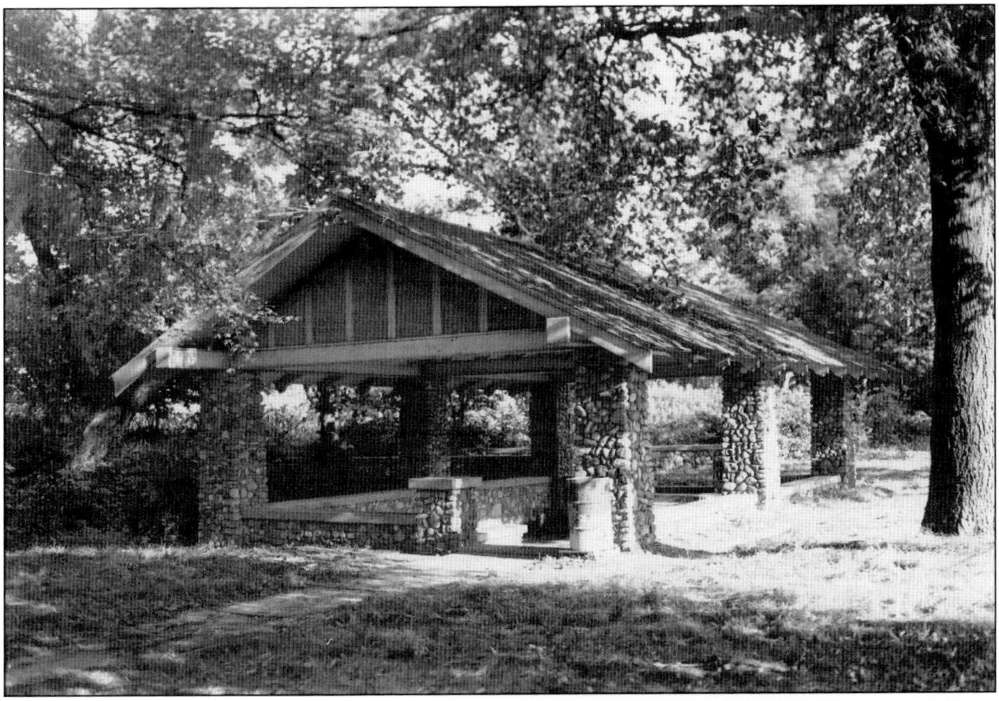

Shown here is the largest of the springhouses constructed on the former sanitarium grounds. Neglect and decay eventually took their toll on the structure.

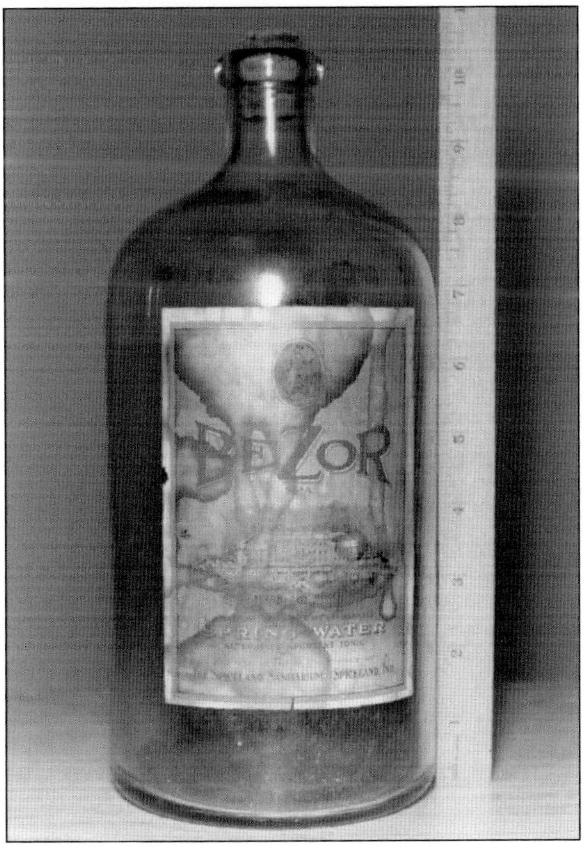

After the sanitarium burned down, mineral springwater was bottled and sold for a time, beginning in the late 1920s. The only surviving bottle from the spa that contains an original label is shown here. It is a prized possession of its Spiceland owner.

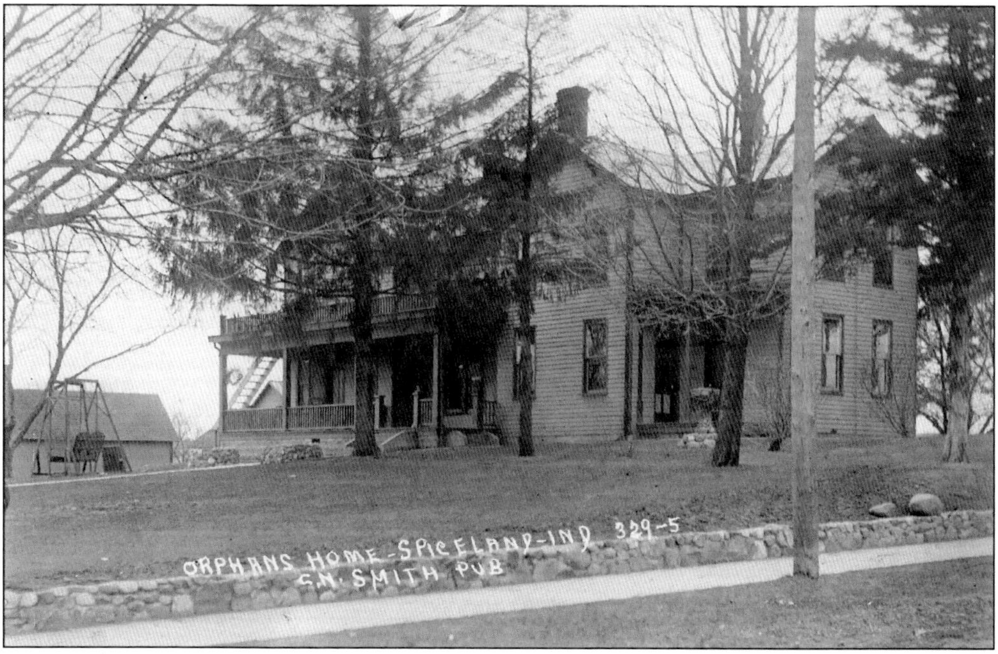

In 1880, the Henry County Orphanage, sometimes referred to as the Spiceland Orphans' Home, was started by Susan Fussell. Shown here is the second home to serve the orphanage. Records of the orphanage are spotty. After it closed, the remaining children were transferred to an orphanage in Indianapolis.

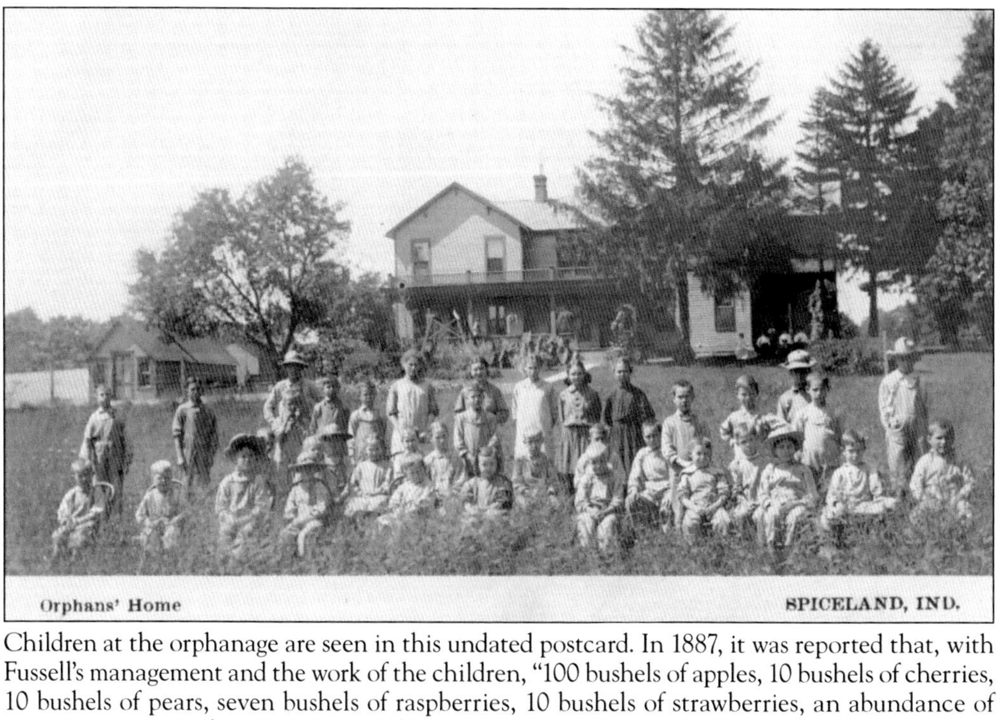

Children at the orphanage are seen in this undated postcard. In 1887, it was reported that, with Fussell's management and the work of the children, "100 bushels of apples, 10 bushels of cherries, 10 bushels of pears, seven bushels of raspberries, 10 bushels of strawberries, an abundance of potatoes, tomatoes, beans, onions, cabbage, turnips, beets, celery, radishes, lettuce, dried apples and 700 hundred quarts of canned fruit" were prepared for the orphanage's use.

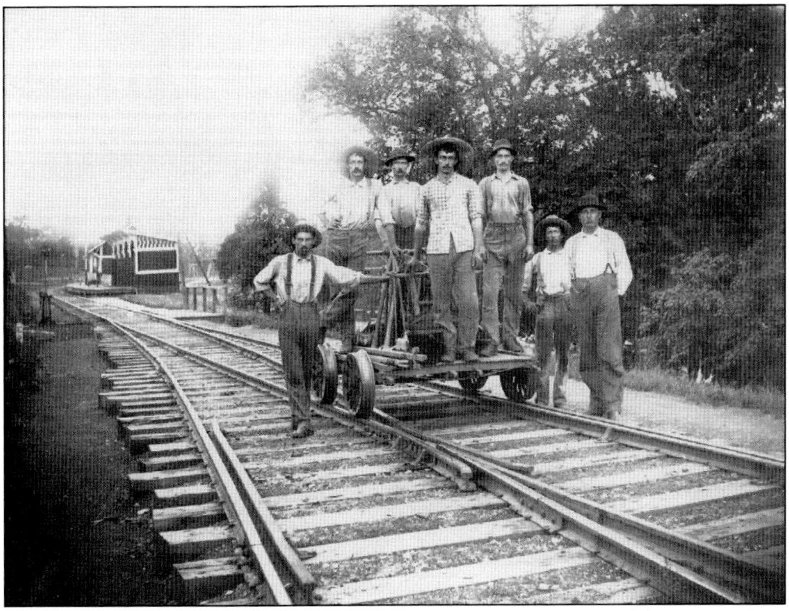

These men were working on the railroad tracks at Spiceland when this photograph was taken around 1900. The only person identified is Joseph Seward, on the far right.

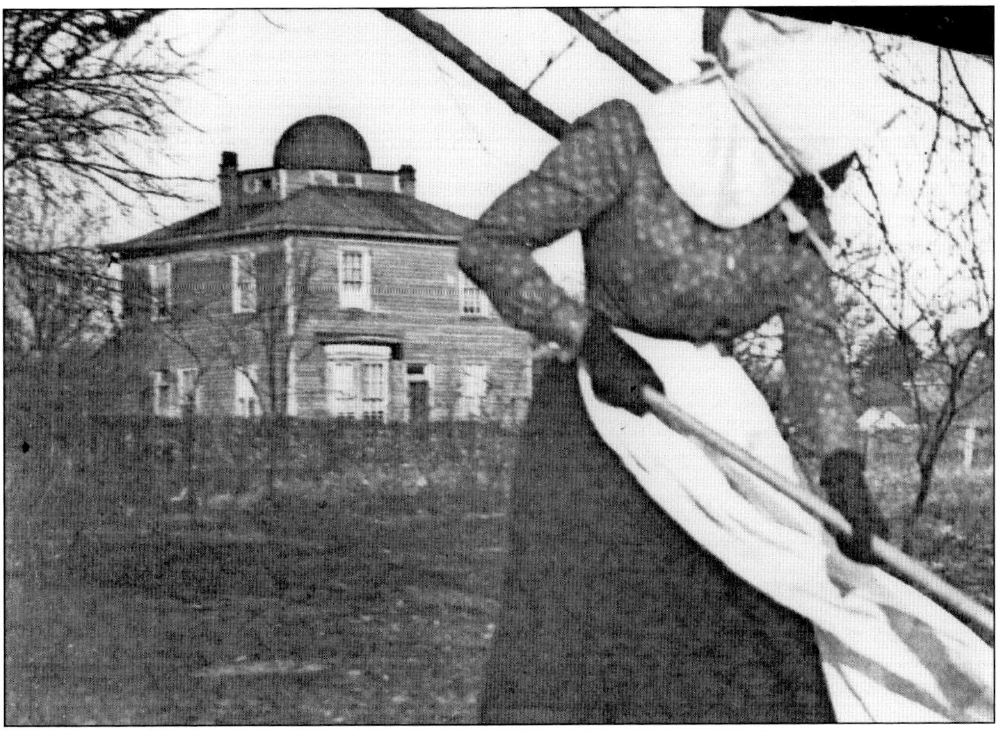

William Dawson (1833–1890) was Spiceland's local weatherman, meteorologist, and astronomer. His home, erected in 1878 and seen here in the background, had a dome-like structure mounted on the roof. Constructed of tin, the dome was made to slide open for viewing the stars, using one of his many telescopes. A cobbler by profession, he began his observations at Spiceland in 1867 and continued until his death. His reports were regularly published in the *New Castle Courier* and the *Indianapolis Journal*, and he frequently wrote for the *Kansas City Review of Science and Industry*, the *Smithsonian* in Washington, DC, and several eastern newspapers.

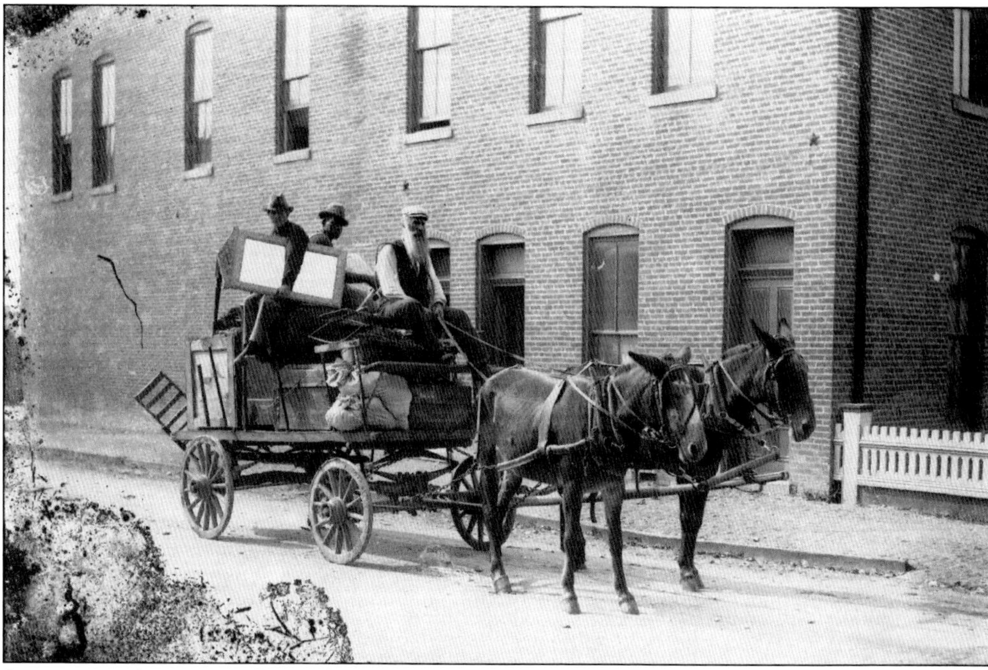

It appears to be moving day in this photograph, taken around 1896 next to Nixon's drugstore on North Pearl Street in Spiceland. It is assumed the fellow holding the mirror did not drop it.

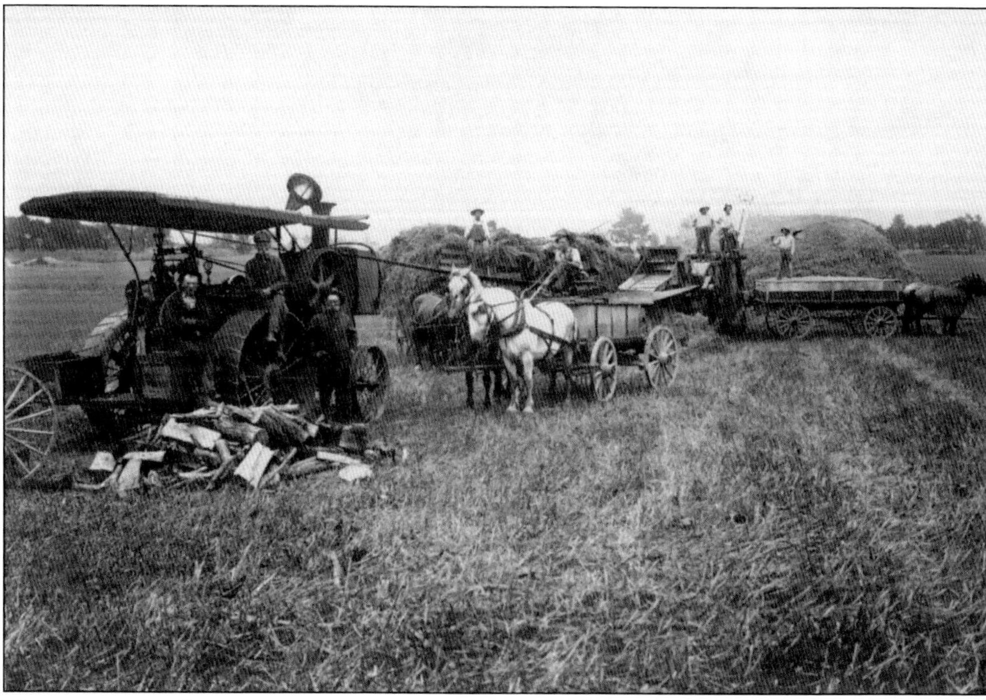

There was a thrill in seeing a threshing machine, threshing grain, and using a team of horses to haul the machine from farm to farm. Alfred Meredith is shown here sitting on the wheel, and standing in front of him is his brother William Meredith. (Courtesy of the Henry County Historical Society Museum.)

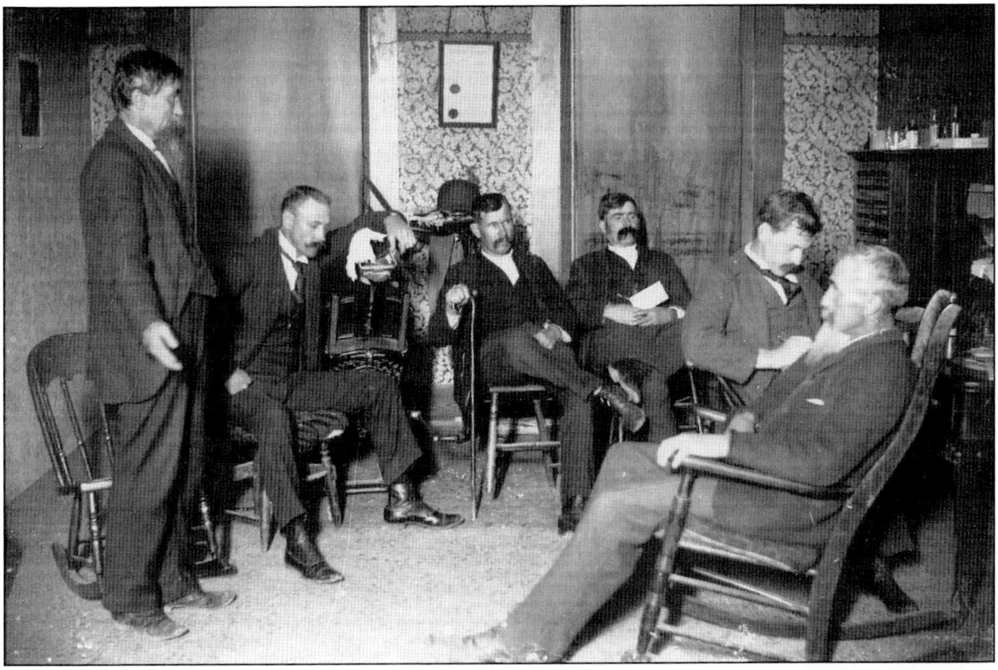

Members of the town board of Spiceland are pictured in 1896. From left to right are Alexander Spencer, Lewis Cloud, John A. Griffin, Tom Gilbreath, Dr. William B. Gordon, and Clarkson Charles. This photograph was taken in Dr. Gordon's dental office. In 1895, a total of 25 streetlamps and posts were purchased, and Gilbreath was paid $6 a year to keep them lighted.

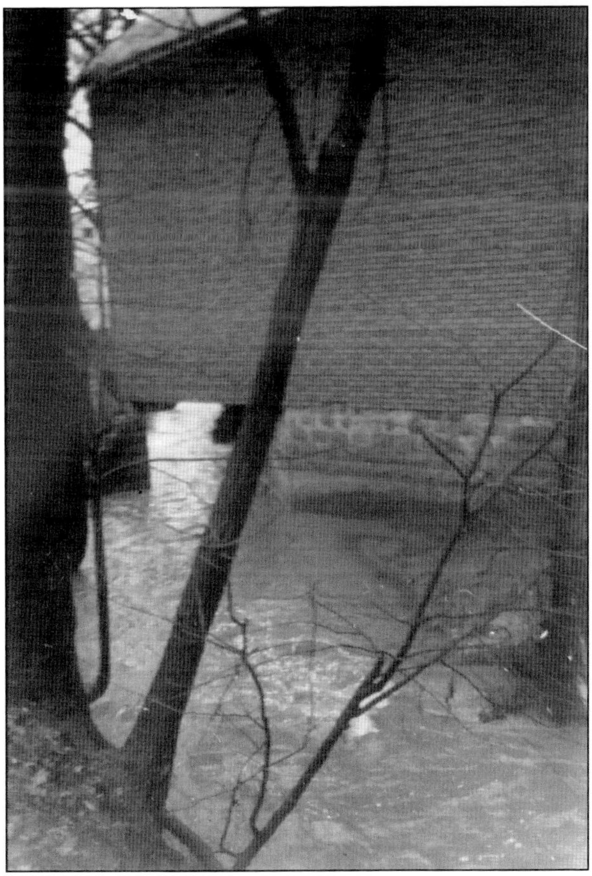

Pictured here is the southeast corner of Lemuel Rifner's apple house, which once served as the Methodist church before it was moved to East Main Street in Spiceland. Note that Brook Bezor flowed under one corner of the building.

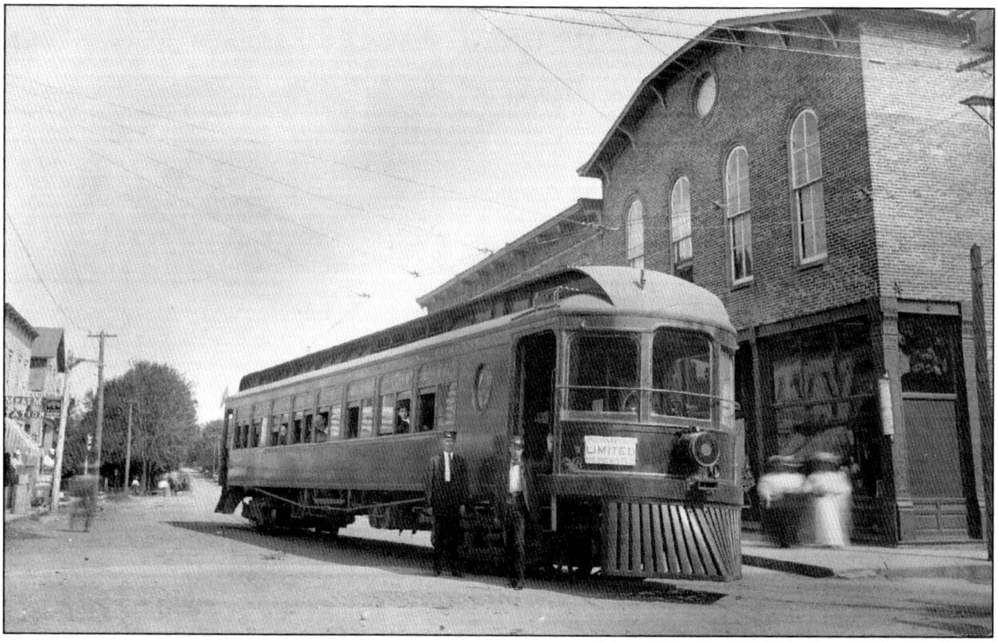

Hoover Hall is shown here on the right, and the interurban appears ready to turn south on South Pearl Street. This car was part of the electric Indianapolis, New Castle & Eastern Railroad, which came from Indianapolis along the National Road (US 40), turned north at Dunreith, and traveled through Spiceland, New Castle, Springport, and Muncie. The line later became part of the Union Traction Company. The interurban era in Henry County ended in 1941, as that mode of transportation could no longer compete with automobiles.

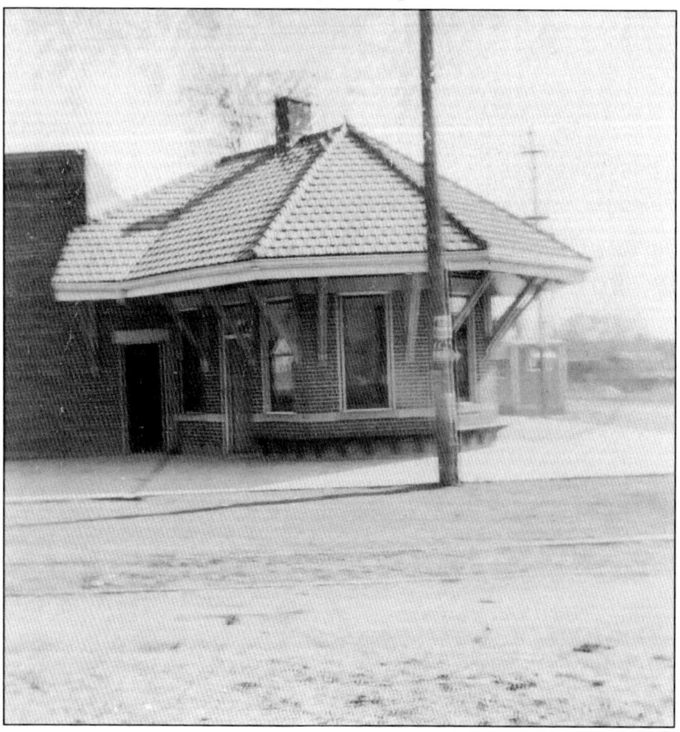

The interurban waiting station at Dunreith is featured here. This building was razed in 1928 for the widening of US 40.

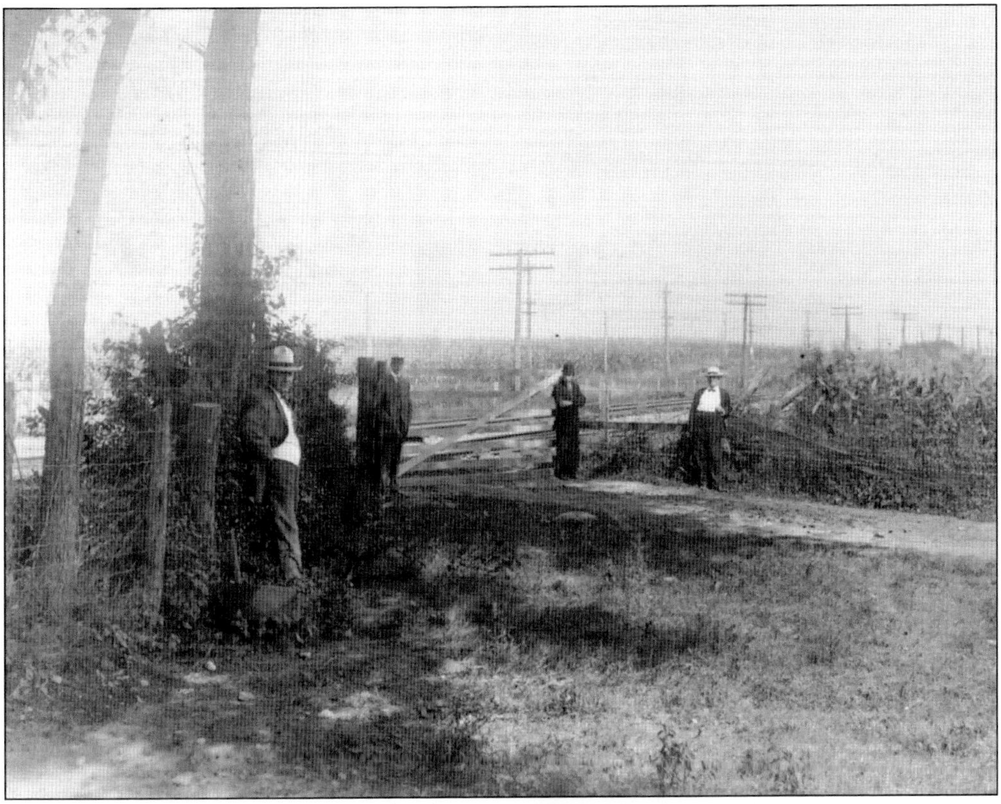

These gentlemen are shown waiting for the interurban at Ogden around 1910. Both the interurban tracks and the railroad tracks are visible in this photograph.

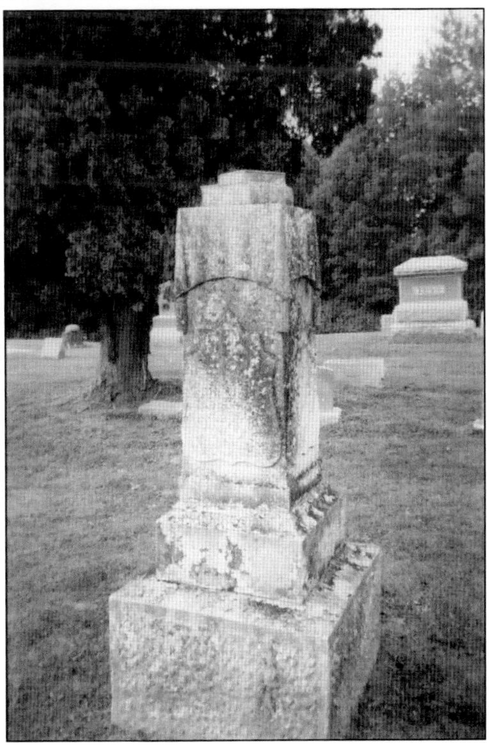

Spiceland's Circle Grove Cemetery contains the tombstone of William W. Wilson, who was something of a maverick in the community. Folks used to refer to him as "Billy Wilson, the infidel," as he admonished everyone to avoid all religions. The long inscription on his tombstone can no longer be read, but it stated that the religious have always been the greatest curse in the world and that all religions are false.

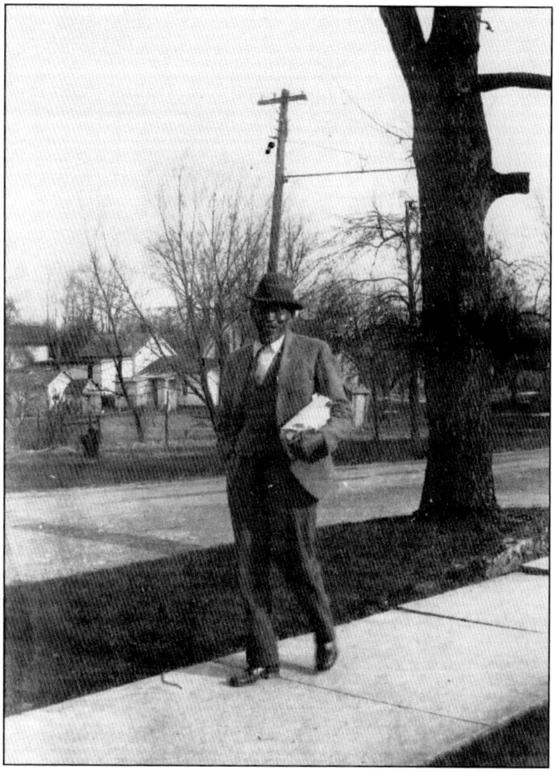

Born a slave, Charles Brandy moved to Spiceland from Carthage in 1880 when he was 21 and opened a barbershop with his brother. When he came to town, he had not received any education. By faithful work and application, he attended school and worked at his trade. With the help of Clarkson and Hannah Davis, Brandy was able to complete the eighth grade.

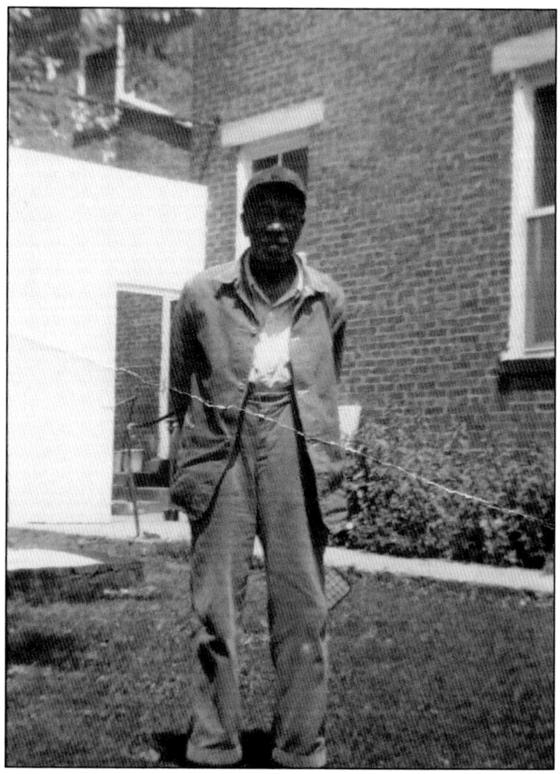

Asbury Charlton was a much-loved resident of Spiceland and one of the town's handymen. His parents, former slaves, wrapped their feet in rags during the winter because they could not afford shoes. Charlton spent his last years in New Castle at the Henry County Home, where he died in 1949.

Susan B. (Hunt) Unthank (1839–1932) was a Spiceland favorite. Born shortly after the death of her father in the 1839 cholera epidemic, "Aunt Sue," as she was fondly called, married Josiah T. Unthank. In cages on their front porch, the Unthanks kept a collection of stuffed birds that attracted the attention of academy students as they walked to and from school. Today, the birds are displayed at the Henry County Historical Society Museum.

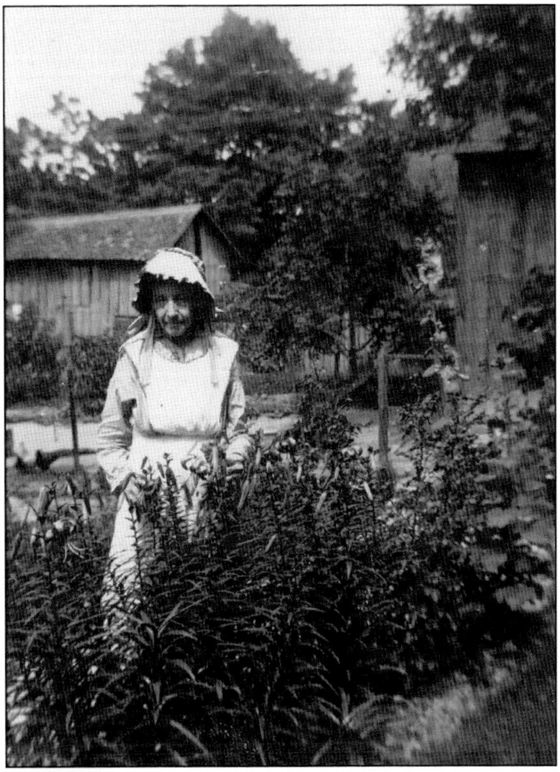

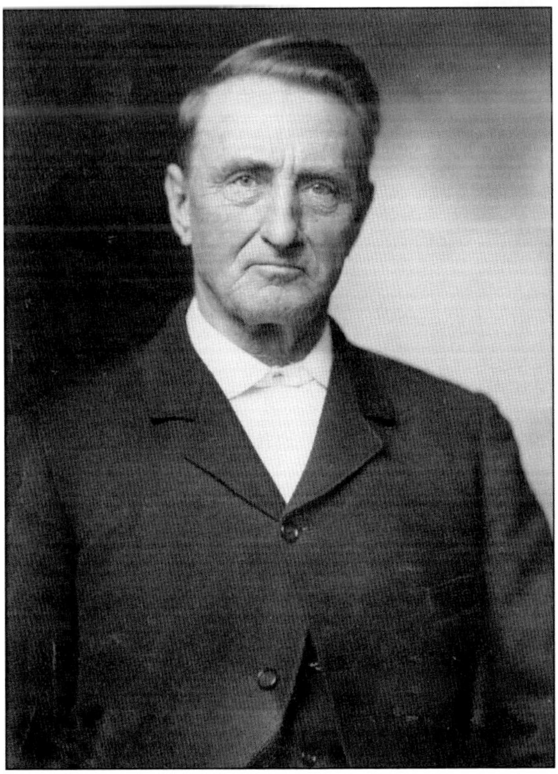

John W. Griffin (1831–1918) was a prosperous farmer living north of Dunreith and one of that town's founders. Very involved with the abolitionist movement and the Underground Railroad prior to the Civil War, Griffin was the last abolitionist in Henry County to pass away.

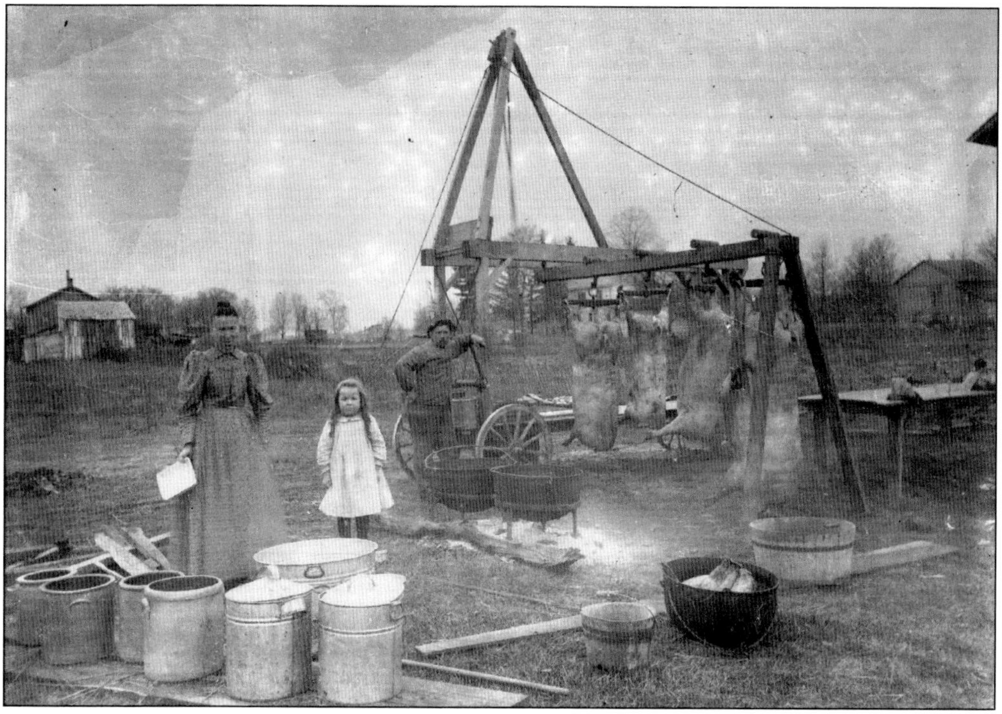

Willis and Josie Hammer and their daughter Lela May butcher hogs around 1900. The operation took place in the vicinity of what is now North Sixth Street in Spiceland.

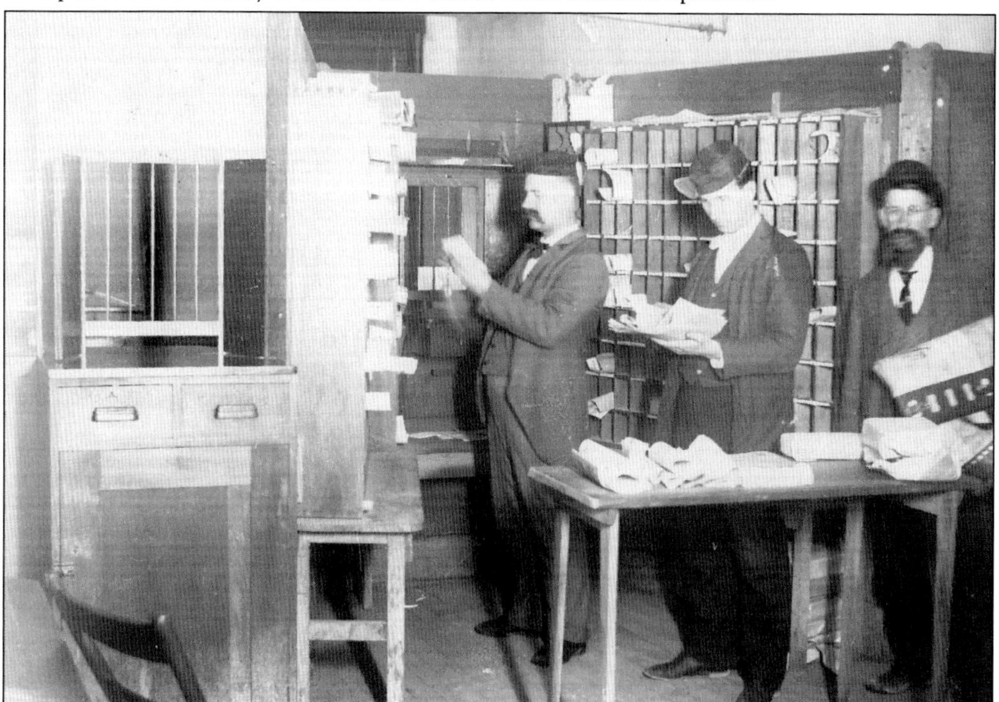

Spiceland postmaster Horace Yergin (left) sorts mail in this 1896 photograph. The gentleman wearing the derby hat is Civil War veteran Alpheus Fawcett.

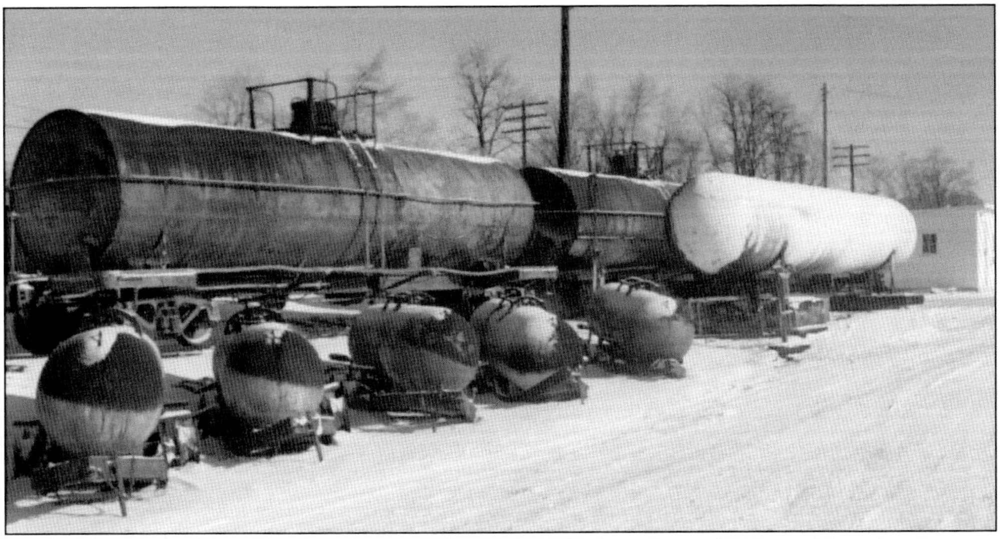

The train wreck and explosion in Dunreith on New Year's night in 1968 was like a bomb going off; it was a miracle no one was seriously injured. The town came close to being blown off the map in a series of weird events that caused damage in excess of $1 million. One business was destroyed, and others were damaged; homes were also destroyed, and others suffered major damage. Newsmen and photographers came from three states, and national television commentators carried news and pictures from the scene for several days. A total of 27 fire departments converged on Dunreith, one coming all the way from Wright-Patterson Air Force Base in Dayton, Ohio. All this came as a result of a westbound Penn Central derailing and sideswiping an eastbound train. The derailment set off a chain of fires and explosions in chemical, ammonia, gasoline, and oil tank cars. Shown here are three tank cars that did not explode.

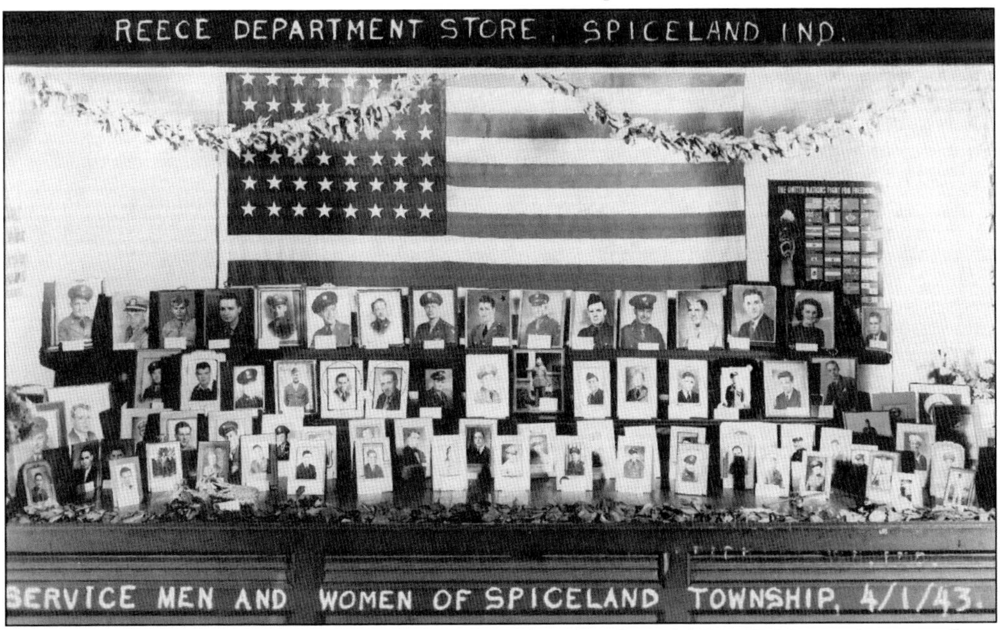

This photograph was taken on April 1, 1943, at the height of World War II. Men and women from Spiceland Township serving in the armed services were featured in a window display in Paul R. Reece Sr.'s department store (now Hoover Hall).

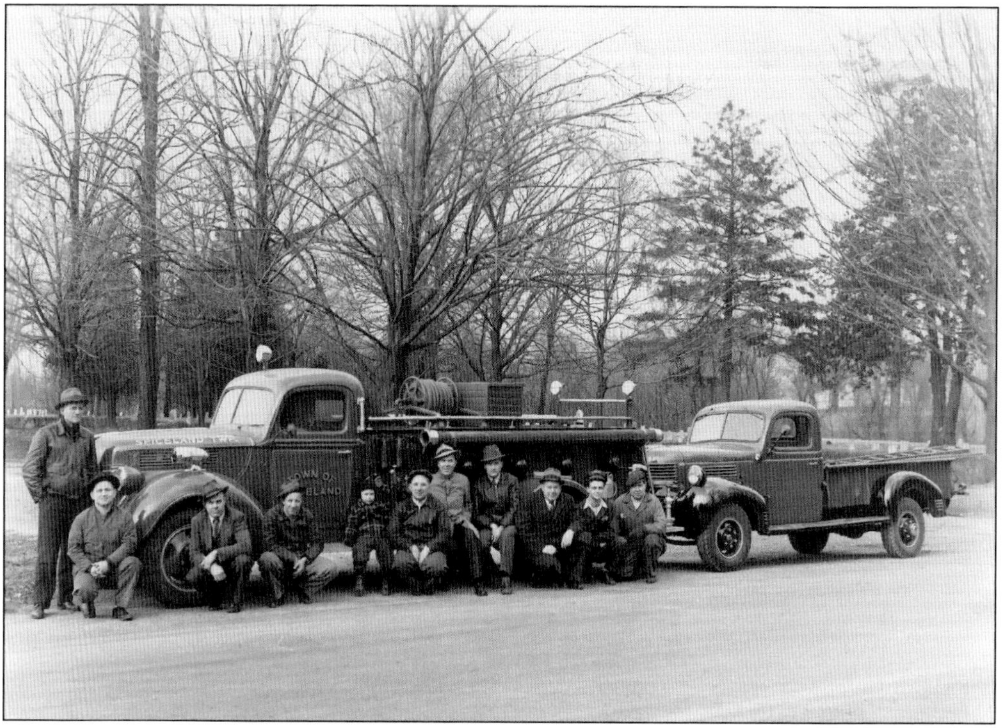

Members of the Spiceland Fire Department are shown here in 1945 with their firefighting equipment. From left to right are Paul R. Reece Sr., Rea Ratcliff, Tivis Smalley, Robert Lockridge, young Marshall Noel, Howard Noel, Ross Allen, Paul R. Reece Jr., Cash Essington, Charles Cooley, and Fred Poer.

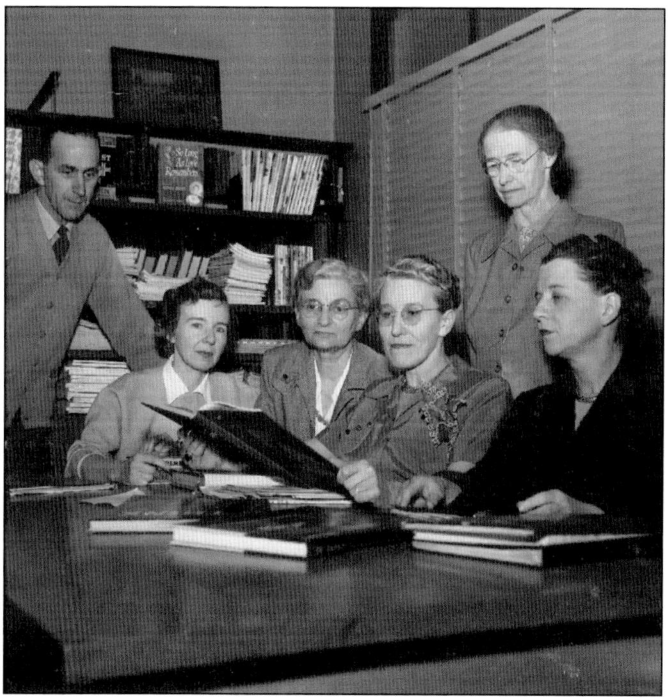

Members of the Spiceland Town-Township Public Library Board are pictured around 1950. From left to right are George Wilson, Harriett Evans, Helen Rockhill, Berniece Eilar, Emma Kendall (librarian), and Dorothy Scotten. Evans served as board president for 37 years.

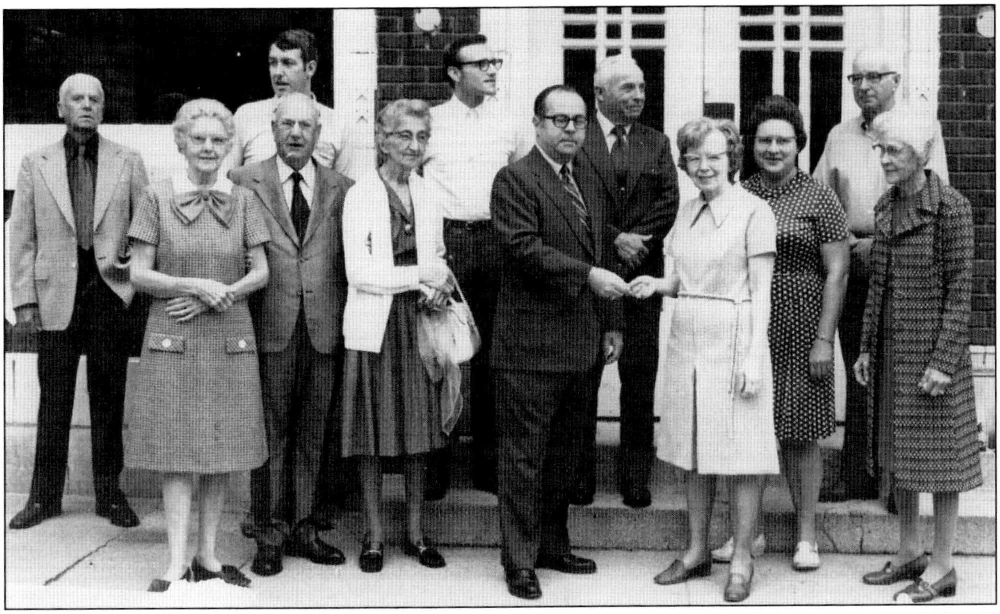

When Citizens State Bank moved into its new branch building in Spiceland in 1972, the old bank building was given to the library. Here, James Maddox, president of Citizens, formally turns over the keys to Harriett Evans, library board president. Others pictured are, from left to right, (first row) Inez Brookshire (library board member), Gilbert Hewit (chairman of the board of Citizens Bank), Florence Bundy (library board member), Esther Applegate (library board treasurer), and Martha Wise (librarian); (second row) Paul Franklin, William Byrket (library board member), Richard Ratcliff (library board member), Wilbur Coffin, and George Cherry (library board member).

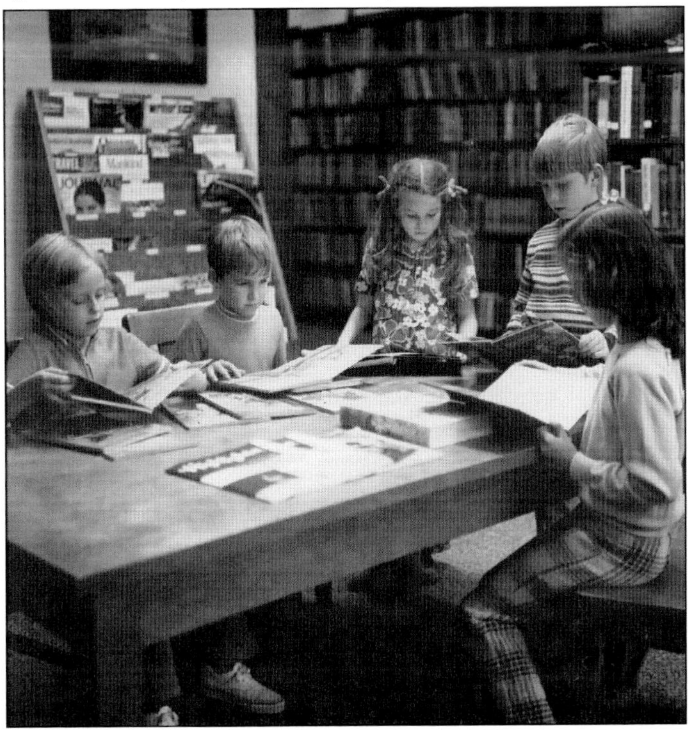

The children in this 1972 photograph, taken in the library, were selected by librarian Martha Wise because of their participation in and their enthusiasm for the summer reading program. The children are, from left to right, Charmaine DeWitt, Robbie Thompson, Lisa Moffitt, Mike Rose, and Cindy Loveall.

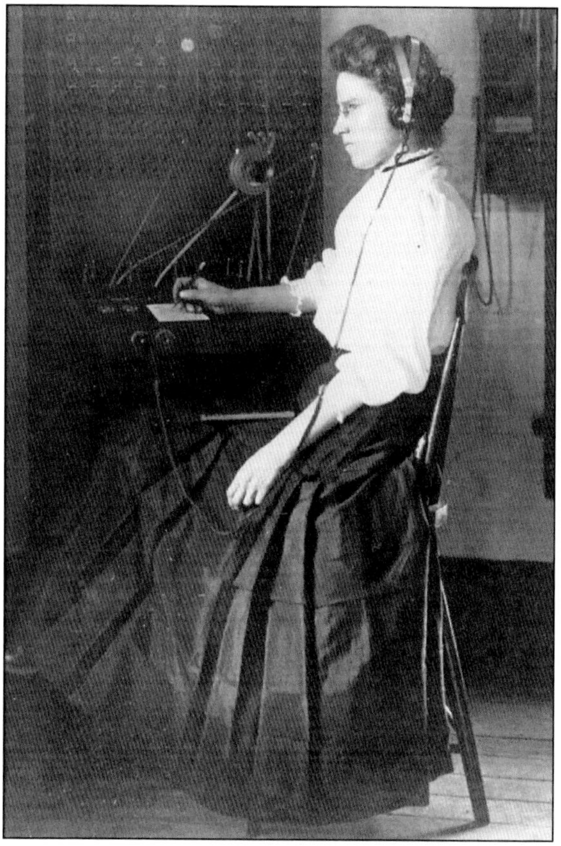

Leora Trabue, Spiceland's first telephone operator, is pictured here in the early 20th century. Other operators over the years were Rubie Cray, Leota Wright, and Nellie Blankenship.

Prior to 1907, these Spiceland Township residents gathered at the home of Caroline Edgerton, located north of Dunreith. From left to right are (first row) William R. Macy, John M. Cude, Caroline Edgerton, unidentified, John W. Griffin, Mary Jane Hall Griffin, and William P. Bundy; (second row) Samuel Exum Unthank, Jason Holloway, Cynthia Holloway, Albert Williams, Jennie Unthank, Arthur Osborn, Elizabeth Williams, William Cory, Virginia Cory, and Martitia Bundy.

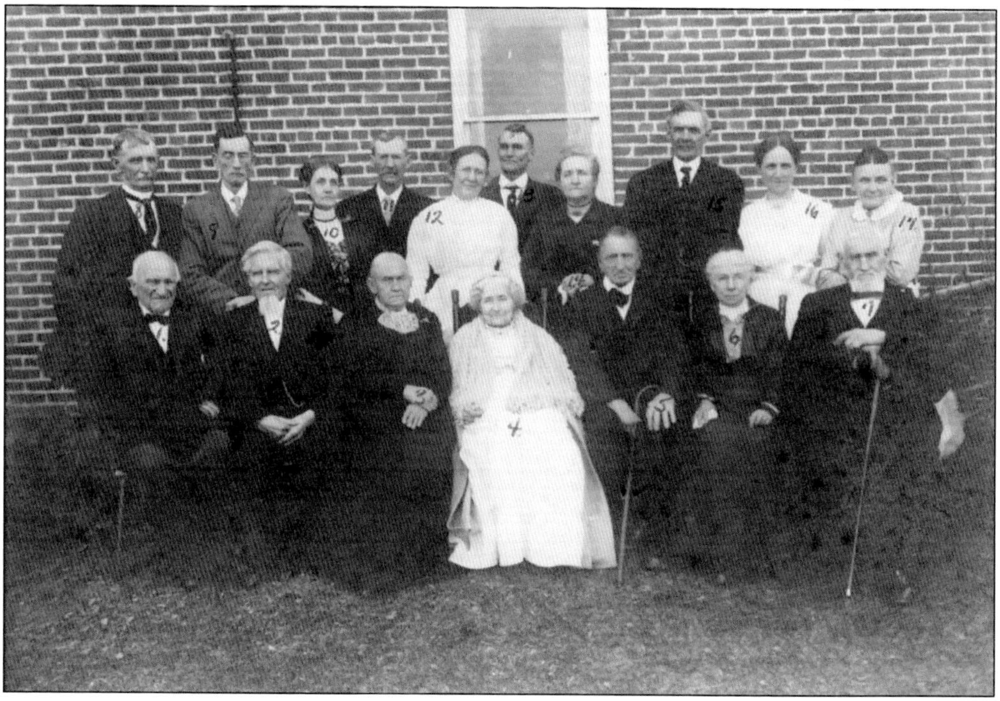

Seven

Just Having a Good Time

Spiceland Township residents are past masters at having a good time. Whether enjoying the annual Freedom Days festival, attending the former school's alumni meeting, attending various faith-related events sponsored by churches, gathering at various watering holes for coffee and conversation, enjoying birthdays and anniversaries at Hoover Hall, or simply gathering in homes with friends, there is a camaraderie that only exists in small-town America.

As the following images suggest, one does not have to have fame and fortune in order to be entertained and have a good time. Fun can be had watching a parade, enjoying music, dressing up at some community-sponsored event, participating in a political campaign, going for a ride in either an automobile or on a bicycle, enjoying the winter weather, lending one's hand in accomplishing some worthwhile community project, or going for a swim. These images, some dating back over 100 years, show Spiceland Township residents enjoying a variety of activities.

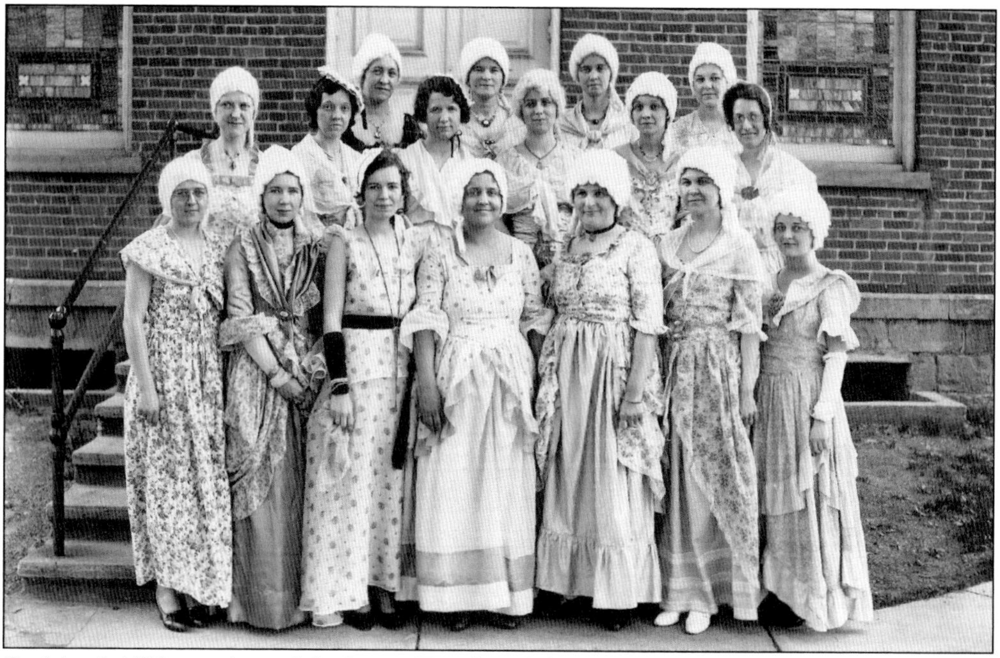

On May 8, 1932, members of the Junior Tuesday Club entertained senior girls at a Colonial tea. Club members are, from left to right, (first row) Edith Elliott, Harriett Evans, Eleanor Gant, Anna Thomas, Erma Pickering, Elsie Brewer, and Melba Powell; (second row) Edith Hoover, Martha Addison, LaVeta Myer, Dorcie Clark, Helen Haines, and LaVon Franklin; (third row) Nellie Stafford, Leslie Hoover, Edna Baskett, and Berniece Moses.

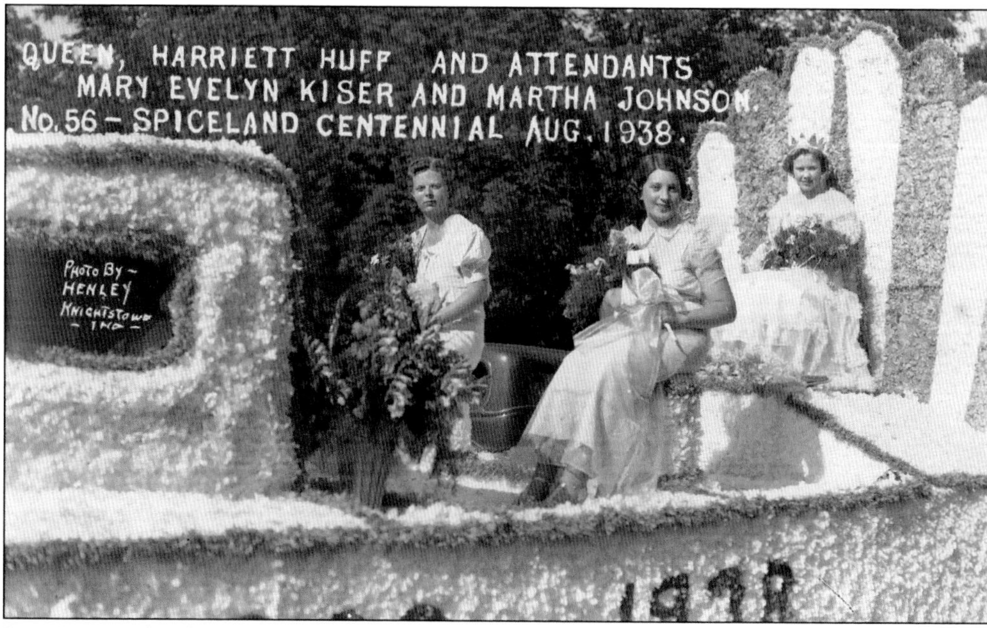

In 1938, Spiceland celebrated its centennial. The community was actually celebrating the 100th anniversary of the founding of the post office, as the town was much older than that. A huge parade was held with floats, bands, and horses and buggies. Harriett Huff (center) was crowned centennial queen. Members of her court were Evelyn Kiser (left) and Martha Johnson (right).

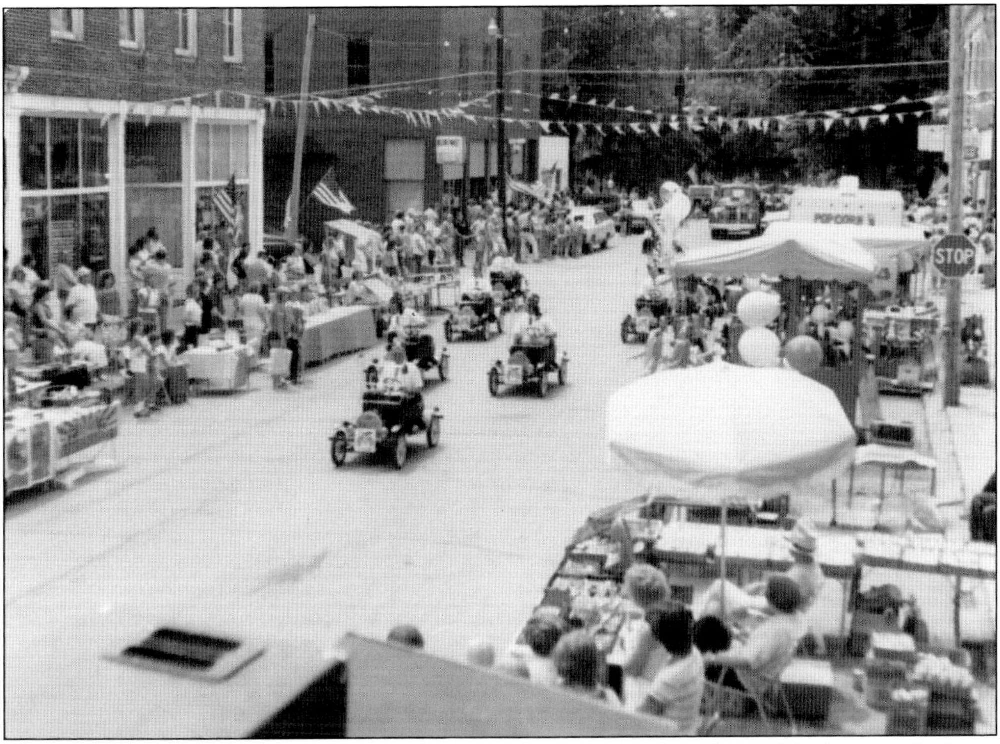

Freedom Days has been an annual event in Spiceland since 1976. This 1979 photograph shows the parade coming down Main Street in the center of Spiceland.

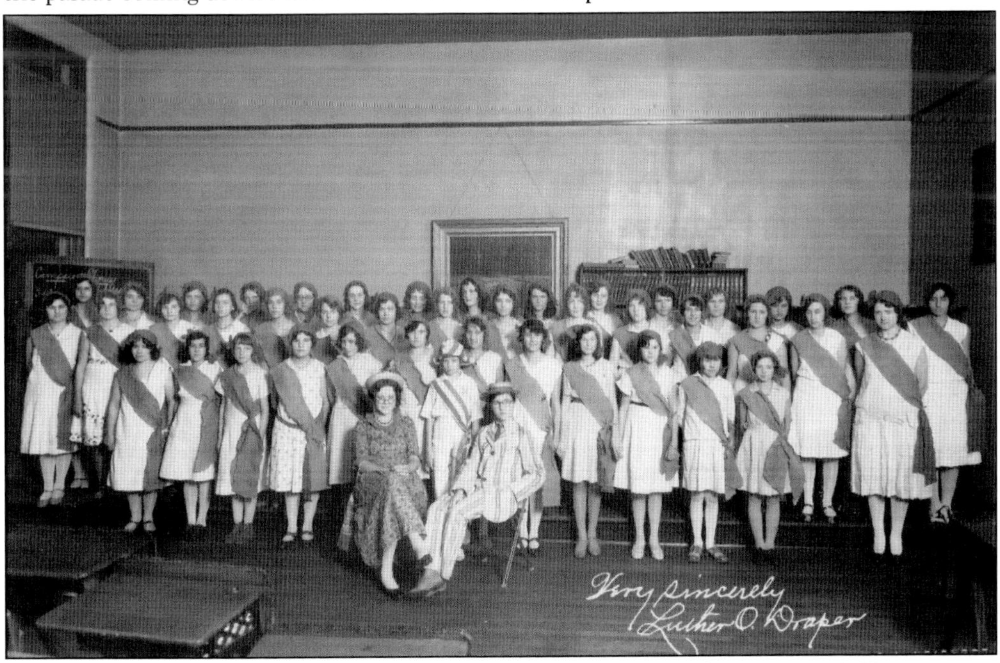

Luther O. Draper was elected to the Indiana State Senate in 1927 and again in 1929. His campaign chorus, composed of Spiceland High School students and community adults, toured the district on his behalf.

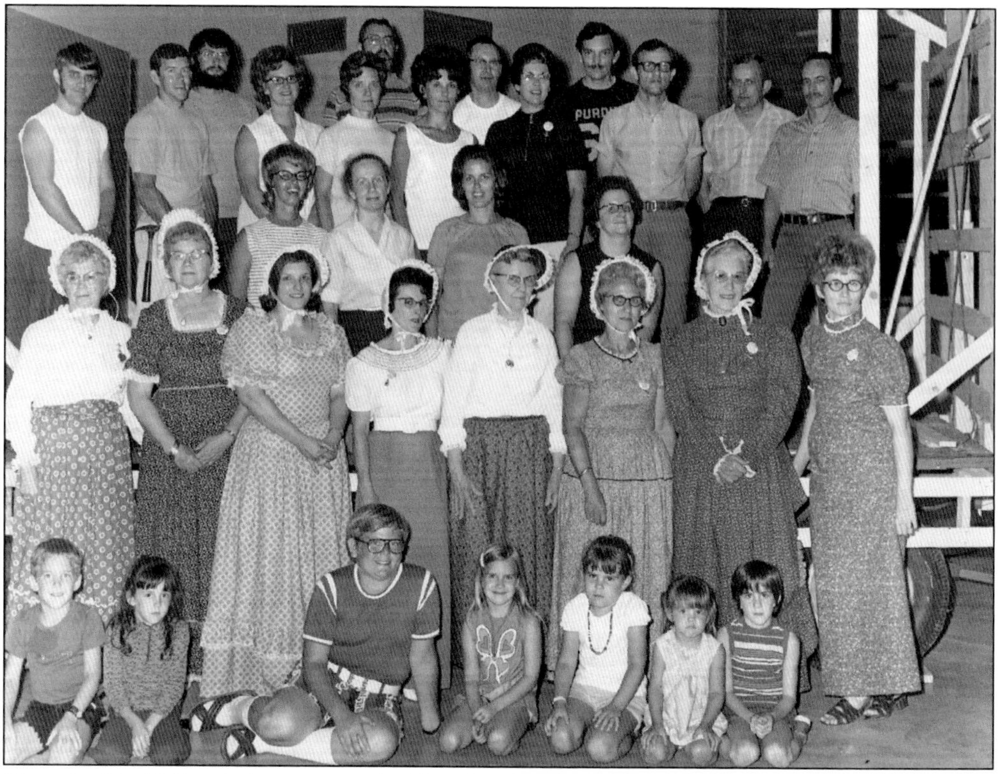

Organized in 1972 to help promote the New Castle–Henry County sesquicentennial, the Brook Bezor Belles and friends were photographed as work progressed on the float the group entered in the parade in New Castle. From left to right are (first row) Rob Thompson, Melinda Thompson, William Carnes, Monica Painter, Linda Bogue, unidentified, and Michelle Painter; (second row) Lucille Catt, Lucille Bryson, Janet Craft, Thelma DeWitt, Doris Noel, Winifred Ratcliff, Berniece Eilar, and Eleanor Painter; (third row) Irene Goodwin, Libby Henshaw, Judy Hicks, and Kathy Painter; (fourth row) Charles D. Brown, Lewis Thompson, Donald Painter, Pat Bogue, Janice Estelle, Walter Clay, Nancy Thompson, Theodore Applegate, Janet Carnes, Jerry Murray, Richard Ratcliff, Max Jessup, and Phil Estelle.

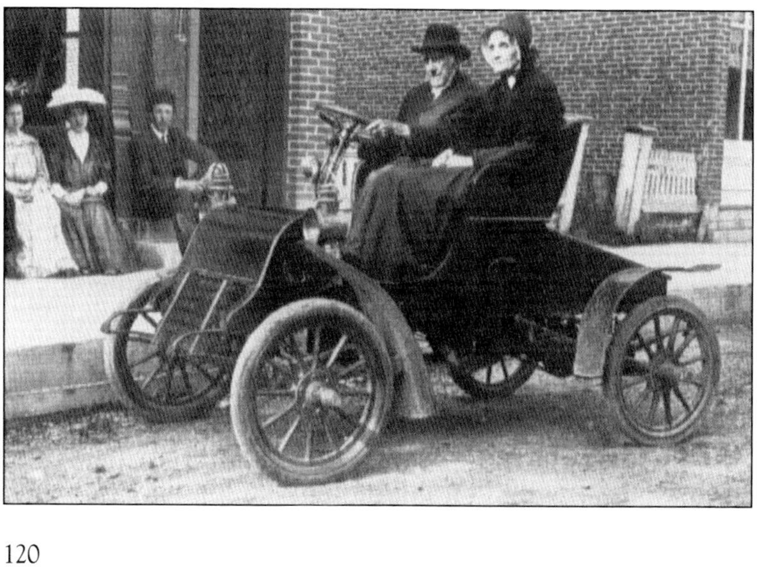

David (1814–1913) and Susanna (1815–1911) Edwards, early residents of Spiceland Township, appear very confident riding in their horseless carriage. This picture was taken in front of the Bank of Spiceland around 1905.

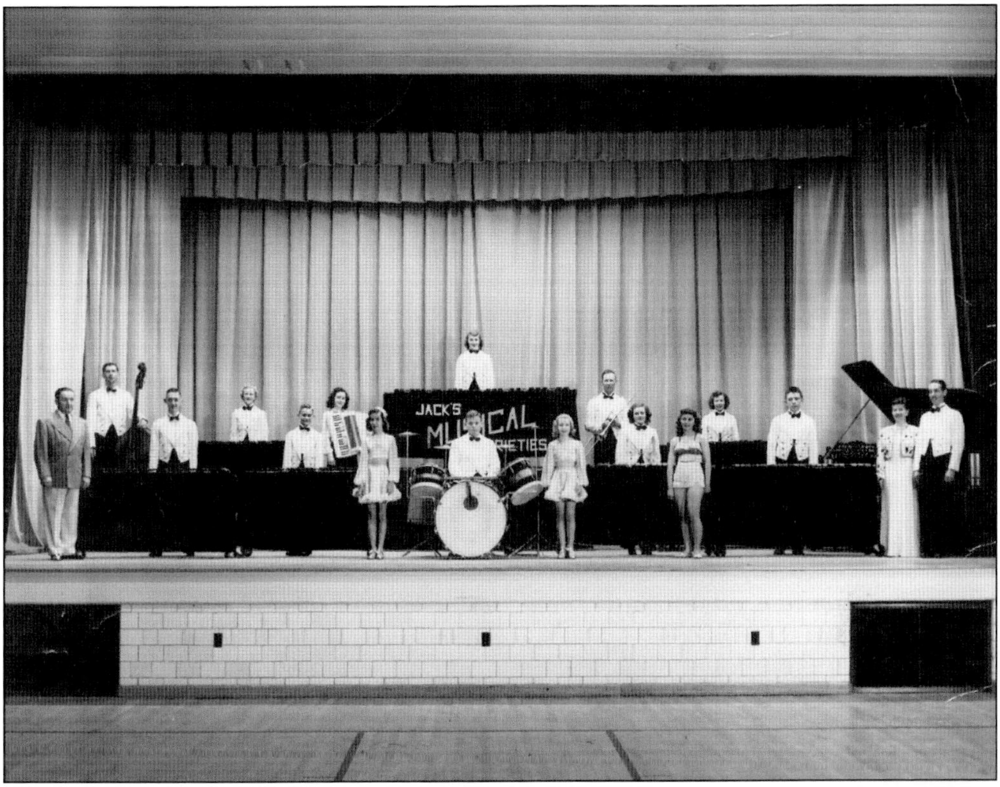

Donald Lee McCoy is seen here (third from the left) with Jack's Musical Varieties in 1950. Starting when he was quite young and extending through his high school years, he entertained multiple groups by playing his xylophone. He graduated from Spiceland High School in 1952.

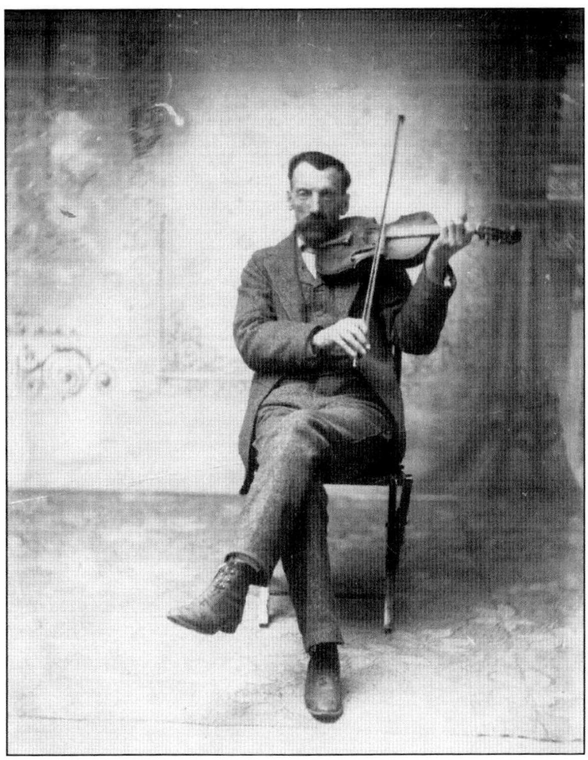

Spiceland bachelor Adolphus "Dolf" Newby plays a tune for the photographer in 1898. His father was one of 52 Spiceland Township residents who served in the Civil War.

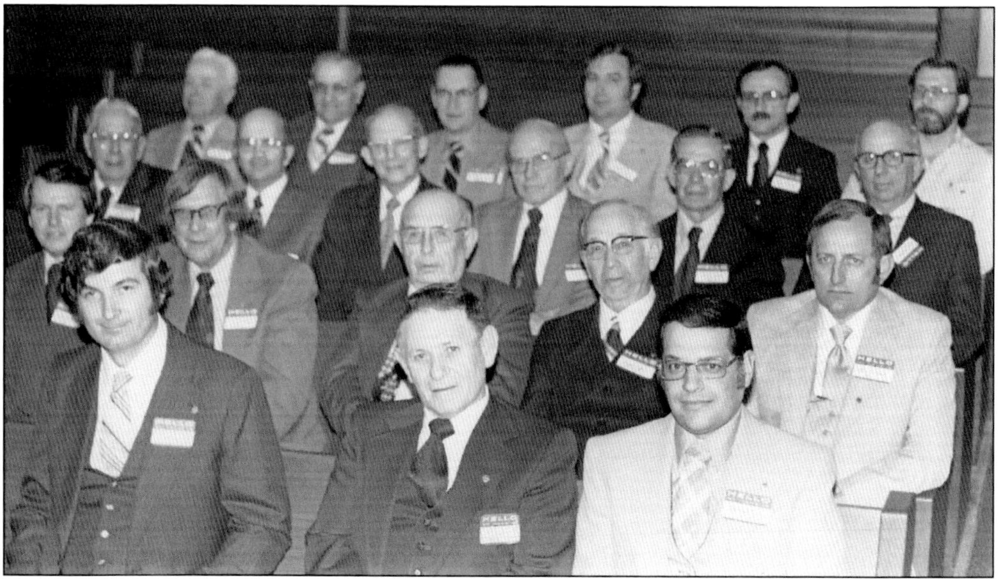

In 1975,a group of 20 former presidents of the Spiceland Lions Club were honored at the 30th anniversary of the club's founding. Seated from left to right are (first row) David Miers, J.C. Neal, and Charles Painter; (second row) Tim Goodwin, James Murray, Ralph Hollinger, Russell Coffin, and Max Jessup; (third row) Cash Essington, Kenneth Pohlenz, James Van Osdol, Kenneth Applegate, George Smiley, and Al Chamberlin; (fourth row) Wilbur Coffin, Lowell Painter, Theodore Applegate, Charles Myer, Richard Ratcliff, and Ronald Smith.

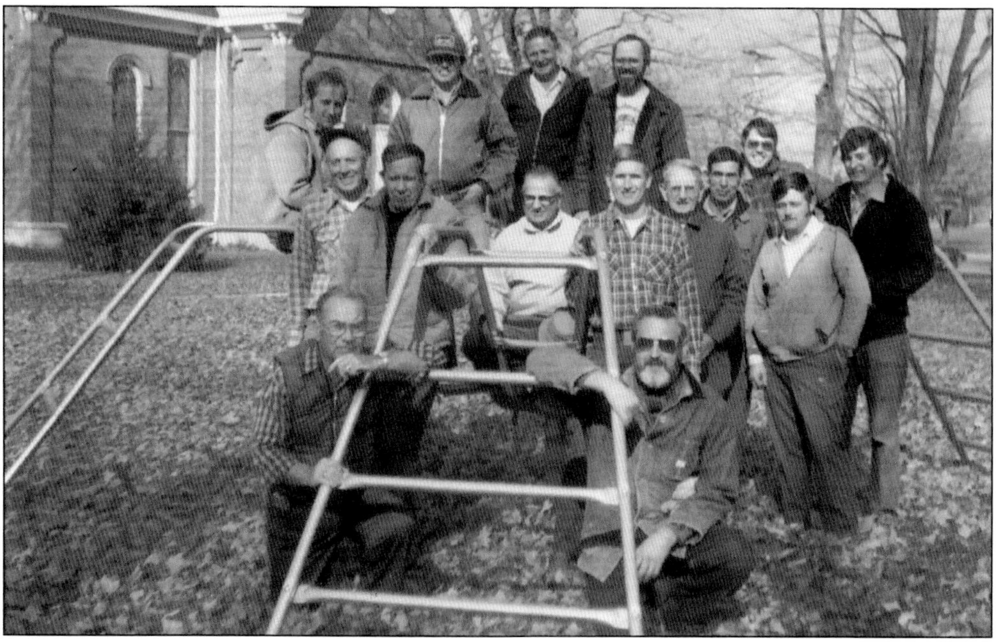

Spiceland Lions Club members take a break from installing playground equipment in the park in front of the Friends meetinghouse in October 1979. From left to right are (first row) Ed Miller and Walter Clay; (second row) Ed Bryson, Robert Taylor, Wendell Painter, Tim Lewis, John Longwell, Willard Acton, John McGuire, Danny Day, and David Miers; (third row) Max Jessup, Tim Goodwin, J.C. Neal, and Gary Robertson.

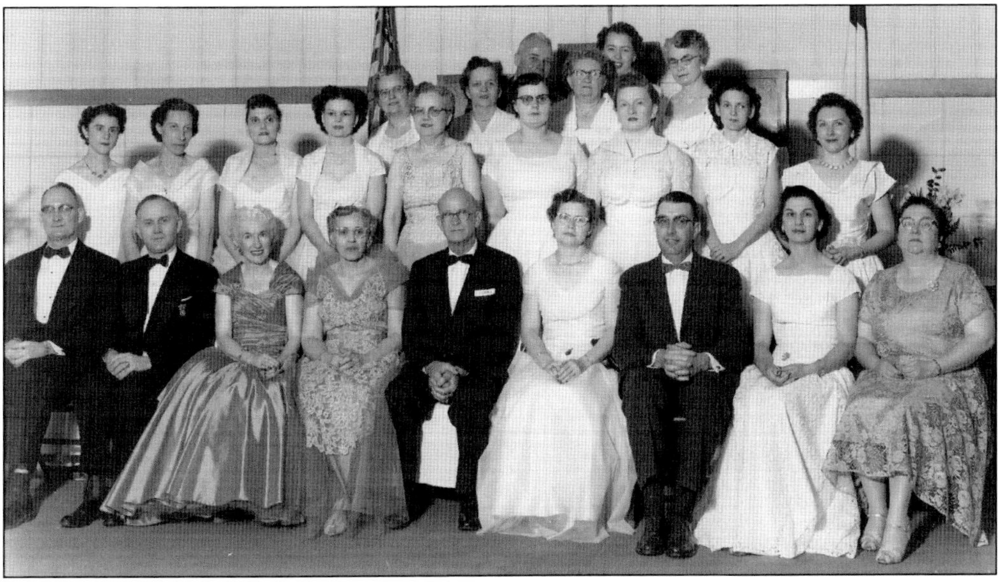

In 1956, Spiceland Chapter 563 of the Order of the Eastern Star held a public installation ceremony, with members from other chapters participating in the service. From left to right are (first row) unidentified, Willard Avery, unidentified, Margaret Harris, Ed Harris, Mary Bina Jessup, Howard Newkirk, and two unidentified; (second row) Leslie Reece, Catherine Noel, Marie Johnson, Marjorie Butler, Agnes Essington, Jonell Green, Mary Jane Estelle, unidentified, and Esther Carmichael; (third row) Gladys Poer, Ethel Newkirk, Wilbur Coffin, Treva Cooley, JoAnn McCormack, and Lucille Catt.

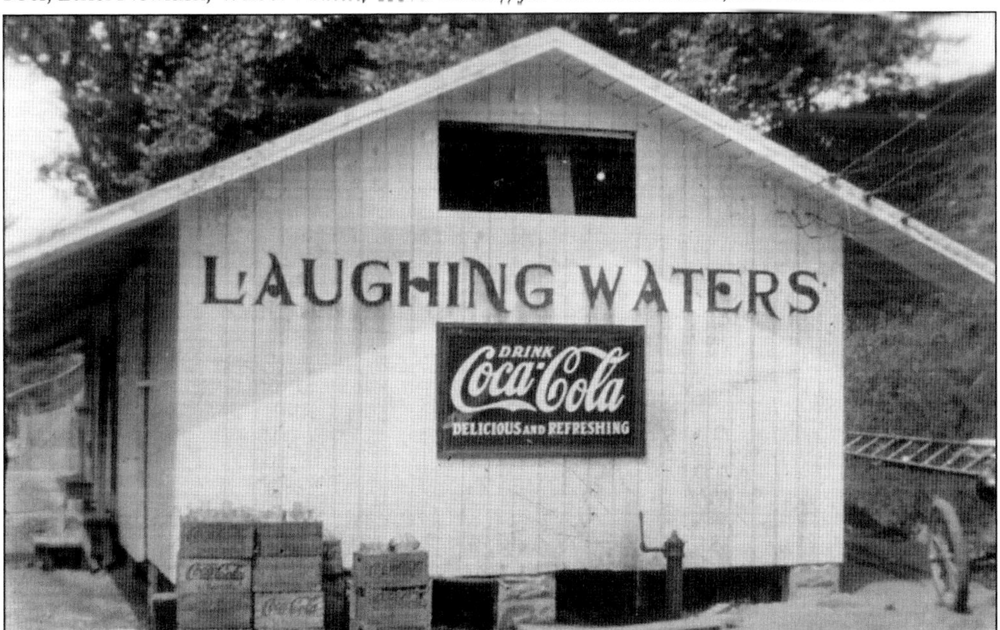

On a hot, steamy summer day in the 1930s and early 1940s, the place to be was the Laughing Waters swimming pool in Ogden. The center of the known world for many area residents, it was the first cement pool built for miles around. Bill Fentress built it around 1930, and it closed in 1944 due to gas rationing and the advent of municipal pools. The pool's concession stand is shown here.

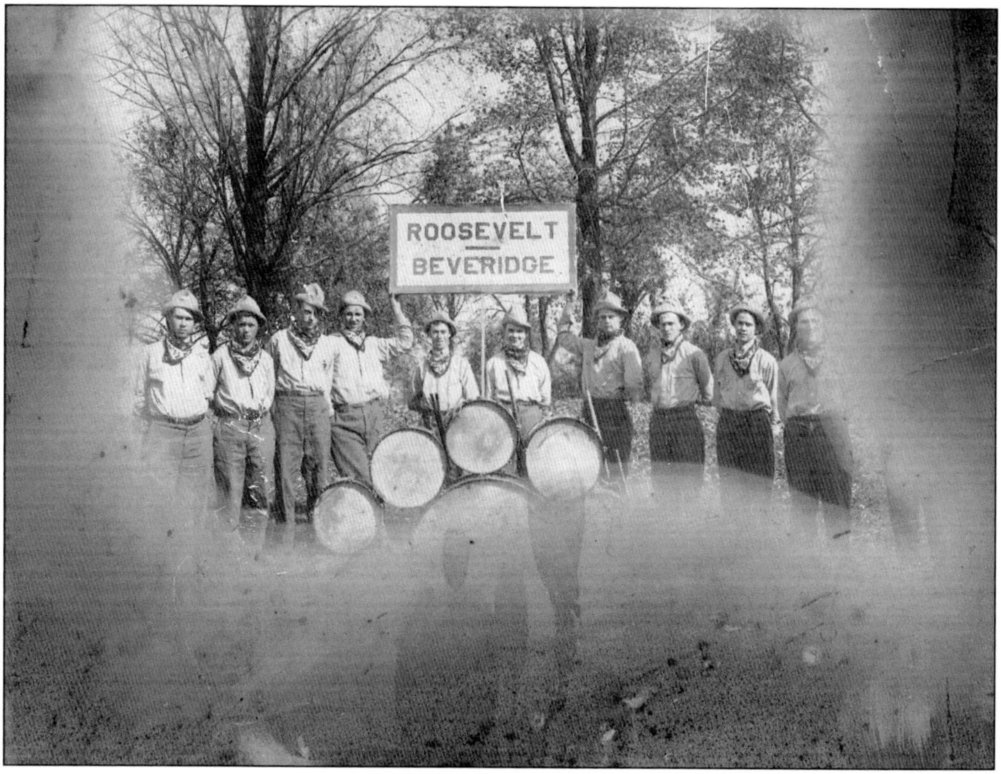

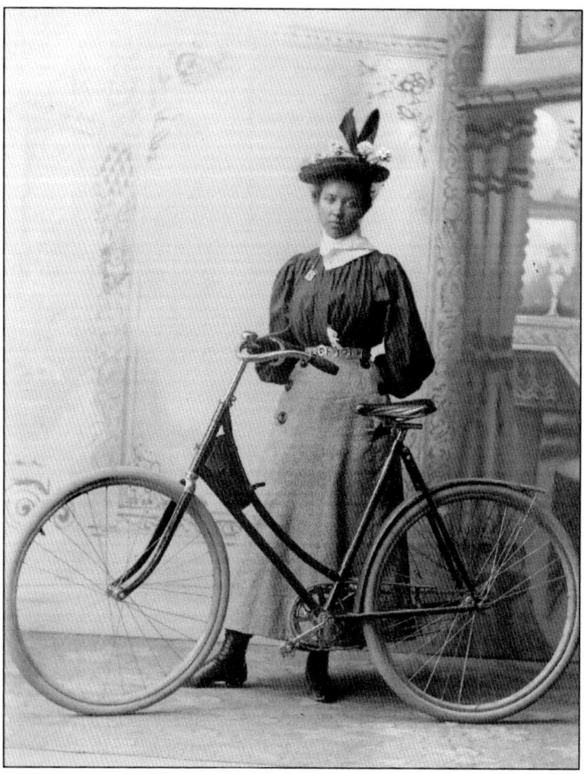

In the election of 1912, a group of young men organized a drum corps in support of the Progressive Party and its candidates. The party was an outgrowth of a split in the Republican Party. Former president Theodore Roosevelt was running for president as the party's candidate, and Albert Beveridge was an Indiana senator seeking reelection. Even though the boys no doubt did their best to drum up support for them, both were defeated. From left to right are Clarence Cramer, Everett King, Floyd Bundy, Cortez Ewing, Roy Brown, Carl Toohey, Carroll Copeland, Iris Hall, Paul Cramer, and Claude Haisley (partially shown).

Cycling was an extremely popular activity in the United States in the 1890s and early 1900s. This unidentified Spiceland cyclist appears ready to hit the unpaved streets for a pedaling getaway.

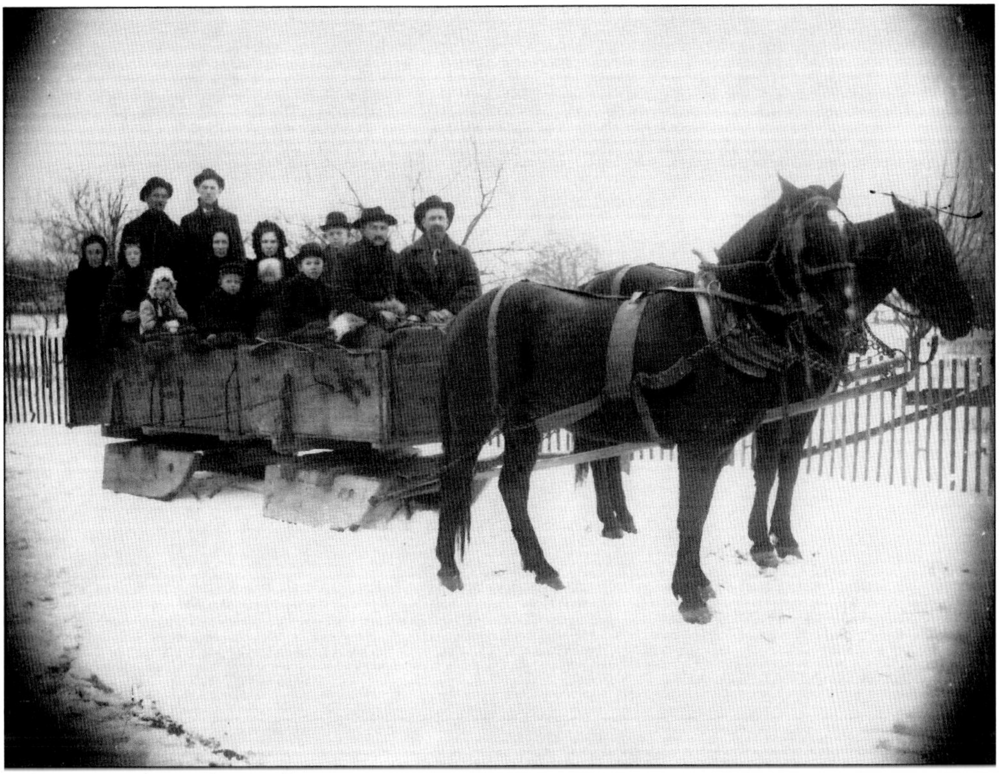

Taken around 1896 by Cephus M. Huddleston, this interesting photograph shows a group of Spiceland residents enjoying the winter weather.

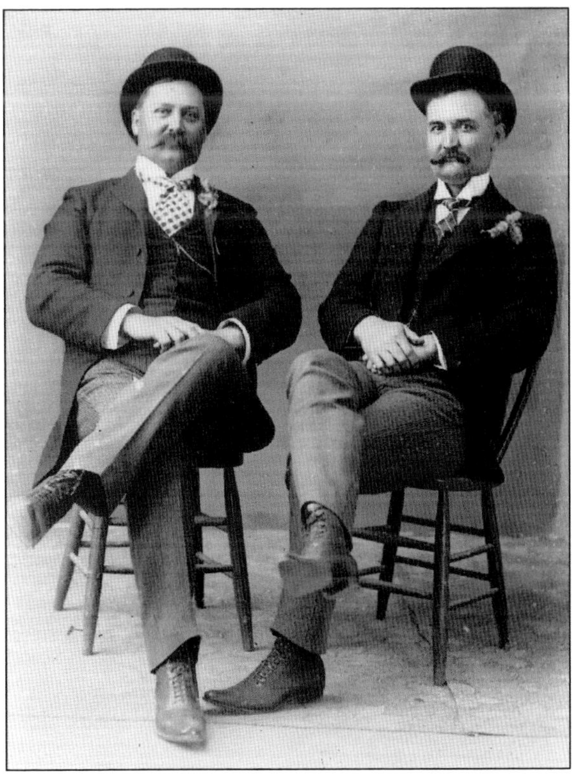

These unidentified Spiceland gents appear ready for action in this 1896 image. One cannot help but wonder where they were going.

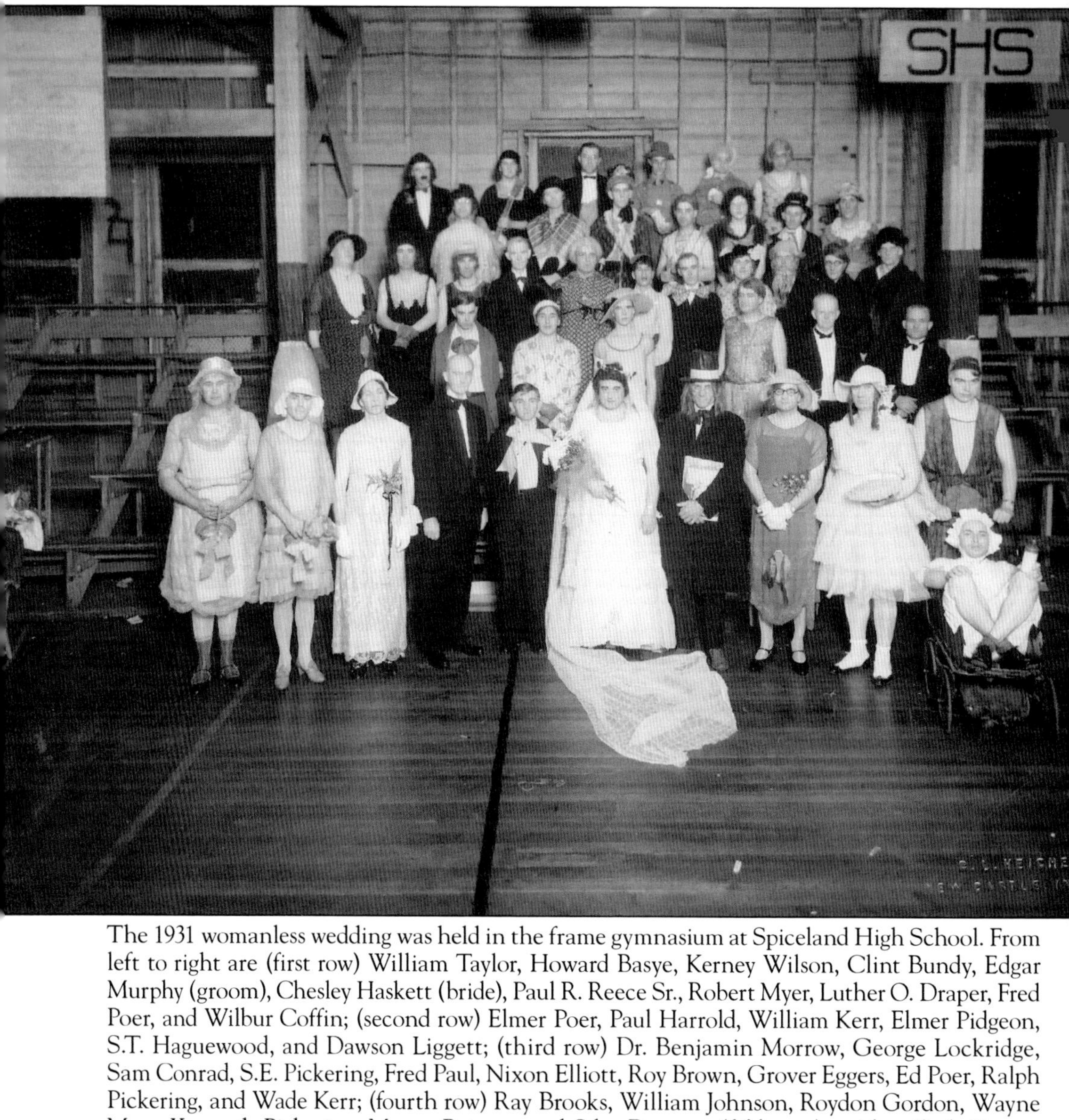

The 1931 womanless wedding was held in the frame gymnasium at Spiceland High School. From left to right are (first row) William Taylor, Howard Basye, Kerney Wilson, Clint Bundy, Edgar Murphy (groom), Chesley Haskett (bride), Paul R. Reece Sr., Robert Myer, Luther O. Draper, Fred Poer, and Wilbur Coffin; (second row) Elmer Poer, Paul Harrold, William Kerr, Elmer Pidgeon, S.T. Haguewood, and Dawson Liggett; (third row) Dr. Benjamin Morrow, George Lockridge, Sam Conrad, S.E. Pickering, Fred Paul, Nixon Elliott, Roy Brown, Grover Eggers, Ed Poer, Ralph Pickering, and Wade Kerr; (fourth row) Ray Brooks, William Johnson, Roydon Gordon, Wayne Myer, Kenneth Pickering, Myron Painter, and Silas Denney; (fifth row) unidentified, George Cartwright, Clyde Mercer, Ralph Griffin, Macy Scovell, and Frank Dillon.

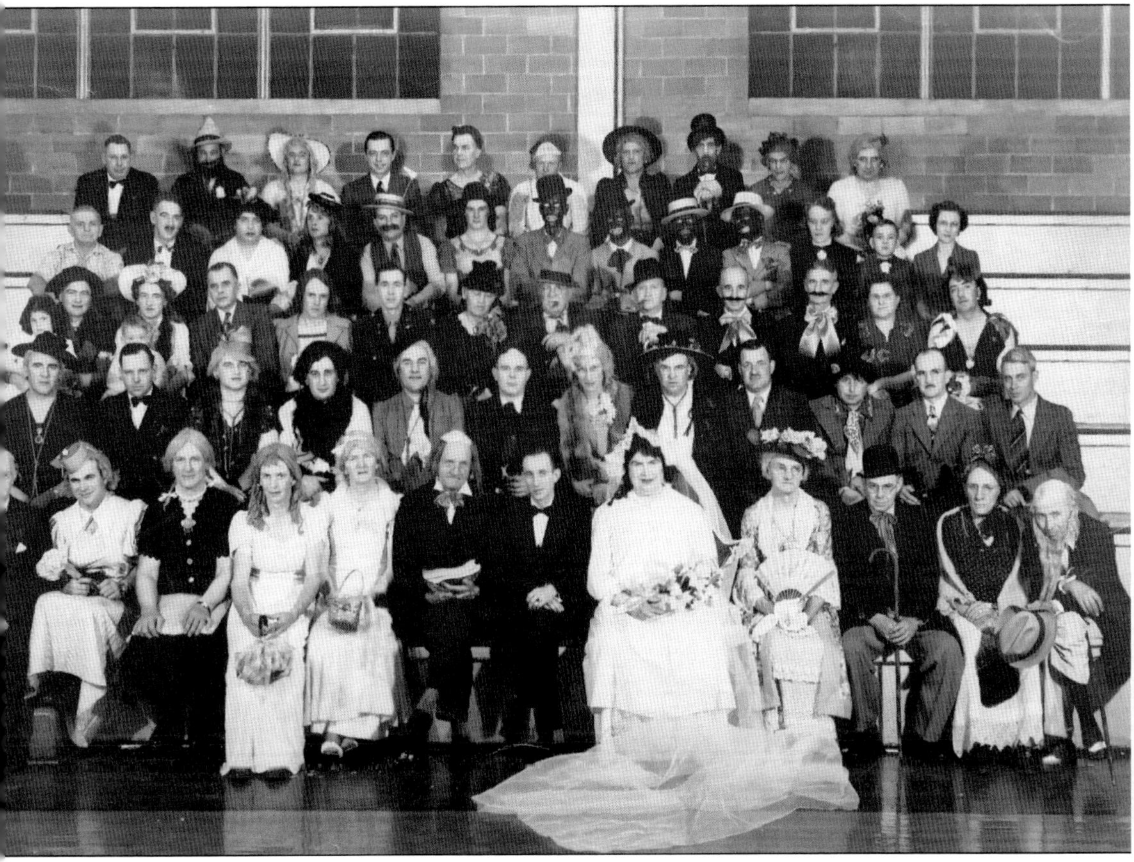

In 1948, the Spiceland Lions Club staged another womanless wedding. The lovely ladies and gentleman shown are, from left to right, (first row) James Knapp, Morris Herbert, Amos Sourbrine, Harold Lockridge, Kerney Wilson, Paul R. Reece Sr., Thomas Evans (groom), Fred Poer (bride), Macy Scovell, Elmer Poer, Ralph Pickering, and Earl Antrim; (second row) Lige Campbell, Harold Walter, Rea Ratcliff, Owen Wissing, Philip Applegate, Tivis Smalley, Howard Catt, Charles Applegate, Ralph Van Hoy, Ralph Hollinger, Jasper Barlow, and Maurice Byrket; (third row) Mary Ellen Painter, Will Kinkaid, Willard Lamb, unidentified child, Orin Pew, Kenneth Applegate, Charles Wilson, Walter Coffin, Fred Paul, Ralph McCoy, Marion Risk, Homer Eastridge, Erma Pickering, and Howard Newkirk; (fourth row) Edgar Murphy, Francis Anderson, Wilbur Coffin, William Coffin, Lowell Painter, Clarence Lefter, Justin Davidson, Richard Coffin, Keith Albion, Byron Coffin, Ruth Donahue, Lynn Barlow, and Winifred Ratcliff; (fifth row) Cash Essington, George Conrad, Marion Griffin, William Kiger, Ross Allen, Edgar Hall, Myer Hoover, Harvey Davidson, Howard Basye, and Howard Noel.

Consistent with our mission to preserve history on a local level, this book was printed in South Carolina on American-made paper and manufactured entirely in the United States. Products carrying the accredited Forest Stewardship Council (FSC) label are printed on 100 percent FSC-certified paper.

MADE IN THE USA